THE LAST
RHINOS

Also by Lawrence Anthony
and Graham Spence

Babylon's Ark
The Elephant Whisperer

THE LAST RHINOS

My Battle to Save
One of the World's Greatest Creatures

LAWRENCE ANTHONY

with Graham Spence

Thomas Dunne Books
St. Martin's Griffin
New York

THOMAS DUNNE BOOKS.
An imprint of St. Martin's Press.

THE LAST RHINOS. Copyright © 2012 by Lawrence Anthony with
Graham Spence. All rights reserved. Printed in the United States of America.
For information, address St. Martin's Press, 175 Fifth Avenue,
New York, N.Y. 10010.

www.thomasdunnebooks.com
www.stmartins.com

The Library of Congress has cataloged the hardcover edition as follows:

Anthony, Lawrence.
    The last rhinos : my battle to save one of the world's greatest creatures /
Lawrence Anthony, with Graham Spence.—1st ed.
        p.cm.
    ISBN 978-1-250-00451-2 (hardcover)
    ISBN 978-1-250-01509-9 (e-book)
    1. Anthony, Lawrence.   2. White rhinoceros—Conservation—Congo
(Democratic Republic)   3. Wildlife conservation—Congo (Democratic
Republic)   4. Rare mammals—Congo (Democratic Republic)
5. Endangered species—Congo (Democratic Republic)   6. Rhinoceroses—
Conservation—South Africa—Thula Thula Game Reserve.   7. Thula Thula
Game Reserve (South Africa)   I. Title.
    QL737.U63 A58 2012
    599.668'096751—dc23
                                                            2011279123

ISBN 978-1-250-03169-3 (trade paperback)

St. Martin's Griffin books may be purchased for educational, business,
or promotional use. For information on bulk purchases, please contact
Macmillan Corporate and Premium Sales Department at 1-800-221-7945
extension 5442 or write specialmarkets@macmillan.com.

First published in Great Britain by Sidgwick & Jackson, an imprint of
Pan Macmillan, a division of Macmillan Publishers Limited

First St. Martin's Griffin Edition: August 2013

D   10   9   8   7   6   5

*This book is dedicated to the courage of Ian Player,
Nick Steel, Kes and Frazer Hillman-Smith and those
other brave men and women who spent their lives
trying to protect and save one of the most magnificent
creatures ever to have graced this earth: the rhinoceros.*

The author condemns past and present governments of Vietnam, China, Myanmar, Indonesia, Thailand, South Korea, Taiwan and Malaysia who have failed to take effective action to end the superstitious use of rhino horn in so called traditional medicine. Their criminal neglect has driven the rhinoceros to the very brink of extinction all over the world.

THE LAST
RHINOS

CHAPTER ONE

It was barely light when the radio first crackled into life.

'Code red! Code red! Come in, Lawrence, come in. Over.'

'Standing by.'

'Bad morning.' The caller paused. 'We have a dead rhino at Hlaza Hill. A female. Over.'

Dread froze my blood. I looked up at the sky above the distant Hlaza Hill, the highest point on the new community game reserve that abuts Thula Thula, my own reserve and my home in Zululand, South Africa. There were no vultures and no gunshots had been reported, a sound that echoes like a thunderbolt across the African wilderness when the wind is right.

'Cause of death?' I asked, fearing the worst.

'Poachers. Both horns are gone. There's blood all over the place. Professional job. Looks like they used an AK-47, or maybe an old military-issue R1.'

I could feel my fists clenching. Rhino poachers – the disease of the wild that was now becoming a pandemic.

'How long has she been dead?' I asked.

'Can't be more than a few hours. They probably took it around midnight. There was plenty of moon to help them.'

'OK, I'll be there now. Out.'

I glanced at the pump-action shotgun leaning against the passenger seat of my Land Rover, reached for the ammunition box and stuffed my pockets with handfuls of SG cartridges.

I hoped against hope that the poachers were still on the reserve.

The green-black flies were already gathering when I arrived at the hill. The air was metallic with the rank smell of blood. The rhino lay uncharacteristically on her side, legs splayed awkwardly at right angles to her stiff body.

I got out of the Land Rover and walked across to the three rangers standing nearby. Nobody said anything. The shock of the kill, the dominating presence of the huge dead creature, stifled our words.

Rhinos have an ancient, eternal beauty. With their massive bodies, clad in thick folds of prehistoric body armour topped by a magnificent scimitar horn, they fascinate like few other creatures. Weighing up to three and half tons and reaching six feet high, they are the largest land animal in the world after the elephant.

In death, there was no trace of that beauty. The regal horns, viciously hacked off with honed machetes – or *pangas*, as we call them in Africa – left the noble face crumpled and desecrated. The eyes gazed vacantly. Pools of blood had congealed around the grotesquely disfigured head. Without its horn, the imposing creature looked as vulnerable as a baby.

I could see my own turmoil mirrored in the rangers' faces. In Africa, the war against poachers is intensely personal. There are two types of poacher: the local tribesman looking for something small for the pot; and the heavyweights, the professional killers, who want rhino horn and elephant ivory, who will shoot a ranger then brag about it. Poaching any animal is a crime, but killing a rhino or elephant is not shooting to feed a hungry family. It's blood money. And it's an intimate, violent invasion of our lives.

'Who found the body?'

Bheki, my most trusted ranger, looked up and pointed at a

young Zulu guard, Simelane, standing a little way off. I beckoned for him to come over.

'*Sawubona*, Simelane,' I greeted him. 'What happened here?'

'*Sawubona*, Mkhulu. I was on patrol when I saw the dead rhino,' he replied quietly, staring at the ground.

'Who was with you?'

'I was alone.'

'You were on patrol out here all alone?' I asked, surprised. Poaching patrols always consisted of two armed men.

'Yes, I was alone.' He was barely whispering.

I was about to press on with the questioning when a loud Zulu voice interrupted me.

'Mkhulu, there is too much blood.'

It was Bheki, down on one knee closely examining the rhino's head.

'There is too much blood,' he repeated. 'That means they were in a hurry. They took the horns while she was still alive. Maybe unconscious, but alive.'

For a moment we just stared at Bheki. Then it sank in. These monsters had hacked the horn off a living animal.

'Which way did they go?' I asked Bheki, who had been at my side in several firefights with poachers over the past decade.

He pointed east. 'Four, maybe five hours ago.'

That meant that unless they were in hiding, they would be almost out of the reserve and heading towards the townships, where we would never catch them. However, that didn't mean we wouldn't try. At the very least, it would give us something physical to do to vent our fury.

'OK, we all know the drill,' I said. 'These guys are probably carrying AKs and we all know what that means. If we make contact and they so much as think of lifting their rifles, shoot fast and shoot first, as we'll be up against automatic fire.'

I looked at the solemn faces. Armed only with shotguns and

Second World War-era Lee–Enfield .303 bolt-action rifles, they were completely out-gunned, but that would not deter these hard, dedicated men for a moment. They would be facing automatic weapons, replying as fast as their wrists could work their rifle bolts. You cannot imagine the courage that takes. I had a pump-action shotgun that was fast and deadly and spread nine lead balls in a lethal cluster. Our weapons complemented each other well. The .303s had a longer range than an AK, and the shotguns at close quarters in thick bush didn't miss. Used in tandem they were a match for the illegal AK-47s so favoured by poachers. 'Bring your own water and keep your safety catches on. Let's go!' We would be moving as fast as we could in thick bush, and I didn't want anyone tripping and blasting the person ahead of them.

The going was tough and by mid-morning we were well off the beaten path, following barely discernible game trails used by the poachers. The sun burned relentlessly, a typical Zululand scorcher, and sweat poured from our bodies, stinging our eyes and drenching our shirts. But hyped up with adrenalin and anticipation, we never eased our blistering pace. If we faltered, any slim chance of catching them would be lost.

It's difficult to remain calm when you see a rhino brutally slaughtered for a horn that consists of little more than keratin, the same fibrous structural protein you find in hair and fingernails. In fact, it's impossible. You're more likely to be consumed by raging fury, but that won't do any good. Rhino horns are used for mythical medicinal purposes in countries across Asia, as part of their traditional healing systems. In traditional Chinese medicine it is believed to cure types of fever, for instance. And the increasing wealth of these economies has created an insatiable demand. Tens of thousands of rhino have been killed in Africa, with several subspecies hunted to extinction. The demand is reminiscent of a nineteenth-century gold rush, and with good reason. On the streets of China or Vietnam, ounce for ounce the horn is more valuable than gold. If you truly want to grasp the situation faced by conservationists, do what a poacher does and look at a rhino and see a three-foot-long horn made of pure gold. Game rangers are in the unenviable and extremely hazardous position of trying to protect solid gold. What should be locked securely in a vault instead walks around on four legs in the bush.

It is not an exaggeration to say that every rhino on the planet is now in mortal danger. Unless something fundamental changes, and quickly, every last one in the wild will eventually be killed.

As we pushed on, we periodically picked up traces of the killers' trail, such as footprints, a small patch of flattened grass, a marked tree or flecks of blood, probably oozing from the horn that the killers would be carrying in a hessian sack. These signs that we were on the right track provided the edge we needed, with Bheki urging us to speed up the chase.

However, Simelane, the young Zulu ranger who had discovered the dead rhino, was starting to worry me. Twice he veered off into the bush alone, following false leads and losing us valuable time. Maybe his strange behaviour was due to the stress of tracking the killers, I thought, as well as the possibility of an ambush around the next corner.

An ambush was my biggest worry. The penalty in South Africa for rhino poaching is a fifteen-year jail sentence and there was no way these professional killers were going to risk being sent away for that long. They knew it and we knew it. If the killers sensed they were being followed and were waiting for us, there is no doubt we would be in a lethal firefight – at close quarters, in thick bush, with minimum visibility and maximum chaos.

Eventually the punishing pace took its toll. I called a halt for a brief rest and sent one of the rangers ahead to high ground to try and pick them out from above.

'Nothing,' came the reply on the radio from a nearby hill. 'I see nothing.'

I could tell by the frustrated look on Bheki's face as we waited that the spoor was now cold. We were too late; and, sure enough, a couple of hours later when we finally reached the boundary fence, all we found was a slash where they had snipped through the wire, carefully avoiding the electric strands. They were well and truly gone.

'Next time,' I heard Bheki whisper as he unloaded his .303. 'We will get them next time, Mkhulu.'

I nodded silently, also unloading my shotgun as we started the long trek back.

At home, I reported the incident, first to the police and then to our local Parks authority, KwaZulu-Natal Wildlife. The latter phone call was tough, as they had just donated the now dead animal to a project I was working on. I was joining my reserve, Thula Thula, with the huge Zulu tribal trust areas to form what we believed would be one of the finest game reserves in the country. It was to be called the Royal Zulu and would be a unique joint venture with local tribes. The project would provide meaningful benefits to poor rural communities through conservation and eco-tourism, giving them a stake in the future of the African wilderness. Thanks to years of apartheid when game reserves had been racially exclusive, many rural Zulus regarded conservation as a 'white man's' concept and had little regard for it. Now we aimed to rehabilitate their traditional spiritual and cultural links to the bush that once were so powerful. We would demonstrate that poaching animals provided food for a week, but protecting them provided jobs for ever. These animals are worth infinitely more alive than dead. We had to get locals to buy into that concept with total commitment, otherwise we as conservationists would start to run out of options – as the horn-less mound of rotting flesh we had just seen confirmed.

KZN Wildlife had donated four white rhinos as part of the Royal Zulu venture to provide breeding stock, and the manager I had phoned to break the news to was understandably un-happy. I knew what was coming next.

'Lawrence,' he said, 'this is really bad. We're worried about the security, man. I mean, you've got three more rhino there and we don't want to lose those as well.'

'I know. I've activated *impimpis*,' I replied, referring to our informants in the local tribes who we paid to collect information about poaching or theft, 'and we're increasing patrols as from tomorrow. I'm going to catch those bastards if it's the last thing I do.'

'Well, good luck. But I think in the interim, we had better get the animals into a safer area until everything settles down. Rhinos are like a bloody magnet for poachers these days.'

'OK, I understand where you're coming from,' I replied. 'But they have just been delivered to us, so how did anyone even know they were here? There had to be a tip-off from your side. How do we know they will be safer with you?'

He sighed. 'That's my biggest nightmare.'

He was a decent man whom I knew well. I also understood what he was saying, but it really galled me to be told that we were going to have to return three rhinos. Our security was by necessity among the best in the area. After all, we had been protecting a herd of elephants for almost ten years. But these days nothing, including one's own life, is guaranteed in the bush when rhino poachers are about.

However, there was nothing I could do. If the Parks authority wanted to take their animals back, so be it. Unfortunately that meant there would now be only one rhino left on the reserve, a female. A German tourist had called her Heidi, and the name had stuck. An elephant had killed her mother some years ago in a tragically unequal battle over who had right of way. She had been crushed by a full-blown charge, and I still remember standing next to the corpse and seeing a movement in the bush some yards away. It was Heidi. Barely weaned, she had watched her mother's awful fight to the death. I approached to see if she was all right, but she ran off into the bush.

Then our other rhino drowned in a flash flood, an unavoidable tragedy, which left only Heidi.

Since then Heidi, who enjoyed grazing with a herd of wildebeest, had grown up with us and become a favourite with rangers and trackers. She had matured into a beautiful creature and loved approaching the game drive vehicles, captivating visitors to the reserve with her playful antics, approaching and retreating, peering myopically and running in the flamboyant, bouncing style of rhinos. We had to do all we could to protect her now.

Yet there was something funny about the Parks Board rhino's death; something I couldn't quite put my finger on. I summoned Simelane, the guard who had discovered its carcass, to my office.

'Mkhulu,' he said as he approached, and we shook hands. Mkhulu loosely means 'grandfather' in an avuncular sort of way, and it is my Zulu nickname. Rural Zulus give nicknames to most people and some can be bitingly accurate in depicting your shortcomings, either physical or social. I was lucky; at least mine was benign. I have a friend who sometimes taps his hand rapidly when sitting. He ended up with the epithet Thathazele, meaning 'the nervous one', and the name stuck. Yet he is one of the bravest men I know.

'I see you, Simelane. Well done on finding the dead rhino.'

'*Yebo.*' Yes.

'How did you find it?'

'I just knew it was there.'

'Did you hear the gunshot?'

He shook his head. '*Aibo.*'

'Did you see any hyenas, or maybe vultures?'

He shook his head.

'But the rhino was a long way from where you patrol, more than a mile off the path. Why were you in that area?'

'I just knew something was wrong. So I went to have a look.'

'But you somehow found the exact place. How did you do that?'

'I just felt it. Things were not right that morning.'

'OK. Thank you,' I said, purposely bringing the conversation to an end.

He left. I was now extremely suspicious. Simelane could have been telling the truth – Zulus sometimes do have a sixth sense in the bush – and he may just have thought something was wrong. But something didn't gel. I knew my game guards well and they seldom left their patrol areas. And if they did, they never went alone.

I called Bheki on his cellphone. 'Stay close to Simelane,' I said. 'Try to get his confidence and see what you can find out about him and the rhino. I don't trust him any more.'

The next day the phone rang. It was the police.

'*Ja*, Lawrence, we may have something,' said the sergeant, whom we had dealt with before. 'The story is that a gang, we think from Johannesburg, came here, hired a professional gunman and gave him a drawing of a rhino's head and where to shoot. X marks the spot, as they say. We're told he was paid five thousand rand [$700 US]. But you can forget about the horn. A Taiwanese ship that has been docked in Richards Bay for the past week left last night – convenient, hey? It'll be on the high seas by now and you can bet your game reserve that the horn was on it.'

? The horn would sell for a fortune in the
ne gang may have come from Johannesburg,
also spoke volumes. This meant we were deal-
ofessionals, the big boys. These were no local
usually only hunted for the pot anyway. No, these
the Boere Mafia – a name given to a predominantly
An   -speaking organization that regarded the sometimes
chaotic post-apartheid South Africa as an easy way to make big
money in hunting and poaching – or a Far East syndicate, getting
marksmen from outside our area to do their dirty work.

'We've done the post-mortem,' the sergeant continued. 'They
used an R1, similar in calibre to an AK. One bullet straight into
the brain from very close.'

That too was interesting. The R1, a locally manufactured semi-
automatic combat rifle, was used extensively by the South
African Army during the border wars before apartheid was
abolished. This could indicate that someone with former army
links had supplied the weapon to the gunman, which again
could point to the Boere Mafia, who dealt in anything from
canned lion hunting, in which caged animals were shot from
vehicles, to ivory and rhino horn.

The next morning I called my section ranger, Vusi Gumede,
and asked him to send Simelane to my office. Vusi came back
ten minutes later.

'Simelane hasn't reported for work today.'

Bingo.

'OK, take some rangers with you and go to his house. Get
him here by force, if you have to.'

An hour later, Vusi returned. Simelane had packed his bags
and fled. Even his wife did not know where he was.

Simelane, who knew the reserve well, had possibly taken the
killers right up to the animal. Maybe he was even the shooter. I
passed the information on to the police.

That evening we went out on patrol. There were just four of us: myself, Bheki and two tough game guards, Thulani and Nkonka. All of us were hoping for a contact. We wanted those poachers badly.

We walked all night along the fences, or sat for hours at lookout points, watching silently, searching for the flicker of a giveaway torchlight, constantly updating each other, whispering on walkie-talkies. But we found nothing. I fell into bed, exhausted, as the sun rose. The next night we were out again.

And the next.

The waxing gibbous moon shimmered like a beacon – poachers love to operate on bright nights. We had been patrolling for five hours and it was now just before dawn, the time of night when spirits are at their lowest ebb. Bheki and Thulani were scouring the bush about a hundred yards away, when suddenly Nkonka grabbed my arm and pointed. I immediately crouched low. He pointed again, and then I saw it: the briefest, tiniest glint of light just down the hill. This is what we had been waiting for. Slowly I thumbed the safety catch off my pump-action shotgun as we moved down to intercept them.

We got into position, took cover behind two large marula trees on the banks of a small stream and waited patiently. The adrenalin was pumping hard when two figures emerged from the dark about thirty yards away, and then they saw us and ran straight towards Nkonka, firing wildly. In an act of incredible bravery, Nkonka left his cover behind the tree, stood up and charged straight back at them, firing from the hip with his bolt-action Lee–Enfield .303. All hell broke loose as the night erupted in a cacophony of blasts and shouts. It went on for what seemed like an age, but was probably little more than ten seconds. I was swinging my shotgun back and forth looking for a target, but from my vantage point it was just shadows, and I couldn't let off a shot in case I also hit Nkonka.

Then it was silent. They had gone, melted into the bush.

'Nkonka!' I whispered desperately. 'Are you all right?'

'*Yebo*, Mkhulu. I am fine.' It was a miracle – he had run into a hail of bullets, returning fire with a weapon that had to be manually cocked every time he fired. And he was unscathed.

'Thank God. Well done.'

Bheki and Thulani came running over. I could see by Bheki's face that he was bitterly disappointed to have missed the action.

'Look,' said Nkonka. He shone his torch at a dark pool. Blood. One of the poachers was wounded.

'Let's go,' Bheki responded. He flashed his torch and followed the spoor as best he could. Every now and again he would lose it and we would double back to pick it up again.

Even with the light of the moon the going was too tough, and the ground too hard to hold tracks, so reluctantly we decided to go home.

The next morning I sent Bheki out to see if he could pick up the spoor again, and he managed to follow it to a hole in the fence where the poachers had escaped. He reckoned there were three of them.

He then showed me something else – one of the footprints exactly matched the trail we had been following a few days before. It was the same gang that had killed our donated rhino. It was just as I had hoped, although I couldn't believe their audacity in coming back so soon to kill yet another animal. They were obviously after Heidi.

Thanks to Nkonka, we had won the firefight with at least one casualty on their side. Now the word was out: Thula Thula was ready for anyone coming after elephant or rhino.

CHAPTER TWO

About a week later, I was at the safari lodge when the phone rang.

It was Julie Laurenz, one of South Africa's top TV journalists, who is based with her photographer husband Christopher in Durban, South Africa's sunny holiday resort situated about a two-hour drive south of Thula. They were doing a story on rhino poaching in Africa and had heard about the one killed on our reserve, as well as Nkonka's courageous firefight. I outlined what had happened and we discussed the general gravity of the situation. Not only is the supply chain to Asia becoming significantly shorter due to Africa's burgeoning trade links with the continent, she told me, but professional gangs are now more sophisticated, darting animals from their helicopters and then killing them with automatic weapons. The horns are ferreted out of the country hidden among legal cargo – or even, it is claimed, smuggled out in diplomatic bags.

As a front-line journalist, Julie always had the latest information. She then gave me some startling news: she had credible reports that there were fewer than fifteen northern white rhinos left in the wild. And those pitifully few survivors were all situated in the Garamba National Park in the Democratic Republic of the Congo – or DRC. The park is in the far north-east of the country, near the border with Sudan, about 2,200 miles away.

I knew the northern whites had been in trouble for a while, but not even fifteen?

'Are you sure that's right?' I asked.

'Yes, maybe even fewer,' she said. 'The park's been abandoned by the authorities. Unless a miracle happens, they are on their way out.'

I thanked Julie and put the phone down. Another major life form gone, I thought, while the rest of the world barely blinked. The northern white rhino had existed for millions of years in a home range stretching across the centre of Africa, through Chad, the Central African Republic, the Congo, Sudan and Uganda. Now, but for maybe only fifteen survivors of a veritable holocaust, they were gone. I was stunned at the news.

In South Africa we have the southern white rhino, like our Heidi, which looks almost identical but is genetically different from its northern cousin. The southern white rhino also nearly became extinct fairly recently. In the 1960s, there were fewer than 500, and those were confined to the world famous Umfolozi game reserve in KwaZulu-Natal.

Then came along perhaps one of the most remarkable conservationists of all time, Dr Ian Player, an absolutely fearless man who, more than anyone else I know, has the wilderness imbued in his soul. Player was the warden in charge at the Umfolozi game reserve at the time, and with a few equally dedicated men he launched Operation Rhino to save the last remaining animals. He showed scant regard for bureaucracy in his quest to save these magnificent creatures, and ruthlessly pursued poachers. Thanks to the courage and vision of one man the gene pool survived. Today a staggering 93 per cent of the world's total number of rhinos is in South Africa.

However, modern-day poaching is now threatening to destroy all his good work.

The image of the butchered rhino on our lands, her face crumpled and her horn hacked off, would not leave me. Knowing that these massacres were getting worse all over the continent pulled some trigger in my psyche. If we could help to save the last northern whites, perhaps we could set an example and just maybe keep the gene pool alive. It would take a few generations to recover, but at least this beautiful species would survive.

I knew I had to try.

By now, in early 2006, the guest lodges at Thula were paying their own way, run by Françoise, my wife, who always pulled us through tough times. Our community projects were working well and the Earth Organization, a conservation group I founded, was expanding internationally. Today it is known as the Lawrence Anthony Foundation and continues to be driven by motivated people who place the welfare of the plant and animal kingdoms ahead of personal gain. However, it all had to be controlled and managed and this new project would take me away for extended periods.

But sometimes you have to go for it in life. If you just sit around thinking, then nothing ever happens. And with that I was seized by a moment of clarity.

I immediately got hold of my sons, Jason and Dylan, who are directors of the Earth Organization in Durban, and explained my thoughts. We agreed to meet the next day.

By the time I arrived at their office, Jason and Dylan had already got things going. They had invited a couple of people from the Earth Organization to attend the meeting: Grant Morgan, a logistics expert, and Marga Marzalek, an administrator. The response was instant; everyone was captivated by the idea of helping to save the rhinos from extinction. We all agreed that this was something we had to do; a noble, urgent and worthwhile project. We started gearing up immediately with research and fundraising and investigating the necessary logistics, authorities and permissions to capture the rhino and move them into a protected area in the DRC or, if necessary, Kenya or South Africa.

We would be going into a lawless part of Africa, where there was no administration to speak of and where civil and tribal wars were rife. The Democratic Republic of the Congo and its neighbours in the Great Lakes region had been in turmoil for three decades. Life there is short, sharp and brutal, and first-class military backup would be absolutely critical. The project would sink or swim on security.

I knew the exact man for the task: JP Fourie, an ex-Special Forces operative with a deep love for the wilderness. Now a successful businessman specializing in aviation, JP had close ties to Africa and the DRC. He knew how to look after himself when the going got tough, but, more importantly, he knew how to avoid trouble.

'JP,' I said when I called him, 'I'm looking at putting an expedition together to try and prevent the extinction of the northern white rhino in the Congo. There are only a few left and then they are gone for ever. We will be going into the far north of the country to the Garamba reserve. It's no-man's-land, security is a big issue and I need a right-hand man.'

'Sounds like fun,' he replied. 'Let's talk.'

Jason and I immediately took a plane to Pretoria, South Africa's pretty capital city in the north of the country, to meet him.

Aged thirty-six, JP was ruggedly good-looking; a well-built six foot two with green eyes and curly brown hair. The discipline of many years as a soldier was complemented by shrewd business acumen, and a warm sense of humour that he reserved for close friends. He was every inch a professional.

He reflected on what was being asked of him: to go into a violent part of the world on a rescue mission that had no guarantee of success.

'These poor bloody rhino,' he said in his strong Afrikaans accent, staring out over the bustling beer garden where we were having our meeting. 'We are not messing around here, Lawrence. This is no cowboy adventure, my friend. I have made some calls and this place is bandit territory. It's in the middle of nowhere. There are no police, no army, no laws, no nothing. It's riddled with rebels, the tribes are unruly and everybody and their brother is armed with an AK-47. I heard that conservation officials were forced to abandon Garamba park completely because of the violence. Guards, rangers, managers, admin staff – they just left, as it was too dangerous for them to stay. It's a poacher's paradise.'

'Yes, I have heard of it.'

'They are busy trying to get back in, but there was no one there for a good while.'

He continued, ticking problems off with his fingers. 'We will need a plane and helicopter for starters, and how do we refuel? There is no aviation fuel for five hundred miles. Supply lines will be long. We can't get guns in so we will have to source them when we get there. That could be arranged.'

He paused. 'It would be crazy to go in through Uganda. Coming in from that direction will take us into territory held by the Lord's Resistance Army. This is a bunch of heavily armed Ugandan guerillas hell-bent on toppling the Ugandan president, Yoweri Museveni. They operate in the north and east of Garamba park, and they are a nasty bunch. No one knows exactly where they are, and if you go anywhere near them they'll bring the plane down. They just wiped out two UN attack helicopters. That means we would have to go in the long way, from the south via Kinshasa. It's probably a nine-hour flight from Kinshasa to Garamba in a small plane, if we can find a pilot crazy enough to make the trip. And once in, we will be exposed on the ground for protracted periods. I said it before; this is wild stuff.'

'That's why we have to do it,' I replied.

JP looked at me and smiled. 'My sources tell me there is another animal conservation group either going in or who have just gone in to help the DRC authorities. I've done my homework. These guys may be well intentioned, but believe me, they will have their hands full. They don't know what they are up against. I mean, if they so much as bump into the LRA, it will be all over for them and for the rhino. Man, I don't even know if we can do it.'

He leaned back in his chair and sighed.

'We can make this work,' I said. 'We have to. If we don't do this, the rhino go extinct. It's as simple as that. This is a one-off chance to do something really important and worthwhile. It's a battle worth fighting.'

'Perhaps,' he said, and then continued, 'We will need a contingent of the very, and I mean very, best fighting men. We have to have assault rifles, H+K MP3s, Berettas, and 20mm grenade launchers at the very least, maybe even RPGs if we can get permission.'

JP looked straight at me. 'The only reason these remaining few rhinos are still alive is because they are deep in the bush and difficult to find. If we bring all those rhinos to one place, the word will get out, and who knows whom it will attract. The horns are worth a fortune.'

'What about money?' he added suddenly. 'This is going to cost a bundle.'

'I think I've got that covered. I will know for sure in a couple of days.'

'Lawrence, are you sure about this? I know you have been into some pretty rough places before for the sake of animals, but this is different.'

'I'm going in,' I replied. 'I must get this expedition together.'

'How long will this take?' he asked.

'Well, we will have to get there and set up camp,' I said. 'Then we have to find the remaining rhinos by helicopter. It's a big area, so let's give ourselves a week for that. Then we have to dart them and get them into a safe holding area, a *boma*, which we have to build near the airstrip. It will need a heavy-lift helicopter to carry them there. Once they are in the *boma* and stable, we bring in a big enough transport plane, something like a C-130, and fly them out. Let's say about three weeks to a month in total. That is if everything goes smoothly,' I said.

JP must have sat silently for a full minute and a half. I didn't say a word; he needed to make his decision without prompting. Then he slowly stood up, looked me straight in the eye and put out his hand.

'OK,' he said. 'If you're in, I am in. You find the money; I will keep you safe while you catch your rhinos.'

We embraced firmly. This was no small ask.

JP loves wildlife and adventure, both of which the DRC project promised in spades. He also had a good relationship with the DRC embassy, which was a vital bonus. Getting a true professional like him to join the expedition lifted my spirits, and I travelled back to Thula with a renewed sense of purpose.

There would be two separate components to the initiative: the expedition itself, and a backup team operating from a home base in South Africa to deal with support and logistics. Jason, my eldest son, would accompany the team on the expedition. JP would handle the security and I would handle the animal side, overseeing the darting and capture, for which we would need the very best wildlife veterinarians. Dylan, my younger son, would remain behind to manage the entire operation and to co-ordinate our efforts. Grant was to tackle logistics and source supplies and equipment. Marga would handle communications and admin.

Jason had some other good news when I returned home. BHP Billiton, the mining group, had taken an interest in what we were doing and committed substantial funds to the enterprise.

The Earth Organization's policy of 'Cooperative Ecology', CO-ECO we called it, was paying off. We believe that the blind demonizing of commerce and industry that defined the green movement in the past has to end. People have to live on the planet. Both sides must develop a better understanding of the use and value of the natural world. If an animal-rights group bluntly opposed mining, then I would expect all their members to stop using metal and glass in their own lives. Respect for biodiversity needs to be ingrained into industry and sensitive areas must remain sacrosanct, but there is plenty of room for cooperation and compromise.

My next stop was with Dr Ian Raper, the very able President of the South Africa Association for the Advancement of Science (S2A3), Africa's oldest scientific association. Ian, who lived in Pretoria, was also president of the Earth Organization's scientific advisory board, providing a strong link to South Africa's universities and scientific community for all our activities.

'This is an absolutely vital initiative,' said Ian after much discussion. 'It's much more important than I first thought, and you can count on me. I will address a letter to the DRC government advising them of our support and involvement, and I am going to speak with our own government. This is more than just a rescue; it must be a long-term joint South Africa–DRC initiative. After the rescue, I am thinking of sponsoring education bursaries where promising students will receive financial assistance in the areas around the park.'

By the time we finished talking I knew it was all really coming together.

Ten days later Jason and I were back in Pretoria to meet JP and Ian, and the four of us found ourselves at the DRC embassy in the office of the very capable Ambassador Bene M'Poko. As is the case with many African leaders, the ambassador was impeccably dressed, his European business suit contrasting severely with my khaki bush atire. There was a sincere and dignified manner about him though, which gave me some comfort as we engaged with him on the subject of the anarchy in Garamba and our proposed rescue.

'The Garamba National Park was completely abandoned recently by our management,' said the ambassador after introductions and the inevitable small talk. 'We are going back in and we already have one conservation group assisting us. But the circumstances are still highly volatile and we can use all the help we can get. The situation with the rhinos is critical and, as you know, we are facing real security concerns.'

He paused to pour tea from a very delicate and very ambassadorial tea service.

'We know of your organization and your work with wild animals in Iraq during the coalition invasion, and we have read your document with interest,' he said, tapping the proposal on the desk in front of him. 'Also, our government received a letter from the president of your scientific association,' he added, nodding at Ian.

He leaned back.

'Your offer of help is most welcome and most timely. I have discussed this with our Ministry of Environment. The initiative is approved, and everything is in place for you to visit the minister in Kinshasa for proper introductions to his department. This will be followed by an immediate fact-finding trip to Garamba, and you will proceed from there with the department. I have spoken with my counterparts in your government and it will be a joint operation between our two countries. Gentlemen, are we agreed?'

We were indeed. Everybody stood up and started shaking hands. Personally, I thought high fives would have been more appropriate, but then we were in the embassy. We had put the project together in record time, and now we had the go-ahead.

I should have realized that things in Africa are rarely that simple.

CHAPTER THREE

I arrived back at Thula Thula just in time for breakfast. My French wife Françoise, radiant as ever, was up waiting for me.

We had met coincidentally while catching a taxi in London twenty years before. Since then she had made a remarkable transition from the streets and bistros of cosmopolitan Paris to the African bush. However, it seems the longer she lives in Africa the stronger her French accent becomes.

Françoise was followed by the dogs. Bijou, her snooty little Maltese poodle, my immediate superior in the household pecking order, deigned to give me a brief acknowledgement. Bijou believed, with good reason, that as far as Françoise was concerned she was the most important life form on the game reserve, and conducted herself accordingly.

Next to greet me was Big Jeff, who did so with considerably more enthusiasm than Bijou. I think Jeff is a cross between a Golden Labrador and a seal, or at least he looks and acts like it. We rescued him from abusive owners and he has repaid us with unconditional faithfulness and loyalty, dispensed primarily from his favourite position lazing near the swimming pool. I was thinking of entering him into the world sleeping dog championships but that would be unfair on other contestants.

And then there was Gypsy, a little black rescue dog we picked up from the Society for the Prevention of Cruelty to Animals. Gypsy was a wonderful mutt, a 'pavement special' as we say,

who had a heart as big as Africa. She slept on our bed and spent
the night purposely angling to get her butt right in my face as a
wake-up present.

As motley a bunch as they were, we loved them all. I have
my two sons from a previous marriage, Jason and Dylan, but
Françoise never had children, and Bijou, Jeff and Gypsy were
her South African family. She treated us all equally, or almost
equally. Whenever I went to the fridge to see what was for
dinner, I was never quite sure which food was ours or which
was the dogs'. Indeed, there were times I just chose the canine
cuisine. Françoise is a superb French chef – the best in the world,
as far as I'm concerned – so no one is complaining.

Max, my magnificent Staffordshire bull terrier who had died
a few years before, was buried close to our cottage. I thought of
him often, of his courage and of the wonderful bush adventures
that we had together. If alive, Max would have been with me
at last week's firefight with poachers, and given half a chance
would have latched on to one of the killers' legs. And Staffies
don't let go.

After an exquisite French breakfast (I have got used to croque-
monsieur and croissants) I fell dead asleep. I would again be on
duty that night and patrols wouldn't stop until we caught the
poachers or they fled the area.

It had been a hectic few weeks, from firefights with poachers
to putting together a plan to save the Congo rhino, and so when
I awoke I decided to take an afternoon off and be alone in the
bush during daylight for a change. I drove into Thula Thula's
remotest section and then abandoned the Land Rover and hiked
down through the savannah to my favourite spot on the banks
of the Nseleni River.

Leaving the security of a vehicle, alone and unarmed, puts
everything into a new perspective in the bush. You're suddenly
completely isolated from humanity and consumed by the living

wilderness. It is a total immersion into a primordial world. Some are alarmed by it, others revel in it. That day it was just what I needed.

The ancient river was moving slowly on its course, pooling deeply here and there, its slippery, muddy banks reaching out of the tangled undergrowth down into the dark silent waters.

A hardcore rule in Africa is to treat any stretch of water as home to Nile crocodiles, so I found a comfortable rock high up the bank overlooking some deep pools, sat down and breathed in the surroundings. It was a gloriously hot African day under an azure sky puffed with the whitest nimbus clouds. Not enough cloud for rain, but just enough to take the edge off the heat. For a second I thought about how long it had been since we'd had a good thunderstorm, followed by a real soaking, but the day was perfect and I refused to worry right now.

You have to sit still at a river until the inhabitants decide your presence is benign. Once you get the nod of approval, everything erupts vibrantly back to life.

Frogs always take the lead. Being right at the bottom of the food chain has its challenges, especially when singing out to attract a mate alerts predators to your hiding place, so they have evolved a very clever defence. Gathered into the reed beds, their loud calls and descants mysteriously echo and reverberate, disguising their exact position from the host of birds, lizards and catfish who would eat every last one if they could find them. It is only the females that can penetrate the canorous deception.

Next out were petite metallic-blue malachite kingfishers, which hovered and zipped in and out of the pools, rippling the water as they dived and sometimes surfaced with a prize tadpole or, if they were lucky, a minuscule bream. Dragonflies decorated in the brightest oranges, blues, greens and deepest blacks flitted on transparent wings.

As always, a hammerkop was stalking the shallows, its

sharp inquisitive eyes glittering hard behind a pitiless beak. This legendary crested brown waterbird builds large clay-and-stick tree nests that can bear a man's weight. A rather macabre Zulu prophecy says that if a hammerkop lands on your roof during a thunderstorm there will soon be a death in the family.

A tiny swirl of water gave away the first croc. He had perceived my arrival and silently submerged his giant reptilian body. I could just see it underwater, a huge shadow beneath the surface slowly moving closer in case I was available for lunch. A chill went through my body. No matter how many I see, crocodiles always evoke a grotesque fascination in me. But so many are dying in Africa as man takes over their habitat that they, too, could soon be on the endangered species list. We protect them at Thula Thula like every other creature. Eventually he decided I was out of range, but patiently hung around in the reed beds on the off chance I might do something stupid like go to the water's edge. It would be the last thing I did.

Two terrapins, *ufudu* as the Zulus call them, waddled into the pool and fiddled around in the shallows looking for worms and other turtle treats. Nothing goes near them, not even a crocodile, for they are basically aqua-skunks, squirting a foul-smelling urine at their enemies that not even carbolic soap can easily remove.

The busy riverine life fascinated me for a couple of hours, easing the stresses of the past few days. Total immersion in the wilderness is the purest and most natural of all therapies, and best of all, you don't have to do anything except be there. The sights and sounds are remedies for the soul, while the scents of the African bush are nature's original aromatherapy.

Then some of the big boys of the Bushveld arrived. A herd of huge, heaving, hot and dusty Cape buffalo appeared far more stealthily than I would have liked. They took ownership of the biggest pool, striding into the water belly-deep to slake their thirst, disdainful of the presence of the crocodile. I quickly looked around and made a mental note of the quickest tree to climb if they came any closer, but they were just getting on with their lives and not interested in me at all.

And sometimes you get really, really lucky. In a side eddy I picked out movement and sat forward in concentration, hardly recognizing the shape, not daring to believe. *Voilà.* It was a submerged python, his long body lying slack and motionless below the reeds with just the tip of his nose showing. He could have been there for days already, immobile, in a demonstration of patience unparalleled in nature, waiting for the right prey and the exact moment. Then he would strike, fast and deadly, instantly wrapping fifteen feet of writhing muscle around his chosen victim and crushing the life out of it in minutes. Depending on the size of his kill, he would not eat again for several weeks, if not months.

Times like this made me realize how vital our conservation programmes among the local community were. Without these educational projects, this glorious world unravelling in front of me could be lost in a few short generations. It still might be.

The lazy afternoon was coming to an end when suddenly something didn't feel right. I had a prickly skin sensation that I was being watched. I have long since given up questioning my gut feelings, nature's inbuilt alarm system, so I immediately sat up and looked around, scrutinizing every tree, bush and shrub for something unusual. Nothing.

Not satisfied, I stood and half turned to look behind me. I instinctively froze dead still. Facing me, less than twenty yards away, were two massive, mud-covered buffalo bulls, dagga boys they are called, arguably the most dangerous animals in Africa – and they were giving me their full attention. I quickly broke eye contact and looked away, forcing myself to remain motionless, frantically calculating my options.

I didn't have any. They were standing too close to my designated escape tree, so that was out of the question. On the other side, the thickly tangled river undergrowth prevented me from making a run for it. My only remaining escape route was down the slippery riverbank, where the crocodile was still waiting. Then, just to hammer home my unenviable predicament, if I somehow made it past the croc, I would stumble into the rest of the buffalo herd.

I did the only thing I could. I turned very, very slowly and walked away from them down onto the riverbank as far as I could safely go, and sat on my haunches, listening for the dreadful sound of a charge from behind, while keeping an eye on the water for the croc.

Nothing happened. They weren't being aggressive at all, just a bit curious as to what I was doing in their space. As soon as I paid them respect, they ambled off to follow the rest of the herd. With my heart thumping loudly, I reminded myself never to leave my rifle behind again. Not to shoot to kill, but a warning shot will often scare off a threatening creature and give you enough room to escape. Yet a firearm is such an alien contraption in these surroundings that I hated carrying one.

The sun was low when I reluctantly took leave of the river and started the trek back to the Land Rover.

In Zululand, there is no gentle easing of day into night, as in the higher latitudes. It's just a brief pause of dusk, a blazing sunset to arrest your soul and then all of a sudden you are in the dark. As the last sunrays quickly faded to salmon pink, I gently came back to the real world and reached forward to key the Land Rover's ignition.

Suddenly I heard a crack like a rifle shot and turned to see the top of a huge acacia robusta tree rocking back and forth in its death throes. It then slowly toppled and crashed down in a roar of timber and leaves.

Elephants. No other animal in the world can do that. No other land creature is that powerful, not by far. The herd was nearby.

I stretched my hand out of the window to feel the air. A gentle breeze coming in from the south-west placed me securely downwind, away from long prying noses. I got out of the vehicle, consciously slowed myself down to elephant mode, and waited. Five long minutes later, I was rewarded when Nana, the glorious matriarch, slowly eased her towering bulk out of the copse of trees, lifted her trunk and tested the air.

I caught my breath, thrilling again at the sight of this magnificent creature who had taught me so much about her kind.

But even in the gathering gloom I could see all was not right. Leaving the herd to feast on the fallen tree, she appeared to be walking out of the thicket at an angle, favouring her right side.

As I watched, the herd's second-in-command, Frankie, emerged behind them and stood next to Nana. She turned towards her, their huge heads barely a foot apart. They stood like that for ages, unmoving, as if meditating. Then Frankie turned slowly, as though she was just letting the momentum of her five-ton weight pull her, and moved into the lead position. Nana followed, the rest of the herd slowly gathering in behind them.

I had never seen that before. Nana was the matriarch, she always led the herd. She was always very visibly at the front. She dictated every move they made.

Had there been a coup d'état? Or had Frankie, by some form of arcane pachyderm ritual, been appointed the new leader?

That seemed highly unlikely. Nana was a respected and admired matriarch and her decisions – always wise and benevolent – were law. Frankie may be the most volatile and quick-tempered in the group, but she never questioned Nana's authority.

I watched as they made their way across the clearing, their colossal shoulders lifting and falling until they were swallowed up by the jagged outlines of the evening bush. It may have been my imagination playing tricks in the dark, but it seemed as if ET, one of the younger cows, was nudging Nana, helping her in the right direction. That too was unprecedented. Nana never needed any form of assistance. Indeed, she was the one who always provided it. In fact, it was Nana who had settled ET when we got her as a traumatized teenager. She had also been earmarked for a legalized kill until we managed to get the hunter's licence revoked. We were just in time to save her life.

Even so, she was in bad shape when we got her. Left alone on a 'Big Five' game reserve as an adolescent, ET had shrieked herself hoarse. She was now almost mute, her vocal chords destroyed, her trumpeting no more than a strange honking sound. We named her Enfant Terrible ('bad baby' in French), as she had regularly charged me when she first arrived at Thula Thula; such was her hatred of humans. Amazingly, Nana had intervened, stopping her with the broadside of her body or with gentle taps of her trunk on ET's forehead until the youngster learned that I was not going to harm her. The irony that she was now helping Nana was not lost on me.

Still, I was extremely worried. What was going on? What had happened to Nana? Was she injured, or ill? The thought of anything going wrong with her, my friend and inspiration for the past decade, was simply too awful to contemplate.

My cellphone was on silent but I could feel it vibrating in my pocket. I took it out and looked at the number. It was a text message from Françoise telling me dinner was nearly ready.

There was no more to be done that night, so I started the Landy and drove off down the bush track, deep in thought. I had decided not to have further contact with the elephants now that they had settled so naturally into the reserve. This was working well with the other elephants, but with Nana the feeling was not mutual. She still tried to come to me whenever she sensed my Land Rover was nearby and I always drove off with a heavy heart. As much as I wanted to be with her, to me it was an iron law of nature that wild animals are meant to be just that: wild. I had only decided to work with them because they had been so disturbed when they first arrived at Thula Thula. If I hadn't done something, the Parks authorities would have shot them. In those days they continuously charged us and smashed through electric fences, shuddering through the pain of 8,000 volts as they snapped the live wires like cotton thread. Throwing caution to the wind, my young ranger, David Bozas, and I had gone to live near them in the bush until I gradually earned the trust of Nana. I finally got her to believe that Thula Thula, with its lush grasses and perennial water supply, was her new home. That she and her family were safe here. They were now one of the finest herds in Zululand.

But something had gone worryingly wrong. Reluctantly, I decided I might have to enter their lives once again.

CHAPTER FOUR

I was up at first light and after downing a steaming mug of strong coffee, I drove deep into the bush to find the herd's tracks.

I'd spent a restless night thinking about Nana, and even a hard three-hour patrol that ended just before midnight was not enough to put me to sleep. The fact that I had just lost four rhinos, one poached and three about to be removed by the Parks authorities, didn't help my frame of mind either.

But first things first – right now I urgently needed to find out what was going on with the herd. I picked them out in the early sunrise moving slowly across open savannah. It was a sight going back to time immemorial – a herd of elephants at dawn in African grassland – and no doubt a common one for our great-grandfathers who strode this continent barely a century ago. It may not be a sight that our grandchildren will be guaranteed to see.

The rising sun was now a gentle scarlet on the horizon and the bush was coming to life all around me. I stopped, got out of the Land Rover and sucked in the dewy air, the crisp tang of an early wilderness morning instantly lifting my spirits. Moving as stealthily as possible, I walked to an umbrella thorn tree about twenty minutes away and, with the breeze wafting gently downwind in my favour, crouched to watch the herd go past.

Pulling out a powerful set of binoculars from my bush jacket,

I zoomed in on Nana. She seemed fine and very much in charge. You could tell by her regal body language that she was the matriarch. Just as human natural leaders can virtually alter the gravity in a room by their mere presence, her authority was pervasive. When she curled her trunk in the air and changed direction the others immediately followed, including Frankie, who was just behind her. I smiled and gave a silent cheer. Last night was just my imagination. She had not needed any help at all.

She then turned, facing me almost head-on, and I zeroed in with the binoculars on her face. Suddenly something jarred. Her expression seemed oddly vacant, as if she wasn't fully registering what was happening. My relief evaporated like smoke. Something definitely was wrong.

Then it struck me. It wasn't an odd expression – it was her right eye. It was marginally closed and seemed to be out of kilter. It made her look slightly confused, although paradoxically she was stepping out with supreme purpose. I kept the binoculars steady as she stopped to pluck a thick chunk of grass.

My stomach sank. The pupil was milky, which meant only one thing. She had a cataract and was going blind.

So that was it. That was why she had needed to be helped the night before. In the dark she was completely blind on one side, so Frankie had taken the lead. But now in daylight she could cope with one eye, so she resumed control. In effect the herd now had two matriarchs; one in the day, the other at night. It was almost like shift work.

I shook my head in wonder at these magnificent creatures. All this had been done without fuss or aggression. There had been no power play between the two senior females. They just accepted reality. Both Nana and Frankie were simply doing what was best for their family. Nana couldn't function at 100 per cent capacity in the dark, so Frankie took charge. She was fine during the day, so Frankie stood down.

The fact that I could see the cataract from a distance, albeit with binoculars, indicated it was quite advanced. That's the problem with so many ailments in the bush – once you find out about them, they're usually getting serious. That's just the way it is. You can't simply walk up to a herd of wild elephants and do an eye inspection on their leader, especially when she stands five feet above you. I had to act fast and get some expert medical advice.

Nana halted and flicked up the tip of her trunk, twitching it like a periscope. A gust had swirled and she had smelled something. I picked up a tuft of dry grass and tossed it into the air, watching it flutter down at an angle. Yes, the breeze had shifted slightly and I was no longer directly downwind. Had she smelled me?

Her demeanour stiffened for a moment, then relaxed and she swivelled towards me. I swear I could see her smiling, which could have been my mind playing tricks, but what certainly wasn't my imagination was that she was now suddenly coming to me. And fast. The Land Rover was a good distance away and I needed to hurry to get to it before she arrived.

As I drove off I could see Nana stop, puzzled at my strange behaviour. You could read the expression creased on her huge brow: why was I running away? Why wouldn't I wait for her any more?

I felt absolutely wretched, as if I was betraying a friend. She was probably wondering what she had done wrong. Keeping my distance was not going to be easy, either for her or me.

Back at home I phoned Cobus Raath, the elephant expert who had brought the herd down in a massive semi-trailered truck from their original home in Mpumalanga in the north-east to Thula Thula. It seemed such a long time ago and so much had happened since then. Nana's original herd members may physically be the same ones that arrived at Thula Thula that fateful day, but mentally they could not be more different from the confused, aggressive creatures that they had been.

'*Ja*, Lawrence, what's happening, man?' It was good to hear his rough Afrikaans accent, so honed by the rugged African veldt that its European origins were barely noticeable.

Then, this being Cobus, the next question he asked was about the elephants. That was the opening I needed.

'Well, there may be a problem with the matriarch,' I replied. 'She's got a cataract in one eye and seems almost blind. Can you help?'

'How bad is it?'

'I don't know. It's already gone milky, so it's probably quite advanced. I'm just hoping it's not as bad as it looks.'

Cobus mulled that over for a moment, then said, 'I've got some veterinary students with me right now doing practical work. Some real live bush stuff on an elephant will be excellent experience for them. Lucky for you, hey? I'll make plans and bring them over to Thula Thula as soon as I can arrange it.'

'A funny thing has happened, Cobus. She's only blind at night, so the second female takes over. During the day when she's OK, she's in charge again.'

Cobus gave a wry chuckle. 'You know, Lawrence, after all these years I thought I'd stopped being surprised by these wonderful animals. But I still am.'

The almost physical weight on my shoulders eased. With Cobus's help we couldn't go wrong.

'When can you come over? I think we have to move fast before it gets any worse.'

'Give me a week to get everything ready. But, Lawrence, if it's as advanced as you think, this could be bad. We can't operate in the bush as there's too much danger of infection, which could be fatal. A cataract won't kill her, but infection might. Obviously, we can't bring her into a surgery. We'll just have to put some powerful antibiotic ointment on. So don't get your hopes up too high. I'll do what I can, but we can't work miracles.'

I put the phone down. Nana would be fine – we would give her the best treatment in the world.

I kept repeating that to myself.

CHAPTER FIVE

Cobus and his veterinary students arrived as planned. There were five of them, three men and two women looking forward to some practical experience in the bush. Vusi and I met them at the gate and we drove out to a ranger I had posted to keep a lookout over the herd.

When we arrived, the ranger shook his head and spread his hands. 'They're gone, Mkhulu,' he said.

'What do you mean, gone?'

'They were here, standing just by the trees.' He pointed about fifty yards away. 'Then ten minutes ago they just ran off in a big hurry.'

'Where did they go?'

He pointed to a lengthy ravine that started about 200 yards away and led to one of the most densely bushed parts of the reserve. It was full of tangled thickets of spiky sickle bush and big-thorned acacias, making it almost impenetrable unless you had an inch-thick hide. Like an elephant.

But still, that was extremely unusual. The herd seldom ventured into the ravine as it was such hard going, even for them. Cobus was listening and echoed my thoughts. 'They know we're coming. They know something is up.'

I nodded. An elephant's incredible intuition was something I didn't query any more. In the past they arrived at the gate with such punctuality to greet me when I returned from away trips that my flight schedule could have been scrawled in some bush diary. It was uncanny and inexplicable, but I have long discarded the belief that human science has answers for the goings-on in the plant and animal kingdoms.

Intuition or insight, though uncommon in humans, is readily observable in nature. 'Anecdotal' is the overused word employed too quickly by critics to wish away natural happenings not yet understood by science. Anecdotal evidence can also mean direct personal experience that science hasn't yet been able to explain. Clive Walker, South Africa's pre-eminent game ranger, states in his handbook *Mammals for Game Rangers* that it appears elephants are telepathic. The legendary Dr Ian Player is adamant that an animal's arsenal of survival skills also includes a form of sixth, or, as he says, even a seventh sense that we don't yet understand. Just speak to any good Zulu tracker and he will regale you with instances of strange animal behaviour that would completely flummox science. This may be scoffed at in the West, but in Africa the spiritual world is very much alive.

'Let's go and find them.'

'It's going to be a long day,' Cobus sighed.

He was right. We followed as best we could in the two 4x4 vehicles and then tried to make our way on foot to get closer. The bush was just too thick; every path had to be carefully negotiated, squeezing through gaps in the thorns that sprang back like daggers once one person passed through. Whenever we got anywhere near them, downwind or not, the herd would move off with alacrity. They were clearly on the run, moving as fast as they could, not wasting any time browsing or grazing. Cobus was right; they knew that we were after them for some specific reason and they weren't going to make it easy for us.

This reminded me of one awful occasion years ago when they broke out of Thula Thula in an attempt to return to their original home in Mpumalanga. We chased them for close to

forty-eight hours until they broke into the Umfolozi game reserve thirty miles north. Then they split into two groups, Nana
leading one and Frankie the other, meeting up seven miles later
with an accuracy that would rival any GPS.

Eventually, at 3 p.m. Cobus said we would have to consider
calling it a day. 'If we don't dart her soon, it's going to be dark
by the time we revive her. Let's try again tomorrow. Maybe
they'll come out of the ravine.'

You could tell by the tone of his voice he considered that
unlikely.

Covered in sweat, scratches and insect bites, we returned to
our vehicles. I got into my Landy and started it. In the distance,
I could see Nana stop. She had heard the engine and recognized
it as my truck. She turned, hesitated and then came trustingly
towards me, while the rest of the worried herd stayed behind,
watching.

Cobus got out the dart gun. He instantly assessed the situation. 'She's heard you and is coming to you. Maybe we can use
this to our advantage. It could be the only chance we've got.'

He crouched down, taking aim as Nana came into the open. I
was holding my breath as the dart gun fired with a harsh crack.

Nana reacted immediately to the alien sound and the sting
in her rump. She swung her huge body wildly, speeding off in
a crashing run, paying no heed to the heavy undergrowth. The
herd followed after her blindly.

Then, as if in slow motion, she slowed and started sinking to
the ground. Through the trees I saw the fluffy red feathers of the
dart jutting from her rump as she came down gently onto her
knees with as much dignity as a five-ton hunk of flesh, bone and
extraordinary muscle can muster. Fortunately, she fell cleanly.
With her weight, a bad tumble could rip tendons and ligaments
like paper.

The rest of the herd reacted immediately as Nana fell and

were soon standing over her, stressed as hell, ears flared, heads reared, searching the bush for answers as to why their matriarch was down. Nana's new baby, Shaka, was particularly affected, running back and forth from one adult to the other, desperately seeking reassurance that everything was all right. My heart went out to her.

We urgently needed to reach Nana and so started making as much noise as we could to drive the rest of the herd away, shouting and screaming and hitting the side of the vehicles like frenzied drummers at a rock concert. It worked, and they reluctantly moved off.

'Let's go, go, go,' said Cobus, quickly climbing out of the passenger seat of my Landy, grabbing his medical equipment and setting the pace on foot, with Vusi and me just behind him, and the excited students bringing up the rear.

We were intensely aware that we had a herd of angry and confused elephants almost on top of us so we had to make sure we had specific escape routes. It was absolutely vital that we could get to the vehicles if we had to and, once in them, could speed off without crashing into trees or anthills.

As we arrived at Nana's huge prostrate body, Vusi moved off a few paces and placed himself on duty to watch the herd, which stood barely fifty yards away.

'Dammit,' said Cobus, down on his hands and knees, 'I can't get to the eye. We have to turn her over.'

Strangely, a five-ton elephant can be quite easily rolled over by just a few people if you know how. The way you do it is by crossing the animal's legs, then simultaneously lifting both the front and back by the legs underneath. Cobus crossed her legs and positioned everybody correctly. We lifted in unison on his call until the huge body rolled over with a thump. The dust hadn't settled and Cobus was already doing the inspection. One of the students placed a twig in the trunk tip to keep Nana's airways open and then started spraying water on her ears and prostrate body to keep her cool.

'We're going to have to work fast,' said Cobus, glancing continuously in the direction of the troubled herd. 'I'm not happy about this.'

He lifted Nana's eyelid for a closer examination of the pupil. Close up, it looked even worse than I feared, the eye clouded over in a murky grey-white film.

'It's bad,' said Cobus, 'but, as I said, we can't operate in the bush. All I can do is treat it with a powerful salve that may or may not cure it.'

Suddenly Vusi screamed as the entire herd, led by Frankie, came thundering at us, ears flapping like a yacht's sails, trumpeting in a cacophony of pure rage.

Cobus jumped up. '*Manne – hulle kom!* They're coming!'

He sped past me at a rate of knots, snatched a rifle from the guard and, while still running, expertly fired several shots into the ground. Gunfire was the last resort, the worst-case scenario, but we had no alternative.

The elephants stopped and turned in disarray at the fearful sound, then crashed back into the bush. Cobus continued running up to the Land Rover, put the rifle down and quickly rummaged through the medical bag until he found the medication he was looking for.

'OK, we've got to do this quickly. This is our last chance.'

We ran back to Nana, mindful that the extremely agitated and aggressive animals were now barely thirty yards away. Cobus squeezed the medicine liberally into her eye and carefully massaged it in while I stood guard with the .303. When the job was done, he grabbed the syringe with the reversal injection, the antidote used to revive her, and plunged it into her rump.

'We've got about ten seconds. Let's move out – fast.'

I knew how incredibly quickly the antidote worked and so

joined the rapid exodus to the vehicles standing about eighty feet away. Doors had barely slammed shut as Nana got groggily to her feet and stood up on shaky legs. A few seconds later, the herd emerged from the trees and surrounded her, relieved she was upright. Shaka, her little baby, ran up and went straight under her stomach. Disoriented, Nana followed the herd into the thicket.

I felt terrible. The day could not have gone worse. I hate firing guns near any animal, even if it is to scare them away. The relationship I had built with the herd could now be in serious jeopardy. Even worse, Nana had specifically come to me when she heard my Land Rover engine and had been repaid with a dart in her rump. The trust had been broken. Perhaps irrevocably.

'Please let me know how it goes,' said Cobus as they packed up and got ready to leave. 'I have a soft spot for these elephants of yours.'

At least we had treated her eye. If that worked, it would have been worth it. But it would take time to discover if that was so.

I left them to settle down for a couple of days as we continued preparations for meeting government officials in Kinshasa, but I wanted to check on Nana's progress the day before we left.

I radioed Vusi to find out where the elephants were. About a mile past the lodge was the reply. That was good news. They would be out in the open near the river, in an area where there were lush riverine grasses. Nearby was a copse of shaded woodland, so after a morning's feast they could escape the heat of the day.

I drove up to them, stopping about a hundred yards away to see how they would react. I had no doubt that they would be pretty upset with me after the darting debacle, but I wasn't prepared for the response.

It was Frankie who first picked up my presence, and immediately drew herself up to her full height and swivelled towards the Landy, ears fully extended. The herd responded to her angry warning signs and started milling around, as edgy as if they were standing on coals, fizzing with nervous energy.

Then suddenly they calmed. It was as though some soothing hand had been placed on them, radiating tranquillity. You could feel it in the air, palpable as a breeze, yet everything was still.

I soon saw why. It was Nana. She had been at the back, furthest from me and the last to pick up my scent. She pushed her way through the herd and walked purposefully towards the Landy. I held my breath, heart pounding. I had the engine running and in gear with my foot on the clutch, ready to rev off if I had to.

She came right up to me, and although I was virtually shivering with apprehension, something made me roll down the window. She put her trunk through the gap, sniffing me and glowing with that almost shaman-like sense of contentment and peace. I could romanticize the moment and say she was forgiving me, but that wouldn't strictly be true. She would not have much recollection of the gunshots two days ago, as she had been comatose from the tranquillizer dart. Instead she was just saying, 'Hello, I've missed you.' I gently eased my foot off the clutch and switched off the engine.

'Hello, my baby. I've missed you, too. I'm really sorry about the other day. We were just trying to fix your eye.'

Now that she was close, I could properly examine her pupil. Everything had been done in such haste when we had tried to cure it. Unfortunately, it still looked bad, the milky film of the cataract already appearing to harden into a glaze. It seemed too far gone and I doubted that the treatment alone could reverse the damage. We had cleaned it up and ensured that it wouldn't get infected, but I feared that she would eventually go blind in one eye. There was nothing more we could do.

After about ten minutes of standing amiably next to the vehicle, she left. The rest of the herd moved off with her. The change was incredible. There was no animosity whatsoever. The electric charge of aggression in the atmosphere had completely evaporated. The herd had seen their revered matriarch go up and lay her trunk on the person in the vehicle whom they believed had been troubling her, and so now all was forgiven. Even Frankie seemed happy as she followed Nana into the bush. There was no doubt the incident was over, another indication of Nana's incredible leadership and generosity of spirit.

I breathed out, stunned at how relieved I felt. If the herd had rejected me, it would have been impossible to start again. The elephants were now truly wild, with only Nana still paying attention to me.

CHAPTER SIX

With Nana's eye problems resolved, if not cured, my attention could again focus on the DRC rhinos.

We had our visas, but flights were full, and JP, Jason and I were only able to get seats on a discount African airline that we soon discovered was not a serious subscriber to the International Air Transport Association's guidelines on safety – to put it politely.

After a chaotic check-in at Joburg airport, we cleared customs and found ourselves in the middle of an agitated bunch of pushing and shoving passengers waiting to board.

'OK,' said JP, taking charge and barging forward to the front of the crowd. 'Follow me. When they open the doors we move fast.'

I was still trying to work out what was going on when suddenly the doors opened and there was a stampede for the Boeing 727. I soon discovered why. Boarding cards meant absolutely nothing. It was first come first served for seats. They had let far too many people on the plane and only those who grabbed seats, shouted loudest and argued hardest – us included – stayed on board. The rest were eventually escorted off the flight. They were actually pulling people from the toilets and pushing them out the door so we could take off.

Despite the confusion, I settled back in my seat, pleased that at last we were on our way to Kinshasa.

We landed en route at Lubumbashi on the DRC–Zambia border, where a batch of passengers disembarked. While waiting for others to board, I walked up to the cabin and asked the pilot if we could get out of the plane to stretch our legs. 'No problem,' he said, glancing at us over his shoulder from the cockpit.

Outside we found another group of passengers lighting up cigarettes right next to the plane while it was being refuelled. A moment later, our pilot came down the steps, pulled out a cigarette and lit up as well. Jason had a camera and started taking photos. Suddenly two armed soldiers ran up, abruptly instructing him that no photos could be taken in the DRC. 'Big security risk,' one wearing wraparound sunglasses warned.

The incongruity was rich; lighting up next to a refuelling truck brimming with high-octane aviation gas was just fine, but taking photos wasn't.

Then another passenger came down the steps and asked why everyone was smoking outside. They told him they had the go-ahead to have a cigarette on the runway. And, in any event, the pilot was there himself, puffing away.

'No, no,' he replied, 'what you must do is pay the air hostess ten dollars and then you can smoke in your seat.'

'But it's a non-smoking flight,' someone said.

We all laughed. This to me has always been the essential difference between Africa and the rest of the world. In Europe, bureaucrats publish endless lists of edicts that tell you not only what you can't do, but also what you can. I sometimes feel I'm in a straitjacket in some of those countries. In Africa, rules and laws are more of a rough guideline to life, especially if you have a couple of dollars in your pocket to share around.

Thankfully the plane managed to take off without the refuelling truck blowing up, and a couple of hours later we were hovering above Kinshasa with the Congo River dominating the landscape beneath us. It moved like a colossal swollen python, the afternoon sun shimmering off its watery scales in shades of gold and brown, dwarfing everything around it. To say the river is massive doesn't do it justice. The Congo is the deepest river in the world and it flows virtually across Africa, crossing the equator twice on its 3,000-mile journey to the sea. At some points this absolutely amazing river is over a hundred miles wide. Only the Amazon pumps more water into the ocean.

A few minutes later we touched down in Kinshasa, scene of Mohammad Ali's epic 'Rumble in the Jungle', the heavyweight championship fight against George Foreman in 1974.

Kinshasa airport is an experience unto itself. There, you have two choices. You can either revel in the adventure or be totally overwhelmed. First you have to make sure you have your obligatory yellow fever card available before you even enter the building. If you forget it, or if it's out of date, it's the initial target for a bribe. Sometimes you hand it in and they come back later and say you didn't. Then you have to pay to get it back.

Inside the very basic building, omnipresent soldiers with wraparound sunglasses and AK-47s slouch around keeping a lazy eye on proceedings. Sweating officials who have long since given up trying to restore order move slowly back and forth among the crowd in the midday heat as if they are walking through treacle. Dabbing their sweating foreheads with damp handkerchiefs, they do little more than scan for bribable passengers. You get nothing unless you pay, not even advice. But they are not big sums of money, so it's always a good idea to get some local currency and keep small denomination notes on you.

As usual the baggage carousel wasn't working, and so passengers simply jumped through a hole in the wall and collected their own luggage. If they could find it, that is. The stationary forlorn queue in front of the lost baggage counter is not somewhere you want to end up, so carry-on luggage that you can hold tight throughout the journey is vital.

Amiable hustlers thronged around us, all pitching different lines: 'Taxi good taxi,' 'I take baggage,' 'Visa, you want visa?'

'Where you stay good hotel cheap for you,' 'You want Coca-Cola, beer?' I swear if you just stood there for half a day you would be approached a thousand times. The DRC's Minister of Environment had sent us a vehicle and, thankfully, the driver somehow located us using a well-honed sixth sense, because it was impossible to find anyone by normal means in that hot, sweaty confusion. We finally left the building only to be confronted outside by hordes of hustling kids grabbing at our suitcases and fighting one another off.

They carried our bags to the parking lot, where their patch of authority ended, and we were met by another horde of juvenile porters who took over. Although there was a gate into the airport parking lot, there was no fence or wall on either side of it. The gate was just a closed portal standing completely on its own. Yet all the kids dutifully remained waiting outside, restrained by a man carrying a long stick with which he dispensed blows to anyone trying to get in. Nobody attempted to go around the gate, which they could do quite easily. It was the weirdest thing.

However, once we passed through it was a free-for-all, and the youngsters swarmed over us to grab our bags – to carry, not to steal. If someone got hold of your case, it gave them instant porter rights and all the others backed off. There was little begging. In fact they would be insulted if they were referred to as beggars. These kids considered themselves self-employed and were among the most aggressive entrepreneurs I've come across.

We finally emerged from the jostling crowds with our child porters and found the ministry car. We tipped the children and eased out of the airport onto what had once been a stately colonial boulevard, but was now an anarchic snarl of vehicles hooting and jostling one another. With a roar our driver revved his car into the shambolic mass.

Welcome to crazy, cacophonous, controversial Kinshasa. I love the place.

CHAPTER SEVEN

The quickest way to make the transcendental leap into chaotic Central Africa is to drive through the centre of Kinshasa.

The city's traffic is a wild free-for-all with no rules or laws, and I mean none, in any shape or form. Traffic signs or lights, road markings, licences or any other semblance of street discipline are non-existent or completely ignored. The sounds of revving overheated engines, the gagging belch of exhaust smoke and the acrid smell of gasoline fumes shimmering in the tropical sun assail the senses like a runaway truck. The confusion is total and overwhelming.

Animated drivers weave decrepit vehicles carelessly in and out of oncoming traffic, giving way – sometimes – to gesticulating drivers from the opposite direction doing the same. Passengers hang kamikaze-style on to the outside of taxis and buses, jumping on and off at will, usually while the vehicle is still moving. Colourfully dressed pedestrians dissolve in and out of the seething mayhem, seemingly oblivious to the dangers. Yet somehow, some way, it all works without angst or aggression. There is actually some strange order, and suddenly you realize that you are not about to be crushed by some ancient chariot, or at least probably not. And at that point you have made the leap. This is flamboyant, carefree Kinshasa.

We eventually made it to the Grand Hotel, a twenty-two-floor white box-shaped building near the mighty Congo River.

'Grand' was more the aspiration than the reality. And the price was eye-watering, hundreds of dollars a night, which is far more than the annual wage for most Congolese. But you have no choice except to wince at the bill and pay up, as there are few decent hotels in this wonderfully anarchic city.

The Ministry of Environment offices were only about half a mile away, so after checking in we decided to walk to our appointment with the minister. The offices are in the better part of town and streets are wide without much traffic, unlike the city centre. We soon realized why: armed soldiers standing in groups outside the stately residences of important political brass did not encourage visitors to the area.

'Don't talk to them and never take photos, ever, in this area,' warned JP. 'They will absolutely lock you up. You can do pretty much anything in this city. But cameras and photos are a big no-no.'

The façade of the 1960s-style office block housing the ministry was much like the rest of the city; not much maintenance work or upgrading had been done for decades. The plaque outside was just a hand-painted sign with the DRC flag, informing you in French that this was a government building. The guards carrying AK-47s were also a giveaway that this was something official. They casually body-searched us and asked for cigarettes before one ambled off to call someone.

An efficient-looking woman wearing an immaculate black-and-white African-print kaftan appeared and greeted us. Quite unusually for Kinshasa, where French is the lingua franca, she spoke good English.

'Welcome,' she said, shaking hands with each of us in turn. 'My name is Brigit. Please follow me. The minister is expecting you.' I liked her immediately.

She took the lead and we were escorted down a private passage into the minister's office. It was a plush room with leather-upholstered furniture and a large desk. Above it was the ubiquitous portrait of President Joseph Kabila. Pictures of animals and maps of various game reserves adorned the walls.

A few minutes later the DRC's Minister of the Environment, Nature Conservation, Water and Forests, Anselme Enerunga, smartly dressed in a beige suit and red tie, came in and greeted us.

'Welcome to DRC. We have been expecting you,' he said as Brigit ushered us to the comfortable chairs. 'We have been fully briefed by our ambassador in South Africa, Bene M'Poko, about this generous offer of support to our government, and we are grateful for your assistance. As you know, the situation in Garamba park is poor. The park was completely abandoned until recently, and we face difficult challenges, especially with the rhino.'

We immediately got down to business, outlining the project, going over the details, asking and answering questions, and familiarizing the minister with both strategy and purpose.

First we would do a reconnaissance trip, where we would work closely with his officials on the ground to assess the situation, study security issues and gain local knowledge. Then we would do an aerial census, during which the rhinos would be darted and tagged with transmitters. The rescue itself would be a carefully planned and executed third phase. The recon would only take a few days. The darting and tagging a week or more, if we could locate them easily, that is, and the capture and rescue another three weeks or so minimum.

An hour later we were pretty much done.

'Thank you,' said the minister. 'It is important that I see the situation on the ground for myself, so I will join you on your reconnaissance to Garamba together with two of my staff. My presence with you will demonstrate to all the importance my government is placing on the project. There may be some local resistance to the removal of the rhinos, but this is something we can deal with.'

'This is understandable,' I replied, 'but the rhinos will in any event always belong to the DRC. All we have to do is get them into a safe holding area and we can plan from there.'

Having the minister join us was a huge advantage, but this meant that we would have to increase the size and cost of the plane we were to hire. I could see JP mentally recalculating his options.

'I have arranged for you to meet with the Director General of the Congolese Institute for National Conservation' – ICCN in the French acronym – 'who will facilitate your engagement.'

We all stood for a photo session with the minister, after which he gave a short thank-you speech, and presented us with an ornate bronze image of the DRC with an eagle wrapped in laurel wreaths overhead.

I heaved a sigh of relief as we left for the ICCN offices with Brigit. Everything was as Ambassador M'Poko had predicted, and we now had the minister's official approval for the rescue.

We were kept waiting for a while at the ICCN offices before we were introduced to the ICCN chief and several of his directors. We then covered the same ground that we had with the minister for their benefit. We explained the South African connection, the invitation from both his ambassador and minister and our offer to help the ICCN put in place a programme to ensure the survival of the remaining rhinos in Garamba.

The response was friendly but hesitant. Were we aware, the ICCN chief asked, that until recently Garamba had been abandoned and that another conservation group, African Parks, had recently gone in to take over? We said yes, but pointed out that they were managing the entire area, whereas we had a specific motive – to assist the ICCN to save the rhino. We were purely a single-issue group. We stressed that our expertise and substantial financial backing would be placed at the disposal of the ICCN; that we were more than happy to work in conjunction with any other group, but that this would be done through his department. Our sole purpose was to assist in an extremely difficult environment.

This was all very interesting to them, but still they hesitated. Although they were polite to us, they seemed somewhat reluctant to push forward with the initiative.

Garamba National Park is absolutely massive, bigger than Israel, with uncontrolled poaching throughout and a rebel army in occupation. A single conservation group acting on its own was not going to be enough to help the ICCN take control of something so large while simultaneously undertaking an immediate rescue of the rhino. I knew what it took to run Thula Thula, which was a fraction of the size.

Why the reticence? we asked. Surely they would grab any assistance, both financial and physical, that they could get, especially with the looming extinction of a major subspecies on their doorstep?

Well, they didn't know. They would have to consider the matter and could not yet give us permission to go to Garamba.

That certainly surprised us. We had just got approval at the highest level – from the minister himself – to visit the reserve immediately. In fact, he was coming with us. Yet here was the minister's own department not quite refusing, but certainly not giving us a green light. Further discussion brought about no change of mindset.

Eventually I threw in the towel. 'We were invited to DRC to assist the ICCN with this matter and we are sure that both African Parks and your department will recognize the value of our offer,' I said. 'We will await your further communication.'

As we left I managed to pull Brigit one side and ask her what was going on. 'I am so sorry,' she said. 'We did not expect this complication. I'll discuss the matter with the minister and let you know.'

'What could possibly be the objection?' I asked.

'It is complicated. Please, be patient with us.'

It was only later that we discovered the intricacies of DRC politics. President Kabila was attempting to form a coalition government from the country's many diverse political parties. The Director General of the ICCN and the Minister of Environment were not necessarily singing from the same hymn sheet. This was true not only for the question of who controlled conservation and environmental issues, but also on a whole array of other policies. Most political parties in the DRC have strong tribal loyalties and the country is so vast, bigger than the whole of Western Europe, that people thousands of miles away in the east have more in common with neighbouring countries than they do with native Kinshasans in the west.

The former guerilla leader Laurent Kabila, father of the president, comes from the far east of the country. He announced in 1995 that he was marching on the capital to overthrow the government of the then leader General Mobutu Sese Seko. Kabila had been trained by Che Guevara and his ragtag army followed the Congo River for thousands of miles from the country's border with Uganda. It took Kabila two long years to march through the jungle to reach Kinshasa with his army, but eventually he arrived and conquered the city. When asked how Kabila had been so successful, the famous reply was, 'They took us completely by surprise.'

We left the meeting somewhat deflated. To be given top-level approval and then be told that even with the minister accompanying us we needed further permission was confusing. We were dealing with an emergency; the future of the rhinos was critical. Many thousands of northern whites had already gone the way of the dodo; how much longer could the final few hang on for?

It was early evening and there was nothing more we could do, so JP said he would like us to meet one of his friends. We caught a taxi to the plushest area of Kinshasa, an elite suburb where the city's movers and shakers lived. Kinshasa is a city of contrasts, with small islands of affluence surrounded by an ocean of poverty. There are a few thousand wealthy ex-colonials, mainly Belgian, who remained and toughed it out after the civil wars that wracked the country in the 1960s. That was the era of white mercenaries, such as 'Black Jack' Schramme, the Frenchman Bob Denard, 'Mad' Mike Hoare and other gunmen who flocked to the area in search of adventure and fortune, fighting the Simba rebels loyal to the country's first prime minister, Patrice Lumumba.

Unfortunately for the DRC – and for the rest of the continent – the hasty independence package from the Belgian colonialists backfired spectacularly in an orgy of bloodletting and rape that has never really ended. It was at the height of the Cold War, with the Russians backing Lumumba and the West backing their candidate, Moise Tshombe. Both Tshombe and Lumumba were murdered and a new strongman emerged, General Mobuto Sese Seko, whose corrupt rule spanned the next three decades. He renamed the country Zaire, but when he was toppled in 1997 it reverted to being called the Democratic Republic of the Congo.

During the first civil war in the early 1960s, many atrocities were committed against nuns, which predictably grabbed headlines around the world. That tended to stereotype Africa in the minds of the Western media, something that remains true to this day. Veteran *Newsweek* correspondent Edward Behr told the story of a BBC journalist arriving at a refugee camp at Stanleyville (now Kisangani) and asking loudly in his posh Brit accent, 'I say, anyone here been raped and speaks English?' (Behr actually used that as the title for his memoirs).

Sadly, the wars and insurrections continue. An International Rescue Committee report estimated that 5.4 million people have been killed in the DRC and the Great Lakes regions between 1998 and 2008, and the use of child soldiers remains endemic. Across the DRC, Rwanda, Uganda and Burundi genocide, civil wars and wars between states resulted in over a decade of conflict, the bloodiest on earth since the Second World War. It wrenched Africa apart, yet most people know very little about it.

The supreme irony is that the DRC is potentially one of the richest countries in the world, with untapped mineral deposits worth about $24 trillion – equivalent to the gross domestic product of both the USA and Europe.

You would not believe that looking at Kinshasa today. In fact, you would think the exact opposite – that apart from Mogadishu, the helter-skelter capital of the failed state of Somalia, Kinshasa must be the most disordered, run-down city in the world. Of its population of eight million, only about one million could be called affluent by African standards. Another two million are making ends meet. Then you have three million living in slums, squalid shanty towns grouped around ramshackle infrastructures where there are at least vague semblances of civic services. Finally there are the remaining two million, who live right on the streets, squatting in cardboard shelters on slabs of pavement that they call home.

That's a staggering number, and for these poor souls there is no infrastructure whatsoever. The only saving grace, if you can call it that, is that the pavements are wide, testimony to the colonial days when the Belgians built massive double-highway boulevards and planted huge trees in the middle. Indeed, in its heyday Kinshasa, or Leopoldville as it was then called, was a model city and the DRC was the crown jewel of Belgium's ruthless colonial ambitions. In fact it was considered not even a colony, but the personal fiefdom of their monarch, King Leopold.

The city is close to the equator and bang in the middle of what was once a rainforest, so there are streams and rivulets crossing roads everywhere. In the myriad tributaries flowing to the Congo River, people wash and do their laundry and their ablutions. In many instances, the rubbish and sewage is piled as high as houses on the riverbanks.

People are born on the pavements in huge numbers. They die on the pavements in equally huge numbers. They have no toilets, no running water and no sanitation. They live in a twilight world, far beyond the comprehension of most Westerners, existing in an arcane black-market economy totally devoid of state control. This is a twenty-first-century city without supermarkets, banks or ATMs, where, despite having the most fertile lands on earth, even eggs and milk have to be imported.

But there is little serious crime. People have no access to banks, so money lenders operate openly on street corners with bricks of notes balanced on rickety tables in the middle of the constant rush-hour chaos. If someone did that in any other city in the world, they would be plundered within minutes – or certified insane. Yet strangely, in Kinshasa they are completely safe.

Even in the expensive areas, the façades of the buildings look shabby. But that only lasts until you open the gates. Behind the huge walls, so high that you can't climb over, lie some impressive mansions.

JP's friend lived in one; a palatial home dwarfed by a tree so colossal, so overwhelmingly entrancing, that I could instantly grasp why some cultures consider trees to be possessed by spirits and worship them.

JP introduced us to his friend Philippe Graca, who was the classic Frenchman, dark and urbane. Philippe's family had been in the DRC for generations, and he knew Kinshasa like few others. At first he seemed stressed, but after telling us what a terrible day he'd had, he suddenly cheered up. I think many of the colonials are starved of fresh company. He suggested we all go out for dinner; it was time to party.

It was a night to remember. We were first taken to a Portuguese restaurant that Philippe said served some of the best cuisine in the world. He was right. We had river prawns the size of crayfish and *chouriço* sausage grilled on coals right in front of us that was out of this world. Top Kinshasa restaurants charge New York prices and Philippe explained that because they had such a small client base, consisting of mainly expats and the Congolese elite, competition was fierce and they went out of business rapidly unless their food was world class.

Then we went to a nightclub typical of Kinshasa, the sort of place that in London or New York would lose its licence in the first hours of the first night due to breaking every health and safety rule imaginable in the West – from fire hazards to overcrowding to sheer decibel pollution. On the dance floor the music throbbed to the rhythms of Africa and locals were gyrating to the latest disco numbers.

Eventually JP, tiring of what he called 'head-banging' music, requested what he somewhat bizarrely believed to be the much quieter lyrics of Led Zeppelin. No problem – and as Robert Plant launched into 'Rock and Roll', JP looked at me, lifted a glass and shouted loud enough for all to hear, 'Now that's proper music.'

Overawed by the South African's sheer size and presence, the disc jockey meekly played JP's out-of-date musical requests for the rest of the evening.

But the final destination was one that I will remember for ever. Philippe took us deep into the city among the pavement dwellers. It was about 2 a.m. There were no street lights, but everywhere you looked there were the remnants of cooking fires with thousands of people sleeping or squatting. The air was thick with wood smoke. He stopped at an intersection and we got out and followed him to where a group of about eight children lived, if you can call it that, on the pavement. The oldest child could not have been more than fifteen. The youngest was a one-year-old baby being preciously cared for by an eight-year-old. They crowded around Philippe, shouting, 'Papa Philippe,' genuinely delighted to see him. They were all barefoot in the manner of those who had never worn shoes, clothed in rags and as skinny as sticks.

Philippe turned and said to us, 'These are my friends. Whatever you do, don't give them money. It degrades them. It makes them dependent.'

I put my wallet back in my pocket. However, the children had a cottage business selling cigarettes, which they kept in a makeshift kiosk. I bought several packets.

Then Philippe clapped his hands and called out in French, 'Let's have some music.'

They all cheered. 'Music!'

The oldest child brought out a battered guitar that only had three strings. One of the other kids fetched just a single steel guitar string tied to a tin can. Placing the tin between his knees, he pulled the string with his teeth, plucking it with his fingers in time with the guitar. He somehow was able to tense the string so it harmonized perfectly. Jason said it was like the duelling banjos from the movie *Deliverance*, the two jury-rigged instruments feeding beautifully off each other. I closed my eyes. With a little imagination I could have been listening to the gypsy jazz guitarist Django Reinhardt. It was that good.

A three-year-old girl got up and started dancing, her rhythm so natural, so expressive, in that tiny little body that I found myself tapping my foot. What could she possibly have to dance about, this dear little thing? She should be sleeping safe in a home with a full stomach on a warm bed, not dancing on a pavement at two in the morning. The other children joined in, clapping their hands, egging her on.

When Philippe had called for music, I initially expected to be bored senseless, watching a couple of kids singing out of tune with a beat-up guitar. Instead we all sat there mesmerized at this fragile expression of life. Never had I seen such vitality, such zest, among those who had so little.

'You know,' whispered Jason, 'you can suppress anything, but you cannot kill the human spirit.'

I suddenly felt a little maudlin. The day had been one of total sensory overload. What chance did this place have? To an outsider, a Westerner, Kinshasa was a colourful, vibrant, albeit poverty-stricken, African city. For those ensnared on the inside it was indeed the heart of darkness. And if this was the capital city, what was going on in the far-flung regions where there was no semblance of law and order? If so many street children had no future, what chance could the rhino, mere animals, possibly have?

The children danced on. They were alive; that is all that mattered. They lived for the moment. They danced when they could, and died when they would.

'When we come back here, I am going to bring that guy a decent guitar,' I said, trying to lift myself.

However, as Philippe drove us back to our hotel, both Jason and I wondered how many of those kids would be alive when we returned. I was later told that there are tens of thousands of street children in Kinshasa and they are often subjected to abuse by the police and public, who regard them as little more than vermin.

It was time to go home. We never thought our mission was going to be easy, but at least now we had an inkling of the massive hurdles we would face. How could the world even think of entrusting the fate of these rhino to such a shambolic country? And how can we expect governments who can't feed their own population or maintain any kind of infrastructure to be curators of the rainforests upon which the entire planet depends for oxygen? It should be the responsibility of the UN or an international body created for this purpose.

'I will speak to Ambassador M'Poko when we get back,' said JP, reading my thoughts. 'Hopefully he can untangle this mess quickly.'

CHAPTER EIGHT

We flew back and the following day I woke up in my own bed, absolutely refreshed.

Thula Thula has a way of putting all problems in perspective. Despite the let-down in Kinshasa, we had made some progress with the rhino rescue, and at least were now on the radar of the DRC's conservation authorities. JP would contact Ambassador M'Poko and I would continue working on the rescue with Jason, Dylan and the team.

I decided to get out for a while, and was on the furthest side of the reserve to check a fence when the familiar sound and feel of a punctured tyre juddered through the Land Rover. Normally not a problem, except this time there was no wheel spanner and I was too low down in a valley to raise anyone on the Landy's two-way radio. It would be a long walk home.

A few hot and thirsty hours later, with the sun high in the sky, I came across a large herd of wildebeest spread out in the savannah, grazing peacefully. I heard the bull give a warning call when he saw me and the herd galloped off, the loud drumming of their hooves echoing through the bush. Taking flight is not uncommon as wildebeest, or gnus as they are also known, are particularly skittish and lone bulls are permanent sentinels, always on the lookout for danger. However, it was strange that I hadn't seen the bull. Then I heard it snort again, this time much closer. I pressed on and as I rounded a corner on the rough bush track I was momentarily surprised by Heidi, who was very close by with her ears and tail up, standing on full alert, staring straight at me.

I glanced at her massive leathery shape, looking for any signs of aggression, then quickly scouted for a suitable tree to climb. But she held her ground and there was no immediate problem. Suddenly the wildebeest call came again from right where Heidi was standing and confused the hell out of me because I still couldn't see the bull. Then to my astonishment I realized it was Heidi. She made the perfect wildebeest warning calls once more and then bounced off after the herd.

Seeing a rhino placing itself on guard duty for a herd of wildebeest, mimicking the bull's warning calls and the herd responding as if the rhino was one of their own, was certainly a first for me. Then I understood. White rhinos are the most sociable of their species and females group together. But as Heidi had grown up as an orphan, she had never known other rhinos. Instead she had been adopted by wildebeest, and repaid them by doing sentinel duty. Rhino and wildebeest eat the same sweet short grass and consequently share the same habitat. Growing up with wildebeest, Heidi had taken on their traits and even learned to communicate with them. I defy anyone to tell the difference in their calls. The wildebeest themselves certainly couldn't.

I remember one time when Nana and the elephant herd deliberately rescued some antelope that we had captured to relocate to other reserves. We had placed the antelope in a holding *boma*, or pen. Nana came out of the bush with the herd in tow, opened the clasp and gate with her trunk and then stood back as they escaped to freedom. We had to spend the next day recapturing the animals, but it was worth every ounce of sweat after watching one species go the aid of another. A herd of wildebeest befriending a lonely rhino orphan was another example of this amazing connection all creatures are capable of.

Over the years I had spent a lot of time with Heidi. Despite her tragic childhood, she was remarkably placid. She was acutely aware of my presence and always seemed to appreciate the company. I desperately wanted to introduce a breeding herd of rhino so she could have a normal social life, but a herd would pull in poachers like a magnet. For the time being she was much safer living with a skittish wildebeest herd, which provided plenty of nervous eyes and ears to protect her.

Heidi was a firm favourite with our guests on game drives, and the rangers would go out of the way to find her. She often wandered right up to the vehicles, which the tourists loved. She was so good-natured that the rangers would also regularly take groups near her on game walks, where they could admire this magnificent creature up close and on foot. For many people visiting Thula Thula, this was the highlight of their trip.

There was one incident when a group on foot was watching Heidi from about thirty yards away and an impala ram nearby barked. The sudden sound gave Heidi a fright and she unwittingly bolted straight for the tourists. Thinking they were about to be trampled into oblivion, they turned and fled while the game rangers screamed and clapped their hands to divert her.

Heidi veered and thundered past, then stopped and watched, looking bemused, wondering what all the fuss was about. One tourist had literally jumped out of his expensive shoes. We found them and gave them back to him, amazingly still fully laced. He must have been running at a hell of a speed to have shed them like that.

Heidi was a constant reminder to me of what front-line conservation was all about. Every time I saw her magnificent horn, I thought of her own safety, of other rhinos dying violently throughout Africa, and of the paltry few remaining northern whites in Garamba.

I got back to the lodge tired, thirsty and hungry as hell, and went straight to the kitchen to scrounge something to eat. Françoise was there with the chefs designing a new menu for the guests.

'My poor baby,' she said when she heard that I'd had to walk for hours out of the bush. 'You are starving; I have some beautiful chocolate chilli chicken for you.' Such are the rigours of being married to a French chef. Whatever happened to good old steak, egg and chips for a hungry ranger?

At about the same time we had received some new residents on Thula Thula. We are a designated release site for injured and orphaned animals, and so we received a galago – more commonly known as a bushbaby – and two genets to release into the wild. The two species could not be more different. Tiny, cuddly bushbabies with their huge eyes, soft grey fur and long fluffy tails are probably the cutest, most lovable creatures alive, while genets, beautiful felines that look like a cross between a weasel and a mongoose, are surely the most devious and cunning creatures ever put on the planet.

The galago was set free first. However, he took one look at the comforts of the lodge, did a swift comparison to the bush outside and counter-intuitively – seeing as he was called a bushbaby – decided he would be staying indoors from now on.

We named him George after the former American president, whom I learned while I was in Baghdad that Saddam Hussein had nicknamed 'baby Bush'.

George soon became a regular at the bar. Françoise, to whom he took an immediate liking, said he was obviously a typical bachelor, staying out all night drinking with his friends. He had a penchant for stealing water out of glasses rather than drinking from his dish, and would leap onto the bar and shove his snout into the nearest glass. However, he could only get a slurp if the glass was full, so he solved that problem by flipping it over with a swipe of his paw and licking up the spilt liquid on the counter.

This didn't overly endear him to guests who had just bought a drink. But he was such a character that they soon forgave him. Unfortunately, George also used to join us sometimes for dinner. I say unfortunately because George had the table manners of a goat. He would leap on the table and shamelessly steal food off people's plates, particularly anything that looked like an insect, his natural cuisine. On one occasion he walked onto a guest's plate, sat in the food and snatched a large prawn. The guest tried to grab it back and a tug of war ensued. George didn't believe in fighting fair and promptly sank his teeth into the man's thumb before scampering off with his prize.

The guest, a famous rugby player and a particularly large fellow, jumped up, grasping his thumb and complaining bitterly about wild animals at the dinner table. But he was a decent guy and soon saw the humour in it. It's not often you get to have a fight with a bushbaby over a crustacean.

After that, Françoise and I tried to persuade George to live up to his species designation and be an actual bushbaby rather than a barfly. But he was having none of it.

Bushbabies have incredibly large eyes, which take up three-quarters of their face. This accounts for their excellent night vision and why they are largely nocturnal. Of course, that also means their eyes are ultra-sensitive to light. One Christmas, George made the mistake of falling asleep under the Christmas tree. Not knowing he was there, Françoise switched the lights on and the sudden multicoloured glare woke a startled George, now considerably alarmed and howling like a banshee. If a bushbaby is three-quarters eyes, the other quarter is lungs, and George could have woken people in Alaska. But the look on his face was so comical as he streaked off for darker corners that we all collapsed laughing. George sulked for the rest of the night, which basically meant that no prawns were stolen or glasses upturned.

Then one night he arrived at the lodge and jumped onto the bar counter, and you could tell he had been in a hell of a fight. His face was swollen, his right eye was injured and tufts of hair had been pulled out. It was obvious the brawl had been over a female and it looked like he had been beaten up big time.

But the self-satisfied smirk on his face seemed to say, 'You should see the other guy,' and he was right. The next night he arrived with his girlfriend, proudly showing off the victor's spoils to us.

George's bachelor days were now over and, like most married men, he was banned from the bar. No doubt there are by now a lot of baby Georges around. I wonder if he regales them with tales of his misspent youth in the drinking holes of Thula Thula.

Genets, although beautiful to look at, have razor-sharp teeth and they were a different ball game altogether. Try to stroke one of them and you could lose a finger. Like George, they too decided that the lodge was much more comfortable than the bush, and spent their days slinking around nooks and crannies looking for trouble and finding it. They are real bandits. On one run around the kitchen they dislodged every tin, container and packet onto the floor. By the time they scuttled out the door, the place looked like a bomb had hit it with an explosion of sugar, rice, flour and salt splattered all over the place.

The staff spent half the time trying to win George's affection and the other half escaping the genets' stiletto teeth. Thankfully the gangster felines eventually started hankering for the wild, and one day they were gone. As beautiful as they were, it was not a moment too soon.

But despite these marvellous distractions – which is what makes living on a game reserve so fantastic – our real focus was on the Congo rhino rescue, and a lot was being achieved behind the scenes. Dylan was pulling everything together and Grant came into his own sourcing and planning food, equipment, provisions, vehicles, fuel, satellite phones, first aid and all sorts of paraphernalia that would be needed for a long haul in the wilderness. He even found us a helicopter and a pilot.

JP was making good progress in recruiting top men for security and I was dealing with some of Africa's most respected wildlife veterinarians to recruit the capture team. It was all coming together beautifully – from our side, at least. Everyone saw the critical urgency and necessity of the project and no one wanted to be left out.

About five weeks later, JP's discussions with the ambassador backed up by Jason's ongoing communication with Brigit in the minister's office finally produced results, and we received an email from the ICCN granting us authorization to visit Garamba. Initially we were thrilled as we saw this as the full go-ahead for the rescue. Unfortunately we were later told that African Parks, who were running Garamba, had said it merely gave us permission to look around, and no more.

Be that as it may, our reconnaissance expedition was a 'go', and now at least we could find out first-hand what was actually going on. Although we had put together an expedition in just a couple of months, it never failed to stagger me how slowly everything else was proceeding when it was so blindingly obvious that we had to move quickly. Every day could be the rhinos' last. The poachers weren't going to conveniently hold off while we dithered.

Brigit told us that the minister may or may not be accompanying us, but that two ICCN officials definitely would be and it was customary that we should bring them a gift. We checked with JP, who said this would be appropriate, so we bought them each a good pair of binoculars that they could use in the wild.

Heeding JP's advice not to take the shorter charter-flight route from Uganda because of the presence of the notorious Lord's Resistance Army, we had to find a private plane and pilot in Kinshasa. However, to get to the far-flung boondocks of Garamba from Kinshasa is about as easy as chartering a flight to Mars. Thankfully Brigit knew of an organization called Mission Aviation Fellowship (MAF), who do aerial Christian missionary work throughout Central Africa, but will take paying passengers. In addition to their evangelical tasks, MAF have evolved as couriers and do vital work ferrying emergency medical supplies and mail to the most remote parts of the country.

Jason contacted them and asked for a special flight. Yes, they said. They would take us and they were available immediately.

CHAPTER NINE

With the charter plane booked for the flight to Garamba, JP, Jason and I flew back to Kinshasa. This time we booked on South African Airways, which does conform to an international aviation code – unlike our previous flight operator.

We met up with Brigit, who confirmed that all arrangements were in place and that both the ICCN and African Parks staff at Garamba were expecting us. Not only that, she was joining us on the trip as the minister's official representative.

Our charter flight was scheduled to leave at dawn the following morning, but first JP and I had something important to do.

The UN had a 20,000-strong peacekeeping army in the DRC called MONUC, which sought to bring stability to a region wracked by wars and conflict. I had been in contact with their senior people for a while, ensuring they were fully briefed on the rhino rescue initiative and at the same time garnering their support for it, which would be crucial. I had arranged to meet with their officers before flying to Garamba.

We arrived at the MONUC military base in the mid-afternoon. On each side of a gate heavily fortified by sandbags and barbed wire stood an armoured personnel carrier sporting a heavy 20mm machine gun. Behind them an armoured troop carrier with auto-cannon added more lethal firepower. All were painted in traditional UN white, manned by soldiers in their distinctive blue berets. They were expecting us and we were escorted into the administration building.

My contact was Laurent Guepin, a Belgian in a senior position in MONUC. Laurent was a friendly, knowledgeable UN executive in his late thirties who fitted comfortably into the character and culture of the United Nations operations in the DRC. We had had a lot of communication and were both pleased finally to meet face to face.

'Laurent,' I said after introductions and cordialities were over, 'the reconnaissance mission tomorrow to Garamba is one thing, but at the end of the day all of this leads to a major rescue operation and the main challenge we face is logistics.'

I smiled to soften the massive implications of my next request. 'From what we understand, the rhinos are in deep bush where there are no roads. We have our own helicopter to locate and dart them, but once they are darted we need a heavy lift helicopter to take them to the holding area. Then we need to be able to fly them to a safe destination. This will probably require a C-130 cargo plane with short landing and take-off abilities. It's the only aircraft big enough to carry the animals and you – the UN – are the only people here who have got them.'

I paused. 'Can you help?'

I tensed, waiting for his reply, for this was a very big request indeed. Helicopters and planes of this nature are serious military equipment and not only did we need them, but we needed them for extended periods in a to-hell-and-gone area on the other side of the country. Just getting them there would be a mission in itself.

Laurent sat back, deliberating on the unusual request. 'And if we can't?'

'Then the northern white rhino will go extinct in the wild. It's as simple, or complicated, as that.'

Laurent wanted to help, but I was asking for the moon. He knew it and I knew it.

'Lawrence, MONUC is a military operation and I don't even know if our planes and helicopters can be used for civilian purposes.'

'Well, why can't we make the rhino rescue a military operation, then? MONUC will get kudos for assisting us. This is a high-profile international issue.'

He stood up, looking directly at me. 'Because the last time MONUC sent helicopters into the Garamba game reserve, in January this year, it was to attack the Lord's Resistance Army, The LRA shot down two of them, killed eight UN Special Forces soldiers and wounded twenty others. That's why. This is a very dangerous area you want to go into.'

'I heard about that,' I said. 'That incident took place in the north of Garamba; we will be operating in the south. But perhaps that's why this could be classified as a military operation?'

'We would have to send in troops to protect the aircraft as well,' he said, as though speaking to himself. 'Whew,' he exhaled deeply. 'This will need top-level approval.'

'So do you think MONUC will help?'

'I'll do what I can. It's shocking that it's come to this with the rhino and I think there will be some sympathy at the top. But first let's talk about your reconnaissance trip. How are you getting there?'

'We're flying in.'

'We will need your coordinates in case something goes wrong and we have to get you out.'

'No problem. I'll have them sent over to you,' I replied, making a note.

'Your satellite phone number?'

JP gave it to him.

'There is a village in the vicinity of your destination by the name of Nagero. Avoid it like the plague, and I mean that literally,' said Laurent. 'The village has had an outbreak of Ebola disease, it's out of control and the area is completely quarantined.'

That certainly got our attention. Ebola is a rare haemorrhagic fever that has jumped species from monkeys to humans. It is one of the vilest diseases on earth. Victims haemorrhage from every orifice – eyes, ears, mouth, nose – and usually bleed to death in days. It's an absolute horror story. There are no effective drugs and there is no known vaccine or cure. In the first outbreak of Ebola in the DRC, 318 people were infected and 280 died. But because it kills so quickly, the virus rapidly runs out of people to infect, so outbreaks are usually self-contained.

'Nagero,' I said, committing the name to memory, but then thought with relief that it didn't concern us as we had no plans to leave the Garamba park.

'Lastly,' said Laurent, 'can you give us a full report on the security situation when you get back? We haven't had anyone up there for a while and we'd like to know what's going on.'

'Absolutely,' said JP. 'We will debrief.'

Laurent later joined us for dinner at a Chinese restaurant, as did JP's friend, Philippe.

'Now, everybody listen,' said Philippe in his rich French accent once we were all seated. 'I know this country well. If you are going into the jungle, there is a critical piece of equipment that you must take, something that can never be left behind on any expedition.'

JP, Jason and I leaned forward, eagerly awaiting some precious snippet of local knowledge. Philippe looked at us one by one.

'A pillow,' he said gravely, as if imparting a deep secret. 'A good pillow is vital. I'm deadly serious.'

'Somebody write that down,' said Jason as laughter boomed around the table.

Later there was a phone call from an official in the Environment Ministry saying that he needed to meet us immediately. I told him where we were.

He soon arrived at the restaurant and asked that I come outside. Sensing something was up, JP and Jason joined us.

After apologizing, he said he had been sent to tell us that the two ICCN officials would have to be paid 'out of office expenses' of $150 a day per person for their services.

That was a surprise. I looked at JP, who simply shrugged and nodded.

'That's fine,' I replied. 'We'll bring the money to the plane in the morning.'

We were up at the crack of dawn the next day. Jason had insisted on buying some backup food for the trip, just a few tins of bully beef, bottled water and bread – and thank God he did, as we later discovered.

At the landing strip we met the two ICCN officials. We couldn't believe our eyes. They were dressed in smart suits and polished, long-toed shoes as if they were going to a cocktail party, rather than one of the hottest and most remote wildernesses in Africa where you're more likely to meet rough men with guns than jet-setters. Brigit, who had travelled extensively in the DRC, at least knew that the trip would be hot and uncomfortable, and was more practically dressed in slacks and a blouse.

'This is an important day for the DRC,' she said to everyone. 'None of us have been to Garamba before, and it is important that not only the management but also the local tribes see us there supporting the rhino rescue.'

We boarded the plane, a ten-seater single-engine Cessna Caravan, and JP, a qualified aviator, took the co-pilot's seat. As we were fastening our seat belts, the American mission pilot dressed in official MAF flying uniform asked us to close our eyes and say a prayer for the journey.

The flight path was from Kinshasa to Kisangani, in the centre of the country, to refuel, and then on to Garamba. The entire journey would take about nine hours – longer than it would take us to reach London on a commercial flight.

We flew across the Congo River immediately after take-off and were soon over the rainforest, the second largest in the world after the Amazon. It was initially breathtaking until I noticed with alarm how much logging was going on. The land was criss-crossed with the scars of mud tracks gouged out of the ground by hulking twenty-wheeler trucks. In some areas all you could see were the splintered stumps of once-massive jungle trees.

Like the human body, Mother Earth has two huge lungs: the Amazon and the African rainforests. Why anyone would be allowed to tamper with the planet's most important life-support systems was beyond me. Were they replanting trees? I hoped so, but in my gut I knew they were not. And what about the many species lost in the collateral damage?

Eventually we were so far away from any form of civilization that even the loggers couldn't get there. Below was a never-ending canopy of forest, impenetrably thick and green, stretching to the horizon on all sides, obliterating any view of the thousands of rivers and streams below that feed the mighty Congo. There were no roads or tracks, and you could only tell a river path by the palm trees that glowed silver in the sun. We were directly over the equator and sweat streamed off us even while flying at 10,000 feet in an unpressurized plane.

'Kisangani coming up,' said the pilot after five hours of endless jungle.

Kisangani, formerly known as Stanleyville, is more than 1,200 miles upriver and is the furthest navigable point from the mouth of the Congo. It's an isolated port city, lying right in the middle of Africa's rich rainforests.

Our stop was brief, just a quick refuel parked among an assortment of military and cargo planes strewn around the runway. I noticed the huge white UN C-130 cargo planes and massive helicopters that were based there due to the current civil wars and the presence of the Lord's Resistance Army. They were the same ones we would need for the rhino rescue, and I thought of Laurent back in the UN offices.

Fully fuelled, we continued flying north-east into no-man's-land. Eventually the jungle below started easing into subtropical bush until we were flying over rolling savannah and woodland stretching as far as we could see.

A little later, we spotted Garamba for the first time. At JP's request the pilot circled so he could get a feel for the area and see if there were any poachers or guerillas around before landing on the rough grass airstrip. There was no sign of humans, but we did see four elephants moving off to the south.

A smashed aeroplane lying ominously in a mangled heap on one side of the runway greeted us as we touched down. The plane had apparently belonged to mercenaries desperately trying to escape a previous insurrection. It was shot down and the wreckage has been there ever since.

Hello, Garamba.

CHAPTER TEN

We taxied up to the simple shed that doubled as a hangar. A four-wheel motorbike came out to meet us, followed closely by a Toyota truck carrying staff from the ICCN, who ran the camp. We were taken to a central thatch-covered patio structure at the main camp, which stood near what appeared to be a parade ground. Across from us was a large double-storey house, and by walking off a little we could see some guest huts strung out along a river, not too close to the water mind you, for this was a wild African river. Further off there was a large building which looked to be an administrative centre of sorts.

On enquiring about meeting the manager, Mr José Tello, who was employed by African Parks to manage the reserve on behalf of the cash-strapped ICCN, we were told they were not expecting us and he was not available. Brigit immediately explained who we were, that she represented the minister and that there were two ICCN officials in our party. As far as the staff was concerned, the news of our impending visit never reached Garamba and consequently Mr Tello was not available.

We were shown to our huts, and, despite the presence of our high-profile delegation in the small camp, we never saw any management officials again until late the next day.

The thatched rooms were crudely furnished: two single wooden beds with a tub of water placed in the corner that served as the hand basin and bath. The toilet was a rustic long drop. The one thing all the rooms did have in their favour were views of the Dungu River, a beautiful clear-flowing stretch of water with a healthy pod of hippo basking about a hundred yards in front of us.

Jason and I dumped our suitcases and were walking over to JP's hut when he grabbed my arm.

'What's that noise?'

Then I heard it, a strange 'whooshing' sound. Even in the dusk you could see the foliage in front of us heaving like an ocean. The 'whooshing' was the noise of a million leaves rustling in unison.

I suddenly recognized the sound from my childhood. '*Siafu*,' I exclaimed excitedly. '*Siafu*.'

I quickly searched the ground to make sure we weren't standing in them.

Jason looked at me quizzically. 'What?'

'*Siafu* . . . driver ants, army ants, safari ants, they have lots of names. I can't believe it.'

There they were, moving right past us in their millions, a living river of ants, pouring through the camp, hell-bent on a hunting expedition. It's a spellbinding phenomenon and I was delighted to be seeing it again. They are the ultimate marauders; a column will attack and eat everything in its path. They can strip a living creature to bare bones within minutes.

As we watched, fascinated, I told Jason of a story I had once heard about an African bush clinic that was directly in the path of a driver ant annual march. The doctors there considered it to be a blessing. The voracious insects only move at about sixty feet an hour, so once the staff knew an army was on its way they carried out the patients, opened all the doors and windows and left. The ants swarmed through the building, rapaciously devouring insects, mice, rats and cockroaches as well as the grime and gore on every bed, basin, utensil, scalpel or operating instrument. They picked the equipment as clean as if it had been sterilized with the most potent detergent. They got rid of every speck of congealed blood and infected matter, in the process consuming all the superbugs and germs. When the ants left the building it was as pristine as if it had been spring-cleaned.

Jason was unimpressed. 'This is crazy! They're only thirty yards away from our rooms. What happens if they come in, or if we walk into them in the dark?'

'You'll soon know all about it. Their jaws are so powerful that the local tribes use the bite to suture wounds. They carefully hold the ant so that one pincer is on each side of the wound and let it bite to pull the wound together, then they break the head off, forming instant bush stitches.'

We were both silent, watching the deadly procession and listening to the chilling music of one of nature's most awesome armies on the move. It struck both of us how remote we really were. This was an incredible wilderness. This was David Livingstone territory. It was as feral a place as you'll find anywhere on the planet. More Europeans or Americans had probably climbed Everest than had been to a place like this. Even Jason, who is quite citified, felt its raw, uninhibited power. The nearest city of note was 500 miles away in another country and on roads so bad that it takes trucks days to get through. Even in the depths of Thula Thula's bush I never felt anything this 'wild'.

We called JP to show him the *siafu* column and he whistled quietly.

'*Ja*,' he said. 'I've seen them before. That'll certainly keep us out of mischief at night.' Neither of us knew we would be breaking that rule the following evening.

JP, Jason and I walked alongside the ICCN officials' cabin. They were both outside, sitting a little way down from their room drinking beers with their backs to the river. It was now dark and I could hear hippos grunting in the background.

Hippos feed mainly at night and account for more human deaths than any other creature in Africa, not counting the malarial mosquito. It's not as though they will just attack you for no reason, but if you get in their way, you've had it. They've been known to bite people in half. The problem is that they come out of the river at night to graze and that's when humans need to be very careful.

'Hey, guys,' I said, wondering where they had found the beers. 'Maybe you should at least turn your chairs and face the river. Some of the hippos are already out of the water.'

I then pointed to the ground. 'Look at the spoor. Not only hippo, but lions and hyena came through here recently.'

That certainly got a reaction. They thanked me and rapidly moved inside, still wearing their designer suits.

It soon became obvious that we weren't going to be fed at the camp that night, and so Jason was the hero of the moment. Dinner was four cans of bully beef, two loaves of bread and bottled water. But seeing as none of us had eaten since breakfast in Kinshasa, we weren't complaining.

That night we made sure our nets were as tight as drums around our beds. There were so many mosquitoes that they must have been colliding with one another and Jason used a whole stick of Tabard repellent. If any part of your body touched the net you got bitten right through the mesh. This was, as he said, Malaria Central.

The next morning we were up at dawn without breakfast. Outside, the ICCN game guards were mustering in military fashion for the day's anti-poaching patrols and JP and I stood watching the drill for a while.

'They're not trained,' said JP, shaking his head as we walked away. 'There's a lot of work to be done with these guys. They can't even march, and if they can't march they sure as hell can't shoot. And out there they will be facing well-armed poachers, not to mention the bloody LRA. By the way,' he continued, 'I got up early and I found a hut full of guns, mainly AK-47s, but they're all broken or useless. These guys have taken on a major challenge and Tello's obviously trying his best . . . but I don't know whether they are up for it.'

We continued on our walk, getting to know the camp, meeting and talking with as many staff as possible, and eventually found ourselves outside the front gate. As we were standing there we noticed a village on the outskirts of the reserve and Jason asked one of the staff what it was called.

'Nagero,' came the reply.

'What?' We stopped in our tracks. 'Nagero?'

The guard nodded and Jason and I shook our heads. The word 'Nagero' was not one we wanted to hear. In my wildest dreams I never realized that Nagero, riddled with Ebola, was so close to the main Garamba camp. In fact, the deadly virus Laurent had warned us about was less than a mile away.

'There's Ebola in the village?' I asked.

The man nodded. 'Near to the village,' he said. 'Very bad.'

'Has anyone come out of there recently?' I said, asking the vital question.

'No one came out of there,' was the reply. 'They cannot.'

I wasn't sure what he meant by 'cannot'. Was it just quarantined and the villagers remained within voluntarily? I doubted it. I also wasn't sure whether I wanted to know the answer. There wasn't much we could do about it.

At around noon, José Tello, the African Parks manager, came down to the camp and introduced himself. I had heard good things about him. He was a veteran of the African bush and I knew we had mutual friends. I was pleased to meet him at last.

In his sixties, he was a strongly built, bearded man, with a craggy face wrinkled from a lifetime in the fierce African sun. He spoke good English with a strong Portuguese accent and seemed suspicious of us, saying he had not been informed of our trip. Brigit did introductions and explained matters and we were led up to the main reception building for our meeting. Garamba's resident ICCN manager was waiting for us outside the office and greeted us with a big smile. He at least seemed pleased to see us.

José took the chair, asked questions and laboriously took down notes of everything that was said, no matter how inconsequential. He was obviously not a formal person and this elaborate note-taking seemed so out of character for this man of the bush that I actually thought he was sending us up. He was dismissive of our project, making it clear that African Parks was doing a good job and really didn't need any help, thank you.

We agreed with him that African Parks was a fine institution and explained that we were a single-issue group, solely focused on saving the remaining rhino. That was our exclusive aim. We would work with African Parks through the ICCN and had no need or intention of usurping their authority in the reserve. Surely with the rhino on the verge of extinction they would welcome all physical and financial assistance? Surely every effort available should be made to save the subspecies?

José shook his head. He didn't know, and despite the high-level presence of Brigit and the ICCN officials, the tone of the meeting was less than encouraging. Brigit shook her head in exasperation.

The only positive overture came from Tello's counterpart, the ICCN park manager at Garamba, who approached us after the meeting was over. 'Mr Anthony,' he said with a warm smile, 'I am very happy you are here. Please stay with us. We need your help.'

'Thank you,' I replied. 'I appreciate your support.'

'Things are bad,' he continued. 'The LRA is a big problem and everybody is worried. The guards are scared to go out and do their jobs properly, so the poachers come in all the time. We cannot protect the rhino with the LRA in the park. Nobody can. It's better we get them out quickly. Don't worry about what happened at the meeting, I want you to help us.'

'Thank you,' I replied, impressed with his sincerity. 'Please let your head office know how you feel because there seems to be confusion here.'

'I will.'

Some real support, at last. I informed Brigit and the ICCN officials, who immediately went across and spoke to him.

A little later I went back to José and asked if we could at least borrow a vehicle to get out into the reserve and look around. He seemed to relent a little and said he would take us out personally.

JP, Jason and myself jumped at the chance and he drove us across the Dungu River, through woodlands into savannah where the long grass *Urelytrum giganteum* is said to be as 'high as an elephant's eye.' In fact, it's much higher, at times growing to an incredible fifteen feet. It was an authentic grassland forest where a herd of elephant could easily graze and you wouldn't even know they were there. The feeling I had experienced the previous night of being in absolute untainted wilderness returned. This was truly old Africa, wild, lush and beautiful, where civilization is just a vague conception. You were on your own, but the result was a sense of endless freedom. Rules and regulations in the modern world meant nothing at all out here. You made your own way. It was a rare privilege. The only sign of civilization was a couple of hastily erected two-way radio towers.

'What about the rhino, José? Do you see them?' I asked.

'Their territory is further away in the north towards the Garamba River,' he said. 'The only way to find them is from the air.'

An hour out into the superb reserve, JP started quizzing José about security, especially about the LRA.

'We haven't had physical contact with them,' replied José, 'but they're around. We've even picked them up on our two-way radios, which scares the guards. I'm battling to get them to do their jobs properly. When I put them out on patrol, all they do is hide for a while and then come straight back. I'm the only one who will even come out this far. But then I can shoot straight.' He laughed, patting his rifle.

The fact that they could pick up the LRA's radio traffic meant the rebels were in direct line of sight of the radio towers. I made a mental note. Perhaps it wasn't the authorities who controlled Garamba, but a terrorist army. Maybe the fate of the rhino was actually in the hands of the LRA.

José started to thaw towards us and we discovered that he was a really decent guy. He was a true man of the bush and, I believe, recognized the same traits in us. When you cut through all the bureaucracy that sometimes stifles conservation, we were kindred spirits.

We came across a big herd of forest buffalo that fled the instant they noticed us. Then, very luckily, we found a lone male Congo pygmy giraffe. 'There are only forty of them left in the world,' said José as we admired the diminutive creature. 'They, too, are on the verge of extinction. It's a bloody disgrace.'

'That really makes my blood boil,' said JP. 'Who the hell would want to shoot a tiny giraffe?'

José nodded in agreement. 'Don't tell me. Poaching has been a huge problem. Most of the wildlife in Garamba has been wiped out, thousands and thousands of animals have been killed. You don't even want to try and count the numbers of animals that are gone with the wind.'

I reflected on his words. A wildlife holocaust had been taking place with barely a murmur from the outside world. Indeed, the drawn look on José's face as he recounted the tragedies said it all. A lifetime spent protecting wildlife, and this is what it was all coming to. This was a man who could remember the old days when the great herds roamed free, when Africa was a glorious place for a young adventurer. My heart went out to him.

'And the northern rhino you are so interested in,' he continued, 'have been slaughtered. There were originally many thousands spread out through Uganda, the Congo and Sudan. Today there are perhaps a handful left, and I don't even know if they can be saved. And all for what? A useless bloody horn whose only real value is to the rhino.'

He pointed into the distance.

'Their last remaining home range is far over there somewhere between the Dungu and Garamba rivers. The poachers can't get in now because the rivers are full, but at the end of the rainy season, before the end of the year, the rivers will drop and that will be the end of them. We can't protect them. They are too far away and the guards won't stay out there long enough. In fact, we don't really even know where they are. We can only make an educated guess.'

That was not what I wanted to hear.

José stopped and looked up at the sky. 'We are missing the sunset.'

So we were. As the day conceded its right to the sky, deep reds, oranges and yellows were being cast all about the heavens in a magnificent, evocative display of African colours. Dawns and sunsets are nature's agents of change. Once they pass, everything is different. And so it was with us that afternoon. As the sun sank our spirits lifted, and we went back to the camp as bats and other nocturnal creatures made their first appearances, and the nightjars started calling. José invited us to dinner that night, an offer we accepted with alacrity as we hadn't eaten all day. He said he would send a vehicle around to pick us up in a couple of hours.

CHAPTER ELEVEN

The chat with José that afternoon had been extremely revealing, much more than any of us realized at first. And I was now extremely concerned.

I had believed that bureaucracy and procrastination were the major obstacles to the rhino rescue so far, but it was fast becoming obvious that perhaps the real threat was the Lord's Resistance Army in the reserve. I had a nagging feeling that this threat was being completely underestimated by the ICCN, who had not so much as mentioned the LRA to us when we met in Kinshasa. I myself had only learned the basics about them, as I certainly had not expected them to be anywhere near us in the camp. But I knew JP had done a comprehensive study on security and so, as we had a couple of hours free before dinner, I called him over.

'JP, you're the expert. What's the real story on the LRA?'

He looked at me and grimaced. 'According to sources in Uganda, they're the worst,' he said quietly. 'The absolute worst. The most savage terrorist army in the world.

'They've been fighting a vicious civil war with President Yoweri Museveni of Uganda for over twenty years, a war that has displaced millions and killed hundreds of thousands. It's the longest-running, most brutal conflict in Africa, with appalling atrocities committed on both sides. Torture, murder, abduction, rape – you name it, they do it all and then some. But the LRA take the cake for utter savagery. They have been known to cut the lips and noses off victims as a warning to others who resist them.'

I sat forward.

'The real story, though, is child soldiers. They have the most barbaric way of recruiting people to their cause. According to reports, the LRA have violently abducted something like ten thousand children from their homes over two decades of war. Their modus operandi is to raid a village, burn the place down, kill any adults who get in the way, and then abduct children. Some of whom, it is claimed, are forced to kill their own parents or other children who resist. Can you imagine that? Then the kids are made to carry all the stuff the rebels have plundered back to the jungle camps. Children as young as ten have apparently been taken. The boys are forced into their army, or killed if they refuse, and the girls are married off to the soldiers – if they're lucky. Otherwise they're used for menial labour or kept as sex slaves for the rest of their lives.

'The leader is Joseph Kony, a self-styled Old Testament prophet who worships a God of vengeance and retribution. He wants the Ten Commandments to be introduced as the law of the land in Uganda. He also has a reputation as a wizard and a clairvoyant, which he uses to control his hugely superstitious followers.

'The second-in-command is the infamous Vincent Otti. If Kony is the spiritual head then Otti is his sword, or more accurately his AK-47. Otti controls the army and is the power behind the throne. He's also responsible for the atrocities. If there is anyone more cruel and vicious than Kony, it is Otti. They say he once attacked his home village in Uganda, killing over two hundred friends and neighbours. Who knows how many deaths and child soldiers he's been responsible for over the years? Kony and Otti are best friends and have been in the bush together from the beginning. They come from the same area in Northern Uganda.

'Kony, Otti and two of their senior generals are among the world's most wanted men by the International Criminal Court at The Hague for war crimes and crimes against humanity.'

He stopped and took a deep breath. 'The LRA are like ghosts. They live deep in the jungle and forests and as far as I know no outsider has ever been into their secret camps and lived to tell the story. They moved into the Sudan in 1994, apparently at the invitation of the government in Khartoum, but that relationship soured. Now they hide out in the DRC, Southern Sudan, Uganda and Central African Republic. They move their bases continuously, and, to cap it all, I have heard they are highly disciplined and absolutely fearsome in battle. When they fight, no quarter is asked and none is given. They kill their wounded.

'To compound this, they're armed to the teeth and have surface-to-air missiles. As Laurent told us, a small group of them recently shot down two UN attack helicopters and wiped out a troop of highly trained UN Special Forces soldiers. The official figure was eight dead, but I have heard that up to forty were killed. They say they cut off the commander's head and paraded it. The LRA drove the UN troops right out of the jungle and the blue berets have never been back. That, by the way, took place right here inside Garamba, just up the road from where we are now.'

'Where are they from,' I asked.

'The LRA are mainly Acholis, the majority tribe in the north of Uganda – a Nilotic people, very different from the Bantu people in the south. Like in so many other places in Africa, there is a huge tribal element that gives an extra grudge factor to the war.'

'What do they want?' Jason asked.

'Well, they want power, but more than that they hate Museveni, a Bantu whom they believe is committing genocide against the Acholis. They hate him with an absolute, implacable loathing.

'Museveni came to power in a coup d'état in 1986, using child soldiers just as the LRA do. It is said he talked openly about using child soldiers, claiming that the West does not understand African culture. You can apparently even see this on YouTube. They say he's as barbaric as Kony and Otti, he just disguises it better. He apparently once said that he would put the Acholis "in a bottle like grasshoppers where they will eat each other".

'Due to continued LRA attacks, the Acholi nation were rounded up by Museveni's government and herded into what they call "protected villages" but were in fact horrific camps, just like the proverbial grasshoppers in a bottle as he promised. Museveni claimed it was for the Acholis' own safety, but the reality is that these crowded camps spread out over Northern Uganda are the most horrible, awful, squalid places to live anywhere in the world. The Acholi call them concentration camps, where almost two million people live in abject terror of both Kony and Museveni, existing on meagre rations barely sufficient to keep them from death's door. Medical care is virtually non-existent and a report last year from the World Health Organization, working with the Ugandan Health Ministry, found that more than a thousand people die a week from preventable diseases. Prostitution is rife, Aids endemic, corruption rampant, families dysfunctional and life expectancy is a paltry forty years. To top it all, Museveni's secret police are everywhere and the LRA claim that anyone even suspected of sympathizing with them just disappears.'

He continued, 'Then there are the children who're called the "night walkers". Every afternoon thousands of terrified kids walk for miles from the camps into nearby towns to evade the LRA. I haven't seen it myself, but I know people who have, and they say that it is the most tragic and pathetic sight, thousands and thousands of frightened children hurrying on the road, some carrying babies, walking for miles to escape the threat of either abduction or mutilation by the LRA. They call them the "invisible children". The lucky ones sometimes find a blanket in the churches, while others sleep where they can, often in bus shelters or on the pavements where they're extremely vulnerable. The next morning they wake up and walk back again to get to school, usually without food. They do this every day. Picture your own kids – can you imagine them having to do that every day?'

We were all silent for a moment. 'This is as wild as it gets,' Jason said.

'It sure is. So now you know why I originally said that this rhino rescue has got to be a really fast in-and-out operation. One reason and one reason only: the LRA.'

Then JP's years of experience in the military really came to the fore.

'I've been studying the situation here carefully,' he said. 'The reason the guards have been picking up LRA traffic on their radios is not because the rebels are out on a picnic. It's because they're busy doing full-on reconnaissance.

'Remember that until the ICCN and African Parks came in, Garamba had to all intents and purposes been completely abandoned. The LRA based in the north will be aware by now that someone has moved back into the park – someone who is arming and training a lot of men. So they are busy finding out exactly what is going on. You and I will never know it, but believe me, they are right here, right now, in the shadows watching as we speak.

'I reckon they've also set up a network of informers in the nearby tribes and I have no doubt that among all the new conscripts we saw on parade this morning will be several LRA infiltrators. They know more about this place than management does. Everything they need is here: food, supplies and, most importantly, weapons and plenty of ammunition, all in the hands of rookie guards. To them it's like a bloody great supermarket. From now on this camp will be under permanent threat. The only thing preventing a raid is that it looks as if new peace talks between the LRA and Museveni are a possibility. The government of Southern Sudan has offered to mediate and have opened a dialogue with the LRA. The LRA don't want to rock the boat – for the moment, at least. If the talks fail, and they will, Garamba will be hit. It's just too much of a prize. So we need to get the rhino out of here before the talks end or break down. Or else we've lost them for good.'

He was absolutely right. 'JP, you're a mamba,' I said. 'Thank you.'

Outside we heard a vehicle arriving to pick us up for dinner.

'Let's have a couple of drinks with José,' said JP, pulling two bottles of Johnnie Walker Scotch Whisky out of his suitcase. 'I need to find out more about what is going on.'

CHAPTER TWELVE

The meal on the spacious verandah at José's farmhouse by the river was simple, spaghetti with bolognese sauce. We'd had no other food all day and were so ravenous we would have put starving hyenas to shame.

Although José had a wife and children in Portugal, he had spent most of his life in Africa, and you could tell he was a hardcore outdoorsman who loved the wilderness deeply. Old Africa hands are a different breed, living months at a time out in the deepest bush and never seeing a white face. If you wanted to meet the complete antithesis of a desk jockey, José was your man. I instinctively knew that if there was anyone who would do his best for the wildlife in Garamba, he would. Perhaps his initial resentment of us was because he distrusted anything that came with bureaucratic approval. I knew exactly how he felt. I also noticed the ICCN officials with us did not particularly impress him, although they technically were his employers. In fact, they weren't even invited to dinner. Brigit was tired and decided not to join us – a sensible move, as it turned out!

The night went on; the first empty bottle of whisky clattered into the refuse bin, and the second was cracked open. By now most of the staff had gone home and Jason, who had wisely refrained from joining the whisky-and-water marathon, decided to go to bed. There were fresh lion tracks through the camp so an armed guard escorted him back to the hut. As he got into bed, he heard the clear bark of a leopard. He rushed to the flimsy window and looked straight into the eyes of a full-grown male leopard sitting just a few yards away. He must have walked right past it. He told me he went to sleep dreaming of prowling leopards, lion tracks outside his door, squadrons of malarial mosquitoes dive-bombing the bed and killer *siafu* rustling in the undergrowth.

But back to José. There were so many unanswered questions in this wild, anarchic area and we were hoping he knew some of the answers. JP picked his moment.

'What the hell is going on in Garamba, my friend? Why are we being given the runaround with the rhinos? Or must I give you some more whisky to get a truthful answer?' he asked with a broad smile on his face.

José laughed.

'I'm serious,' said JP. 'Let's cut the crap.'

'All in good time,' said José, pouring more drinks. He was in no rush – this was probably one of the few times he'd had visitors since arriving in Garamba and he was going to make the most of it.

He told us he had spent some time in South Africa and had done work on lions with the famous Dr Ian Player in the Umfolozi game reserve. When he heard that Ian and I were friends, he was visibly impressed, and this I think finally convinced him that we weren't just a bunch of well-meaning bunny-huggers. I then retold Ian's story about how many years ago in Zululand the young game rangers were sometimes out in the bush for months on end without female company. They would return to camp unwashed, sweaty – and hopeful. But, as Ian would say, 'the *nthombis* [girls] were not interested and the baboons were too fast!' After that and a few more strong whiskies, which José dispensed liberally, he finally loosened up.

'You want to know what is going on? I'll tell you, but don't take offence. You're wasting your time trying to save the northern white rhino, my friends. They're gone. Instead you should repopulate this area with southern whites. There are plenty of them in South Africa. Let's rather do a joint programme to bring them in here.'

JP and I looked at each other. This was certainly news to us.

'But the information we have is that there're still fifteen left,' I said. 'If we can get those out of here, we can get a breeding herd going.'

He shook his head. 'Even if there are fifteen left, which I doubt, the gene pool is too small. You're chasing rainbows.'

Was this the real reason there was no appetite for a rescue in Kinshasa? José was African Parks' man in charge and the fate of the last few northern white rhinos must have been very high on the agenda when they took over Garamba. Had they already given up? I had a bad feeling about this and shook my head in frustration.

'José, this is a subspecies that is going extinct unless we move our butts. If there is just the tiniest chance of saving them, we must take it. Let's not worry about head office crap right now. Will you help us?'

'Of course. I'm not going anywhere. Head office is thinking of doing an aerial survey to count how many are left.'

'"Thinking about it" – well, I suppose that's a start,' said JP facetiously.

José shrugged. 'I am afraid that's the way things are. I have a lot on my plate.'

'We haven't got time to just "think about" anything,' I countered. 'We have to bloody well do something – immediately. We have to find them, then dart and tag them, and then we go back and bring them in. We can do it in just two quick operations. Otherwise they are gone, I tell you. Gone!'

'Well, good luck to you,' said José, glass held high in a toast.

'You get your approval from the powers-that-be and I will help you.'

Eventually we ran out of water. All water on the reserve came straight from the Dungu River and had to be purified. Happily, I thought that was the end of the session. But no; José ordered the last remaining member of staff on duty to go down alone through the bush to the river in the middle of the night and get another bucket, which he dutifully – and very bravely, I must add – did. I certainly wouldn't have, not in the dark with the crocodiles and hippos I had seen in the river, or the lion moving about.

Then José boiled the river water and again topped up our glasses, mixing the whisky directly with the water coming out of the kettle. He didn't waste time waiting for it to cool, although how cool it would get on a humid African night I do not know. Steaming hot water and whisky virtually slap on the equator in the bush is not an experience I will forget, and certainly would not want to repeat.

Eventually at about 4.30 a.m. we ran out of whisky as well as tepid river water. José was still as steady as a statue, lamenting the fact that it was difficult to find good whisky or good friends. He obviously put us in that camp, as we did him.

'JP, the sun is coming up. The plane's leaving in an hour and a half,' I said. 'We've got to try and get at least a bit of sleep.'

José offered to drive us back to our huts, still complaining about the whisky running out. The man had the constitution of a buffalo.

He dropped us off and JP was walking – or, more correctly, weaving – towards his hut when suddenly I heard a string of lurid expletives followed by a loud, 'Bloody hell, they're all over me!'

He was hopping around, shouting and frantically slapping his legs.

'What's the problem, man?'

'Ants! And the buggers can bite!' he said, stamping his feet.

The *siafu* column was returning from its hunt and he had walked right into them. I rushed over, albeit slowed by whisky. Thankfully JP was now out of the path of the rampaging ants and was rubbing the multitude of bites on his burning legs, muttering curses. We both started laughing and staggered back to our respective huts. As I collapsed into bed, I fortunately was still aware enough to make sure the mosquito netting was tight.

We were due to leave at 6 a.m., and our pilot had warned us that his entire schedule would be out of sync if we were fractionally late. In fact, he would leave without us.

In what seemed like a split second later, I was shaken awake by Jason and told the plane would be taking off in ten minutes. I felt rotten, but not nearly as bad as JP, who definitely didn't want to wake up at all.

'I like it here,' he groaned when we got to his room. 'Come back for me in a couple of weeks. I still have to get revenge on José.'

JP had valiantly matched José drink for drink – all in the line of duty, you understand – whereas I, like a wuss, had secretly poured some of mine into a rather forlorn flowerbed nearby. He had also fallen asleep with a bare leg sticking out from the netting and it was an angry red mass of mosquito bites, which were doubly painful on top of the *siafu* attack. He was in bad shape, but looking at him it seemed to me to be more than a heavy night's drinking. He didn't seem well at all. He's got malaria, I thought.

We somehow got him up and then we saw José's Land Cruiser still parked where he had dropped us off, the charismatic Portuguese ranger fast asleep, snoring behind the wheel. The driver's door had been wide open, beckoning to the plentiful carnivores. Perhaps it was the smell of whisky on his breath that kept them at bay.

JP started laughing and walked over and shook him awake. 'Thanks for everything, mate,' he said. José was human after all, and a really good guy.

Once on the plane, JP gave up and curled on the floor among the baggage at the back. It was stiflingly hot and I could see the sweat pouring off him.

'JP,' I said, going over to him, 'I think you've got malaria.'

'Probably. Nothing we can do about it. Relax and let me sleep.'

Malaria, which is carried by the anopheles mosquito, is a potentially fatal disease and I was genuinely worried. Symptoms include fever, violent shivering, sweating and nausea – all of which JP was showing. But he was right; there was nothing that could be done. He was experienced enough to know he would have to tough it out until he got back to South Africa for treatment.

On the way, the pilot announced we would be making an unscheduled stop to drop off and collect mail at a convent in the middle of nowhere. Below us was what seemed like a runway, cut as thin as a piece of string into the rainforest. We slid between the giant trees and landed. As we stopped, dozens of eager children came running out of the little school, followed by the nuns. A plane landing was a big event and they were not going to miss it. They crowded closer when we set down, and as we descended the stairs they were pressing right around us, giggling with excitement.

'Isn't this great?' said Jason. 'Look how happy they are to see visitors.'

Suddenly the laughter stopped and the expression on the cherubic faces changed to absolute panic. Behind me I heard a roar and swung around to see JP standing at the top of the aeroplane stairs. His shirt was out, his hair was sticking up like a clogged rake and sweat was drooling off his chin from the malaria. He is a huge man. He looked like an apparition from Dante's *Inferno*.

'Hey, Lawrence,' he bellowed at the top of his voice. 'Let's show these people what a real South African *babelaas* [hangover] looks like.'

As he spoke, he went down onto the grass runway and lay there, arms outstretched, laughing out loud. The children crowded around the nuns, grabbing at their robes in alarm. Thankfully Jason walked over to them and made a joke of it all, which got them laughing again.

I looked at the bright faces before me and thought of both the LRA and Museveni stealing children just like these away from their parents on days just like this, and the unimaginable horrors they inflicted upon such innocence.

We helped JP back into the plane, where he resumed his position on the floor. It was only when we returned to South Africa that we found out he did indeed have malaria, which, because of the incubation period, he must have contracted before the expedition. Malaria attacks the liver; how he managed to match José drink for drink is staggering. Anybody else would have been out for the count, but then JP is not anybody else.

The trip to Garamba was a turning point for us. The LRA was a big problem but at least we knew what we were dealing with. One thing I knew was that the aircraft used for the rescue would attract attention, and anything flying over one of their patrols could be shot down. Additionally, we needed to prepare for the possibility of a ground attack, and I knew JP was already doing that. But how do you fight against a terrorist army? Hold them off for a while with a contingent of good men, possibly. But take them on in battle? No way.

There was another idea forming in my head but it would mean shaking hands with the devil himself. No way, I decided.

It was so over the top that I immediately discarded it. There had to be another option.

The good news was that José believed there were still some surviving rhinos, and I knew there were some in the Dvůr Králové Zoo in the Czech Republic to provide genetic diversity.

Perhaps we could still pull the rescue off. But that was only if we got crucial support and approval from the ICCN and African Parks without any more procrastination. Spring is when the rivers fill up again and protect the rhinos. As José had said, once the poachers could cross the drying rivers and get into the rhinos' territory, that would be it.

We landed in Kinshasa, thanks to the pilot's skill as well as perhaps to the prayers offered beforehand.

'You know something,' I said to Jason as we joined the untamed traffic into the city. 'This is really weird, but it seems we have just arrived home and landed in the lap of luxury.'

Jason laughed. 'We're back in the real world.'

It was true. Compared to the feral yet magnificent paradise of Garamba, Kinshasa was indeed civilization.

None of us ever thought we would say that about this chaotic capital.

CHAPTER THIRTEEN

When I arrived back home at Thula Thula, the elephants were near the gate. They hadn't come to meet me this way for some time and just being close to them lifted my spirits, their welcome making the stresses of the past few days seem almost trivial.

There they were: Nana, Frankie, ET, Marula, Nandi and their various offspring we had never named and never would. They were wild. But there they all were at the gate waiting for me, for some reason that I don't think we could ever fathom, or need to. Perhaps there was no reason; they were just there.

I stopped and got out of my car. Nana came forward and slowly lifted her trunk to my chest. The sheer size of her blotted out the sun as she stood there, wrapping me in a bubble of contentment, and for a few moments I had never felt better or more alive.

It also gave me the opportunity to look carefully at her eye, hoping that the treatment had worked. To my dismay, it hadn't. The eye was still milky. But there was nothing more we could do.

Eventually they left, and as they moved away I picked out Heidi, a speck in the far horizon. I reached into the Land Rover for my binoculars and focused on her grazing complacently in the Zululand grasslands that had been her ancestral home for aeons. Watching her reminded me of her cousins on the run for their lives in Garamba. How such incredibly powerful creatures could be so vulnerable was a crime against the universe. The tragic futility of it all was what really got me. The rhino's brilliant million-year evolutionary effort to build up three tons of muscle, bone and horn to defend itself meant nothing in a modern technological world that didn't care a fig about them. The fact that our grandchildren may never see a rhino in the wild again was a pivotal reason to continue to try and save them.

I knew what we were up against in the Congo. The logistics alone were mind-numbing and the odds of pulling off a complex rhino rescue in such a remote area were slim indeed. We had to be creative about what we could do and what we planned to do. Queensberry rules would go out the window – we had to be as clever and cunning as jackals if we wanted to succeed. There would be no second chance if we failed.

I drove up to our cottage, where Françoise was waiting on the lawn. She jumped up and gave me a huge hug as the dogs scrambled around my legs, yapping excitedly. I often wonder what I put her through with some of these journeys, going to crazy places that just months ago we didn't even know existed. She always accepts my expeditions and escapades with total support and understanding, which gives me the wherewithal to continue.

She had a surprise for me today.

'David is here. He's come back for good,' she said, taking my hand and leading me inside. 'And guess what? Brendan's come over for a visit. They're down at the lodge.'

We drove to the lodge and even before entering I heard their animated voices in the lounge.

'Elephants really busticate trees,' said Brendan Whittington-Jones.

'What is it with you and all these fancy words?' David Bozas responded. 'Yesterday the elephants were anthropomorphic, today they busticate. Do you just make them up as you go along?'

'Busticate is a real word, it means to break things apart. It's where the word bust comes from. And anthropomorphic means human-like,' retorted Brendan.

'So why don't you just say so? You're starting to sound like a nerd. Actually, I'm beginning to think you are a closet nerd.'

'And you? What about you? You still think Elvis is the King. Who still thinks that? I'll tell you who – nobody. I mean, you actually think the Black Eyed Peas are a vegetable.'

'Well, Elvis would never have said busticate. It's a bloody stupid word. And of course he is still the King,' David retorted. Then he added, 'And he's still alive. He was seen in a supermarket in Memphis just last year.'

They both jumped up, grinning broadly as I walked in. I noticed George the bushbaby, on one of his return visits, had already taken a shine to David and was sitting on his shoulder. David tried to remove him as we shook hands and got a sharp nip for his efforts.

'You little bugger,' said David, sucking his finger. George gripped him ever tighter and then, seeing Françoise, immediately made a long hop across to her shoulder and tucked himself in against her neck.

David was back from Afghanistan, Brendan had popped in to say hello and they were already arguing like a married couple. It was as though they had never left.

David Bozas was the fearless young 'can do' ranger who was with me when the troubled and then very dangerous elephants first arrived (as told in *The Elephant Whisperer*). I had recently bought Thula Thula and we had many wonderful bush adventures together, establishing the reserve and settling Nana and her herd. He had left four years before to attend the prestigious Royal Military Academy at Sandhurst in England and, after graduating as an officer, did a tour of duty with the British Army in Afghanistan, seeing a lot of action. Now he was back with us permanently. David is a natural leader and a man of the bush to his marrow, never happier than when out in the wild with a pile of problems to solve, animal or human. The last time I had seen him was in the smoke of London, where he had been a true fish out of water. We had met for a quick drink at a Soho pub called the Dog and Duck and, as I was ordering a round, David – a strapping, exceptionally good-looking young man – had come up to me and said that the people were 'real friendly' around here.

'Just a second ago, this guy came up to me and asked if I wanted some coke. I said, no thanks, you were busy buying me one.'

A good friend, Nick Thomas, was with us and he and I roared with laughter.

'He was actually trying to sell you cocaine – and probably chat you up at the same time,' wheezed Nick in between guffaws.

David was outraged. How dare anyone try and sell him drugs? We explained that in Soho, one of London's trendiest quarters, anything goes.

'Well, not with me,' retorted David. 'If that guy comes back again he's going to get properly thumped.'

Now, I could tell just by looking at the energized expression on his face that David had truly come home to Africa.

Brendan Whittington-Jones was my former head ranger and had been my right-hand man during a rescue mission at the Baghdad Zoo after the coalition invasion in 2003. The zoo, the biggest in the Middle East, had been the site of the key battle for the city between the Americans and the Iraqi Revolutionary Guards, the forces loyal to Saddam Hussein. When I arrived, hundreds of animals had died in their enclosures or been plundered for food. There was a blind bear cowering in her cage, paralysed with terror from the thunder of bombs she couldn't see, while all animals without teeth or claws to defend themselves had either starved to death, died of thirst or been killed and eaten by rampaging mobs. I got Brendan over to help me, and with a handful of incredibly brave Iraqi zoo workers and crucial assistance from a US Army captain, we managed to save the remaining animals and get the place functional again. Happily, the Americans invested millions in the facility, and today it is one of the showpieces of the city. (The story of the Baghdad Zoo rescue is recounted in my first book, *Babylon's Ark*.)

Brendan was now back in Zululand doing research on the highly endangered African wild dogs in the neighbouring Um-folozi game reserve. A good-looking young man, slim but well built, with red hair, I have never met someone so at ease with himself and so gloriously oblivious to issues he considered inconsequential. The fact that when he was head ranger at Thula Thula he shared his bed with a dog and an epileptic warthog called Napoleon – then wondered why he didn't have a girl-friend – says it all. But that was Brendan.

'Françoise says you went to a party last night,' I asked. 'How was it?'

'Good. But that damned drive back is getting to be a bit of a hassle.'

'What do you mean?'

'Well, I got tired driving home and decided to have a bit of a sleep in the reserve. But my legs were cramped in the Land Rover so I got onto the loading bin at the back and dropped the tail flap for a bit more space. I was fast asleep when I felt some-thing pulling me off the back. I woke up and a damn big hyena had his teeth around my boot. He obviously wanted me to go home with him.'

'And then?'

'What do you think I did? I gave it a hard kick in the snout and told it to bugger off.'

'Did it?'

'Yes.'

'And then?'

'Well, I went back to sleep, of course.'

'Did you close the tail flap?'

'Nah, I was too tired.'

'The hyena was lucky you didn't discuss your thesis with him,' chirped David. 'You would've bored him to death with all your big words.'

It was great to have them back. David would be working with me again and Brendan would be close by, as Umfolozi was less than an hour away. No doubt there would be more conversations about 'busticating' and whether Elvis was still alive.

It was also just the tonic I needed to unwind before tackling the rhino issue again. I was scheduled to visit the DRC in a week or two for what could be one of the most important meetings of my life.

CHAPTER FOURTEEN

On the surface, our preparations for the rhino rescue were going as well as could be expected. And we were lucky that Dave Cooper, the famous KwaZulu-Natal wildlife vet, had agreed to join the project. Dave was a good friend, but more importantly he was probably the top rhino man in Africa. I also had positive discussions with other competent wildlife veterinarians who were keen to help.

In fact, the only cause for concern so far was bureaucracy. Jason had been in contact with African Parks to get the go-ahead for the rescue, but they referred us to the ICCN, who in turn referred us back to African Parks in an ongoing, extremely frustrating merry-go-round. So we briefed Ambassador M'Poko, who made some enquiries and came back saying everything had been resolved and that we would receive an invitation from the environment minister to visit him and attend the annual CoCo-Congo conservation conference in Kinshasa.

JP, who had recovered from his bout of malaria, Jason and Dr Ian Raper made up our delegation and we travelled to Kinshasa in high spirits, expecting to get the final go-ahead now that we had been to Garamba. I mean, who would veto major assistance in saving a species from extinction? We purposely arrived a day early to meet with the minister, but first we needed a catch-up with Laurent Guepin at the United Nations' MONUC compound.

Laurent welcomed us and then introduced us to some of his colleagues and seniors including Bill Swing, the head of MONUC. The fact that a rhino species was going extinct on their doorstep had struck a chord. They had done their homework and there was a strong interest and willingness to help. What was now needed was a formal letter from the minister confirming government support for the rescue.

Laurent had achieved incredible results. He had taken responsibility for an extremely difficult request and done everything he could to make it happen. He was obviously a man with vision and this was a huge breakthrough indeed. I started daring to dream that we could pull it off – that the last remaining wild northern whites could indeed be saved.

We hailed a decrepit taxi outside the MONUC compound and made our way to the environment minister's office, where he greeted us effusively, praising the assistance from South Africa for the rescue initiative and for getting MONUC's support. He concluded by handing us a formal government-endorsed letter of approval for the project, exactly what Laurent had requested for his file. We went straight back to MONUC with the letter. Things were looking up.

Laurent had the best news for us imaginable. They were on board and going to provide not only the aircraft we desperately needed to airlift the rhino to safety, but also a contingent of soldiers to protect them. We would, of course, have to fit in with their timing, but they were fully committed to the rescue.

By now it was late afternoon. The city's few relatively modern hotels were full because of the conference and we were forced to book into a shabby guesthouse. It started badly when Ian turned on the basin tap in the bathroom and the water squirted out of a dodgy joint in the piping and hit him in the knees. What a dump – but then we had more important things on our minds. It was at least a roof over our heads.

That night we ventured into the *Mad Max* city, as Jason called Kinshasa, for a superb Chinese dinner. The only problem was that there were no taxis when we came out late at night, so we braced ourselves for the mile or so walk back to the guesthouse. We weren't a hundred yards from the restaurant when a family sedan pulled up.

'Taxi,' the driver called out.

'Yes!' shouted JP and we all climbed in. In Kinshasa, we discovered, every car is a potential taxi. This driver was going to visit relatives but picked up anyone along the way who wanted a lift and charged them, as did pretty much every other car owner in the city.

The next morning, after being kept awake by a local reggae band screeching the same three songs outside our windows until 4.30 a.m., we proceeded to the conference at the Memling Hotel in the city centre.

It was an ostentatious affair, contrasting starkly with the deprived city outside, attended by business-suited delegates and entourages who had flown in from all over the world. We found our seats, and a little later I was given a brief opportunity to address the conference from the podium through an interpreter. I outlined the rhino rescue plan and confirmed the minister's support, to a smattering of applause.

Much later in the day we were summoned to a meeting with the ICCN. Attending were the ICCN Director General and José Kalpers of African Parks, while Brigit represented the minister. Also present were representatives from the International Union for Conservation of Nature (IUCN) in Paris and the United Nations Educational, Scientific and Cultural Organization (UNESCO). To my delight, José Tello had come all the way from Garamba and greeted us warmly. This was a high-powered delegation and I allowed myself the luxury of believing that common sense would prevail and we could kick-start the rescue mission.

I was wrong. It was one of the most depressing meetings I have ever attended.

Before talks even began, we were called aside by the ICCN and, with African Parks officials looking on, sanctimoniously informed that were we had no right to meet the environment minister or to participate in any Garamba operation without the sanction of the ICCN. We were reminded that there was already an agreement in place between the ICCN and African Parks regarding Garamba National Park.

Taken aback at this censure out of the blue, we reiterated that we were well aware of the agreement and that our involvement was a direct result of an invitation by the environment minister himself through the DRC's ambassador to South Africa. It was not some random idea that we had concocted just for the hell of it.

This seemingly logical explanation obviously made no impression, so I continued in a more formal tone. 'The ICCN says our participation in the rescue must be at the behest of African Parks, but African Parks just keeps referring us back to the ICCN, and vice versa. We were getting nowhere, so we went back to the ambassador in South Africa for advice on protocol. We were advised that the correct diplomatic route to the ICCN is through the minister. That's exactly what we did.'

I added that we had a letter from the government formally requesting us to initiate the rescue in conjunction with the ICCN. Did this not mean something?

Well, obviously not. Whatever we said, it seemed to us that the ICCN and African Parks were not in the slightest bit interested – despite official government decrees on our behalf.

This attitude continued into the meeting, where bureaucracy rather than action appeared to me to be the main item on the agenda.

At last we came to the all-important rescue. African Parks

started by telling delegates that a fixed-wing aircraft aerial survey was being planned.

We immediately supported the plan for a census. Not only that, we were pleased to offer the use of a helicopter, a Bell Jet Ranger, already at our disposal which was perfect for the job. It would cost them nothing.

Our offer was rejected out of hand. I have no idea of their reasons for this.

I was stunned. 'On what possible basis would you use a fixed-wing aircraft instead of a helicopter for the census?' I asked. 'The situation is critical. As soon as the rhino are located they must be darted and implanted with a tracking device so we can find them again later for the rescue. You can't do that from a fixed-wing – you have to use the helicopter. Also, if the bush is thick you may miss some of the animals in a plane flying overhead. With a helicopter you have both speed and manoeuvrability. You can hover when you need to.'

Well, that rationale went down like a lead balloon. They wanted a plane instead of a helicopter.

So I tried again, trying to hammer home the obvious. 'If you do that, you are going to have to find them twice; once to count them, and then again later to rescue them. It's a huge, difficult, dangerous area to search. When we find them we have to grab the opportunity to dart them immediately so we can implant transmitters into their horns to find them for the rescue. You may not get that chance again.'

I shook my head in exasperation. 'It just doesn't make sense not to use a helicopter.'

The delegates looked at me, faces like stone. They were going to use a fixed-wing plane, no matter how many holes we punched in their argument.

Then they moved on, discussing dates for the survey to be conducted some time in the future.

Again I interjected, to the obvious displeasure of some delegates. 'That's far too late; we must act now. In fact, right now. The rhino are between the Dungu and Garamba rivers.' I stabbed at an imaginary map. 'According to your own men on the ground in Garamba, the fact that these rivers are in flood is the reason – in fact, probably the only reason – that any of them are still alive. Once the rainy season ends, the rivers will drop and the poachers will be able to cross over and get to the rhino. And that will be the end of it.'

One delegate dismissively brushed aside my argument. 'But our next meeting will only be after that. We can't just decide now.'

It was utterly incomprehensible. In other words, it was a mere inconvenience that the dry season – a certain death sentence for the rhino – would arrive before their next get-together.

I put my head in my hands. I could not believe what I was hearing. The rescue was off the table; dead and buried by an avalanche of bureaucratic obstinacy. I was shaking I was so angry.

The meeting ended and as we moved off I overheard someone say facetiously, 'The problem is that Mr Anthony thinks he loves the northern white rhino more than we do.'

I turned to see a few of the delegates smirking.

I shook my head. They hadn't done their homework. Why else would they refuse government-approved professional help with the wolf on their doorstep? Garamba was an extremely dangerous place. If the ICCN and African Parks genuinely understood what they were up against, and what the LRA was capable of doing, they would be laying out the red carpet for us – or, for that matter, anyone else crazy enough to risk their lives and money to go out on such a project.

It seemed to me that the only people who actually understood what was going on were the ICCN's manager at Garamba and his guards, who were now actually abandoning patrols and hiding. They knew what they were up against, all right.

It was then that the reality of what had just happened struck me. I knew then, with blinding clarity, that the fate of the northern white rhino had been sealed in stone at that meeting. That unless a miracle happened, the species would go extinct in the wild. Not because of poachers or the LRA, not because of these very real physical threats, but because of the curse of so many conservation efforts: hubris and self-interest.

I found myself slipping from anger into apathy. It took a supreme effort not to walk away from that building, away from Kinshasa, and to return to the sanity of Thula Thula where I could do some constructive work.

Ian, usually a calm, extremely rational man, was riled. 'I fully expected scientific evidence to be presented at a meeting of this nature. They have substituted sentiment for scientific research, and the results are predictably illogical. This has to be one of the most inept meetings I have ever attended,' he fumed.

JP and Jason shook their heads dejectedly.

'Well, the rescue is off,' said JP. 'It's a waste of time reporting back to the minister. All we can do now is go to Bene M'Poko in South Africa and see what he says.'

The delegates moved through to the lounge and restaurant area. Soon afterwards I saw Laurent from MONUC walk into the restaurant. I called him aside for a debriefing.

He was shocked. 'That's ridiculous. I can't believe what you're telling me.'

'We can't believe it either.'

We chatted for a bit, and then in a last-ditch attempt to restore some sanity I walked across to where the other delegates were sitting.

They stopped talking as I approached and looked up at me. I took a deep breath and said, 'If for some reason you need confirmation of the United Nations support for our initiative, the key MONUC people are sitting over there and you are welcome to speak to them.'

I pointed out Laurent.

A little while later I saw the IUCN representative go over to Laurent and have a brief conversation. As soon as she left, Laurent beckoned me over.

'I just want you to know that the IUCN representative asked if we were supporting your rescue initiative. I said yes. She then asked if the planes and equipment were also available to them.'

I stared at him. 'You're joking! What did you say?'

'I told her our arrangements were with you. We were satisfied that your proposal was viable and that we would not be changing.'

'I cannot believe it,' I said. 'We have placed ourselves, our finance, our equipment, our resources – everything – at the disposal of the ICCN in any event. Why would anyone try and sneak in through the back door to get something that has already been offered to them absolutely free and on a silver plate?'

'Let's see if they come back to you.'

They never did.

We packed our bags dejectedly and flew back to South Africa, where a couple of days at Thula Thula started to bring back some much-needed perspective.

If the world lost the northern white rhino, it would be the largest mammal since the woolly mammoth to go extinct. This was not just my problem. This was an international crisis playing itself out on a stage much bigger than all of us. The rhino didn't know and didn't care about politics, status or bureaucracy. And nor, I vowed, would I.

Unforunately, the only solution I could now see was an idea so radical that I was originally too shocked even to consider it.

The problem in Garamba was simple: the guards were too scared to do their jobs properly. The reason was the pervasive presence of the LRA in Garamba park.

But what if that threat could be removed? Was that even possible? Could the LRA – one of the world's most reviled and dangerous rebel armies – even be contacted?

I swallowed hard.

CHAPTER FIFTEEN

About a week after the disastrous CoCoCongo meeting, I got a call from JP in Pretoria. JP is as tenacious as a bull terrier, and he wasn't going to give up on the rhino rescue, no matter what the conservation authorities in the DRC said.

'Lawrence, I've been speaking with Ambassador M'Poko, and he's accepted our invitation to visit Thula Thula to talk about the problems with the rhino rescue. Is this weekend good for you?'

'Perfect,' I said.

'Good. He's coming with his wife and three children. We'll arrive on Friday at lunchtime. I'll bring them down in my plane.'

'Excellent,' I replied. 'It's going to be an interesting discussion.'

We checked that our bush airstrip was free of new termite mounds or burrows, both of which can be deadly if they snag a wheel and flip a plane over. Then we collected some firewood and placed it near the runway. We didn't have a windsock and the smoke from a small fire served to give pilots wind direction.

We also checked that the herd was nowhere nearby. Our elephants really have a thing about aeroplanes. I once saw Frankie charge a small plane just as it was taking off. The aircraft was taxiing down the runway trying to build up speed with this huge angry elephant in full pursuit, hell-bent on destruction. The pilot couldn't believe his eyes and it certainly gave him some serious incentive to get airborne. Luckily, he got up and away just in time. He never came back again, for some reason.

On Friday, JP and the M'Pokos arrived on schedule and Jason, Dylan, a couple of rangers and myself watched as JP came in low, buzzing the airstrip to drive off any animals that might be lurking nearby and interfere with the landing. He then lined up his approach and cleared the trees at the far end of the runway. Then, as he touched the ground, the plane suddenly slewed violently to the left.

I could clearly see JP in the cockpit, neck muscles protruding like whipcords as he desperately fought the controls. My heart jumped as the plane viciously veered left again. A split second later the wing caught a tree and the now uncontrolled plane sped off the runway and plunged into the bush with a deafening crash that could be heard for miles. I gasped at the terrible violence of the impact, fully expecting to see a fireball soar into the sky, incinerating JP and his passengers in an instant.

Then it was still. Eerily still. We started running.

As I sprinted I saw out of the corner of my eye a herd of panicked zebra bolting, followed by three giraffe. A large flock of hadedas lifted into the air, calling loudly with their distinctive 'hah-dee-dah' cry.

The group of us reached the wreckage and clambered frantically over smashed trees and uprooted vegetation to reach any survivors. But I feared the worst. No one could live through that high-speed smash.

Miraculously, the plane was still upright, lying on its belly between the splintered carnage of broken trees. There was no movement in the cabin and I grabbed the handle and started wrenching at the buckled door.

My fears were realized. The bodies inside were all still.

Then JP stirred, shook his head and, leaning across from the pilot's side, put his shoulder to the door on the inside, helping me. The extra muscle worked and the crumpled door came off at the hinges. Next to JP the ambassador started trying to unbuckle his seat belt. Behind him on the back seats nobody moved.

'JP, we must get out quickly!' I whispered to him in a hiss, trying not to panic the passengers.

'I know,' he replied lucidly as he started climbing out. 'I'm OK. Get the others out.'

'The other doors! Open the doors!' shouted Jason, and within seconds we had yanked all the doors open and pulled everybody out, stumbling in our haste to get away from the plane that I feared may still explode at any minute.

'Is anybody hurt?' JP called out, going from one passenger to the next, making sure they were all right.

Understandably, they were shell-shocked, but for people who had just come out of the sky and smashed into the bush at a near-fatal speed, they were handling it well. It was a miracle no one was seriously injured. The ambassador had a pain in his foot and that was all. His wife and children were dazed but fine. What had saved them was that despite the front and rear of the plane being completely crushed like a concertina, the passenger compartment was intact.

What was equally astonishing was that the plane did not catch fire. Smashing into a cluster of trees with a tank of highly inflammable avgas is tempting fate.

The rangers helped everyone into the game drive vehicles and took them to the lodge, where Françoise, who had heard about the smash thanks to the animated chatter over our two-way radios, was waiting with the French panacea for all of life's ills: champagne.

The French method worked perfectly. After everyone had settled down, JP came across and slapped me on the back with the force of a bazooka.

'We made it this time, *ou maat* – old friend.' This would not be the first time JP had escaped death by a fraction in his adventurous life.

I nodded. 'Only you could have pulled that off and got your passengers out alive. What happened?'

He shrugged. 'As we touched down we lost our undercarriage and hydraulics. It was a tough one.' That's about as close as JP will get to admitting he stared death in the face.

'Well, everyone made it and you are OK. That's all that counts,' I said, then mock-frowned. 'Well, not all – you damaged my trees. Are you going to pay me now or later?'

JP roared with laughter.

Despite the drama, later in the evening we were able to sit down with the ambassador and update him on the disastrous CoCoCongo meeting. Bene M'Poko was an astute diplomat and he was clearly exasperated by what he was hearing.

'This is all completely unnecessary,' he said. 'I will continue to do what I can. I'm travelling to Kinshasa shortly and will speak with the minister and the president about it.'

'Thank you,' JP replied. 'You've always been most helpful. Someone is going to have to take responsibility if the world loses these rhino.'

The ambassador nodded. 'Indeed.'

Perhaps there was still some hope.

While I was waiting to hear if the ambassador was able to influence the rescue, I had one last hand to play. African Parks was founded by a successful Dutch businessman and conservationist by the name of Paul van Vlissingen. Perhaps if we could somehow get to meet him, he would see reason and break the impasse. Fotunately he was in South Africa, and to his great credit he accepted the meeting despite being extremely ill.

The meeting took place at the Marakele game reserve in the far north of South Africa. I was unable to attend so Jason and

JP agreed to meet him. Somehow though JP got lost which left Jason to do the very important presentation alone.

'He was a man with a big presence and I liked him immediately,' Jason told me afterwards. 'I recall explaining matters for about fifteen minutes or so. He waited for me to finish speaking, then he lit a cigar, looked at me, and instantly agreed that we could do the rescue in conjunction with African Parks and the ICCN – which is exactly what we had been proposing all along. That was it, finally it was done.'

African Parks were on board at last. This was the best possible news and we immediately contacted the ICCN and informed them of African Parks' decision. A few days later we received a response saying that they agreed to the rescue provided African Parks agreed.

But they have agreed, we replied.

And with that the ridiculous merry-go-round started again and we were unable to make any more progress.

CHAPTER SIXTEEN

I was driving to our rhino rescue centre at the Earth Organization's headquarters in Durban to give a report back to my team when my cellphone rang. It was David Bozas; he had just taken over operations at Thula Thula and he already had his hands full.

'Hi, boss, we have a bit of a problem here.'

'What's up?'

'At about ten this morning we found a baby elephant wandering around all on its own. A male.'

'How old is it?'

'Can't be more than a few hours. He must have been born early today. Still has the umbilical cord attached.'

'A few hours old and it is alone?' I said, surprised. 'That's impossible. The mother must be close by.'

'I've done a full search and there isn't an elephant within a mile,' he replied.

'That's unusual. What's his condition?' I asked, trying to work out what had happened.

'Stressed and weak, but not injured – just standing around, lost. We found him in a small gully. I have a couple of rangers standing by in case hyenas arrive. I'm going to bring him in.'

'OK, phone our vet, Leottie Morkel, and ask her if she can come out and have a look. Tell her to bring a drip.'

'Sure,' said David. 'I'll also arrange for bottles and the milk mixture.'

Bringing in a baby elephant, which basically means grabbing it and taking it somewhere safe, is not as easy as it sounds. At just a few hours old, it may be vulnerable, but it still weighs about 240 pounds and will strenuously resist being handled.

However, I knew David was highly competent and would do everything possible to keep the baby calm and alive. It was great to have him back.

He first blocked off the bottom of the gully with rocks and dead branches and then, after putting a foam mattress and blanket in the back of the Land Rover, he slowly reversed into the opposite end, trapping the baby elephant.

He and his three rangers quickly grabbed the little guy, gently but firmly, and after much pushing and pulling from the humans and squealing from the elephant, they managed to ease the baby blimp into the back and quickly slam shut the flap. Two rangers then held him down on the mattress until he relaxed a little.

So far, so good. Despite having had nothing to drink since it was born, David thought the baby was still strong enough to survive. Leottie was on her way with a drip, and all that was now needed was to get it to our house where it could be treated.

But something niggled both David and me. Elephants do not neglect their babies. They are without doubt the finest mothers I have ever seen, humans included. Yet this one had for some reason been rejected, and it wouldn't last half a day among predators whose full-time job is to dispatch the weak and infirm. I have seen other animals abandon babies, but there is always a good reason for it, such as a deformity or incapacitation, which in the unforgiving African bush means a death sentence in any event.

However, I had never seen elephants abandon a baby. Once before, we had a baby born with seriously deformed feet, but even then the herd refused to leave it. For twenty-four hours they tried to get it to stand. Eventually we had to snatch it away to try and treat it. Sadly the infant, whom we named Baby Thula, eventually died.

David carefully reversed the Landy out of the gully and began a slow, gentle drive up to the house with his precious cargo.

About halfway home he crested a hill and saw the herd browsing in a glade a mile away. Still puzzled as to why the healthy baby had been rejected, he had an idea. What would happen if he took the baby back to the herd?

It was a tough decision. The risk was that if for some reason unknown to humans the elephants ignored the baby, it would be too close to the herd for the rangers to gather it back safely and it would die. But if it worked?

He thought it through carefully and, deciding to put his faith in the wonderful maternal qualities of elephants, called the other rangers together and explained what he wanted to do.

He said they would approach the elephants upwind so that they could smell the baby and then, depending on the herd's reaction, take a decision on whether to release it. If the elephants picked up the scent and came to them, they would offload the baby quickly and get the hell out of the area. If they ignored the baby, the rangers would take it home for the vet to examine.

There was no margin for error, as David needed to get right up to the herd. Any delay in offloading the struggling and no doubt loudly squealing infant and they could have enraged elephants around them in a flash. And that's one thing you never do – get between an elephant and her baby.

With dread knotting his stomach, David tested the wind, drove off the road into the bush and headed straight for the herd. Fifteen bumpy minutes later he stopped, swung the Landy around and started reversing towards them, trying to get the elephants to pick up the baby's scent. But they continued to ignore him.

He kept edging closer and closer until one of the rangers on the back called out, 'Hey, David, you're nice and safe in the cab

– so don't worry about reversing the rest of us into the middle of some angry elephants!'

They all laughed but David ignored them, getting even closer, almost willing the smell of the baby to waft over to the herd and straining his neck to see if there was any reaction.

Suddenly Nana froze and her trunk swivelled towards the Land Rover. 'Nana's picked up something,' said a ranger excitedly.

David stopped immediately, turned off the engine to kill any smell of diesel that might be tainting the baby's scent, and got out of the vehicle.

Nana was standing absolutely still. Except for a tiny flicking of her trunk near the ground, she could have been a statue. Then she lifted her head and took a measured step towards them, then another.

'She's coming,' said David in a loud whisper as he bolted for the back of the Landy and dropped the tail flap. 'Go, go, go!'

There is nothing that galvanizes anyone more than being too close to a huge elephant that has taken a sudden interest in you. The rangers, two on the back of the Landy and two on the ground, started shoving the baby, desperately trying to get it off before Nana arrived.

Then, disaster – the baby suddenly squealed loudly and with that Nana lifted her trunk and upped her pace. It squealed again. 'They're all coming now!' shouted David. 'Hurry, guys, hurry!'

Trying to get 240 pounds of protesting baby elephant off the back of a vehicle in record time is no joke. Eventually, just as Nana got virtually to within spitting distance, they slid the baby off the back onto the ground, coaxed it onto its feet – and then there was a wild scramble as the rangers leapt into the back of the vehicle, clawing at anything to get a grip as David wildly accelerated off. He swung the Landy in a wide circle and turned to face the baby, which was now squealing at the top of its voice.

As soon as Nana reached the confused baby, she started sniffing and caressing him with her trunk. She then pushed her huge legs against the tiny body and emitted a long low stomach rumble.

By now the herd was close and the rangers noticed one of the adult females start pulling away from the others in her haste to get to the infant.

'It's the mother,' said David. 'Let's see what happens.'

The mother arrived, put her trunk out and smelled every inch of the baby's body, as if she couldn't believe what was happening. She then pushed Nana away and stood over the baby, who immediately found a teat and started suckling.

The rest of the herd arrived and the older females also started touching and smelling the little one, wrapping it in a warm cloak of affection. It was beautiful to watch. The rangers broke out into a loud cheer.

Nana then did something unusual. She slowly turned towards the Land Rover and stood unmoving, staring directly at them for a long time, before turning back towards the mother and child.

David told me that he has no doubt whatsoever that Nana knew exactly what had just happened. And that she was thanking them.

But why had the baby been abandoned in the first place? Given the incredibly caring welcome it received from Nana, the mother and the rest of the herd, there is no way they would have deliberately rejected it. So what did happen?

I think it's this: on rare occasions, baby elephants are stillborn, and this one probably didn't move after birth. Eventually the herd left, thinking it was dead.

Miraculously, it wasn't. There can be no other explanation.

CHAPTER SEVENTEEN

'So,' I said to Jason, Dylan and Grant, having arrived in Durban.
'The rescue really is off. Those bloody pen-pushers in Kinshasa
have lost the plot.'

Around the table heads were shaking in disbelief.

'The problem is some of the biggest conservation organizations in the world were at the Kinshasa meeting, and they are
going to defend their position,' said Grant.

'I have no interest whatsoever in their point of view,' said
Dylan. 'I am thinking about it from the rhinos' point of view.
They're intelligent enough to know exactly what's going on.
Humans keep arriving out of nowhere bringing with them ex-
plosions, fear and chaos, and each time more of them die. The
survivors must've witnessed hundreds of their own being killed
by now, and they will be stressed out of their minds.'

'Their own?' said Grant, amused. 'People will say we're being
a little bit anthropomorphic?'

I remembered Brendan's use of the word – 'human-like'.

'Anyone who doesn't believe that animals are aware that they
have family and friends, and care about them, must also be a
paid-up member of the Flat Earth Society, or still think the sun
revolves around the earth,' replied Dylan disdainfully. 'I mean,
how switched off can you be? How can anyone still believe
animals don't have emotions? They're alive and emotions are a
response to life. I've seen warthogs that are more intelligent and

more responsible than some people I know. Not to say better parents.'

I changed the subject, finding a way to lead up an announcement that was the real reason I'd called this meeting. 'I've spoken to JP and we agree that the biggest risk to the northern whites is the LRA in Garamba park, which frightens the rangers and prevents them from patrolling effectively.'

'Apart from the bloody bureaucracy,' added Dylan.

'Let's not forget JP's assessment that if the peace talks between the LRA and the Ugandan government fail – and he believes they will – Garamba is a sitting duck,' said Jason. 'I spoke to him again today and he was very pessimistic. In fact, his prediction is that it's just a matter of time before the main Garamba camp will be attacked. He's talking of a full-scale military assault.'

The others nodded.

'What if we could somehow remove that risk – or at least reduce it?' I asked. 'What if we could get the LRA to back off? Get them to agree to leave the Garamba rangers and camp alone? Then there's at least a chance the rhino can be saved from extinction.'

'And how do you propose we do that?' snorted Jason. 'Go into the Congo jungle, find Joseph Kony and Vincent Otti, the International Criminal Court's most wanted terrorists, and ask them very nicely if they would please be kind enough to stop killing people and scaring everyone?'

He paused and looked at me strangely.

'I don't believe it!' he exclaimed. 'That's exactly what you're going to do, isn't it? You have lost it. This time you have finally lost your tiny little mind.'

But Jason was right. He had hit the nail on the head – I was planning to talk to the Lord's Resistance Army. Well, to try to.

'Everything starts with a plan,' I said, 'and what's the

alternative? No one is interested in us in Kinshasa any more, and I no longer have any doubt that the way it's going, these rhinos are going to go extinct in the wild.'

To contact one of the world's most shadowy and reviled organizations, or at least contact the political wing, turned out to be easier than I expected.

I phoned Julie Laurenz, who had first told me about the plight of the northern white rhino, to see if she could help. Julie is always ready to go armed only with cameras and courage where others fear to tread. She jumped at the chance.

'Let me do some investigations,' she said. 'I may know someone I have worked with before who can help. I'll get back to you.'

She phoned back a day later.

'Good news,' she said. 'We have a contact. His name is Frank Nyakairu, a Ugandan reporter who has been writing about the LRA for years.'

Peace talks between the LRA and the Ugandan government had started in mid-July 2006 in Juba, the decrepit capital of Southern Sudan. That's where Frank was, and he said he would try to help, but we would need to get there right away.

I put down the phone and immediately booked flights to Juba via Nairobi in Kenya for Julie, myself and her husband, Christopher.

The next day we flew from Durban to Johannesburg and encountered our first bit of bad luck – the customs authorities in Johannesburg wouldn't allow Julie and Christopher onto the plane without Sudanese visas. They insisted they must get visas through Khartoum, the Sudanese capital, which was impossible. Khartoum was deep in the Muslim north, which had been embroiled in a bitter civil war with the Christian south for many years. Not only would getting a visa from Khartoum take for ever, but it would also be far more likely to get us into trouble at Juba, the southern capital, than having no visa at all.

I didn't have a visa either, but for some reason customs officials seemed quite happy to let me board the plane. To aggravate matters, the airport had been hit by an electricity blackout and none of the money exchangers or cash machines were working. This meant that not only had I lost my travelling companions, but I also had no cash, and US dollars are essential in much of Africa, where credit cards are worthless.

I eventually decided to hell with all this and went back to the airline and told them that they knew as well as we did that it was impossible to get a visa to Southern Sudan, and it wasn't really a South African problem as we were routing through Nairobi. Eventually, they relented – and at that moment the electricity kicked in. We bolted for the money changers and managed to grab a handful of crucial dollars moments before the gates closed.

Five hours later, we went through the same tedious rigmarole in Nairobi, with Kenyan customs mimicking their South African counterparts and refusing to let us board the plane to Juba without visas. I painstakingly talked my way through the whole procedure once more, returning to the counter time and time again. Eventually I think the officials got bored with it all and let us through.

A few hours later, after flying north-west over vast, open bush with not even a hint of human habitation, we landed at Juba Airport feeling conspicuously vulnerable without visas – ironically, the same 'visas' we'd fought tooth and nail to travel without.

There are two rules in these chaotic towns of Africa. First, cash is king; and second, it must be late denomination US dollars as many of the older denominations have been forged! As soon as we walked into the arrivals hall, a reasonably maintained white-painted building, I knew what I had to do. In the centre of the throngs of passengers waiting to have their passports stamped was a hard-looking man in military uniform sporting teardrop sunglasses and carrying an AK-47. I walked up to him.

'Excuse me,' I said quietly, wallet in hand. 'May I speak to you privately?'

He looked me up and down disdainfully. Then he noticed the wallet. He nodded and I followed him into a little room at the side of the hall. Two hundred dollars went straight into his pocket. A moment later our passports were stamped. We were through, no questions asked.

For another $100 we found a cab to take us on the short ride into the centre of the city. However, calling it a city might give the wrong impression. Buildings that hadn't seen a lick of paint since they were built in the early twentieth century somehow still stood, defying Newton's laws of gravity, while long-horned cows wandered through the dusty rubble-strewn streets. A magnificently truculent piebald bovine refused to get out of the way for us. You had to be a local, or a long-horned cow, to understand the arcane traffic rules.

Juba has a mysterious, unsettling character; it has the sense of being a lost town, cut off from the world both by distance and by its own peculiarity. It is also a place where the military holds sway and life is cheap, where anything can and does happen. I instinctively switched my wallet from my hip pocket to a zip-up pocket on the inside of my bush jacket. I moved my toes and took heart from the $500 I had hidden in each sock for an emergency. I would have been a lot more comfortable if I had at least a small pistol.

Juba is also the pothole capital of the world. We had already avoided a few of the monsters when we came across the mother of them all, a crater that was deeper than the roof of the taxi. The driver glanced at us and plunged the old taxi recklessly down into the abyss with us frantically holding on. Eventually we reached the bottom and followed the rutted track, which itself had potholes, to the other end. Then he started revving the engine and we literally ramped back into the sunlight and onto the road again.

Our taxi driver told us that the Uganda–LRA talks were being held at the Juba Raha Hotel, which was fully booked. However, he knew of another hotel nearby and would take us there.

He eventually dropped us off at a building with the word 'Hotel' outside. It was a misnomer, being just a basic structure that charged $200 a night for a tiny prefabricated room. Juba is a hub of UN activity due to the civil wars in both Sudan and Uganda, and the locals raise their fees accordingly for cash-laden multinational bureaucrats. When I complained about the raw sewage flowing through an open trench in front of my room, the receptionist gave an apathetic shrug. Maybe they would fix it tomorrow, was the best I could get out of him.

After dumping our luggage, the taxi took us to the Juba Raha Hotel. Heavily armed soldiers were positioned at the entrances, while others cradling AK-47s patrolled the grounds. There would no doubt be snipers on surrounding roofs as well. The LRA were in town and nobody was taking any chances, especially as Joseph Kony had once lived in Juba not too long ago.

We talked our way into the hotel professing to be a TV crew, a claim backed up by Julie and Christopher's cameras and business cards. Once in, we met Frank Nyakairu, the Ugandan journalist, who led us to a spacious outside terrace furnished with plastic garden furniture. In the corner was a dilapidated bar and fast-food counter. There was obviously a break in the talks as the terrace was packed with well-dressed delegates and officials sitting or standing around in groups, apparently debating the afternoon's proceedings.

'Wait here,' said Frank after we had ordered a snack. 'I'll see if I can find someone from the LRA.'

I surveyed the scene over the top of my sandwich, excited by the thought that I was finally in the same place as the Lord's Resistance Army and could shortly be meeting representatives of this terrifying and controversial group.

Ten minutes later Frank came back. He had bad news. 'The LRA delegation is still inside. I spoke to them but I am afraid they don't want to meet anyone.'

Julie and I glanced at each other.

'I am sorry, but they are suspicious of everything. I'll try and speak to them again tonight. Let's meet here tomorrow at about nine a.m. and see what we can do.'

The next morning we were back at the hotel as agreed, but unfortunately Frank was busy. So the three of us found a table with a good vantage position and sat and waited.

Eventually there was another break and I asked a passer-by if they by chance knew where the LRA delegation was. He pointed to a group standing on the opposite side of the garden. My heart jumped; there they were, right in front of me.

I took a deep breath and walked over and introduced myself to a man who appeared to be the leader. He ignored me completely. I couldn't believe it. He wouldn't even look at me, just kept staring straight ahead, unmoving. Apart from the fact that they all stopped talking, there was not the slightest acknowledgement of my presence from anyone.

Again I tried to speak to him, again no result. Not even a flicker of emotion. And that was that.

There is nothing like being rebuked by silence, so I sat down alone at a nearby table wondering what the hell to do next. My options seemed limited. In fact, catching the next plane out of this hellhole seemed to be the most attractive proposition. So far the position was this: we had been forced to bribe our way into the country; the people we had come to see were not interested in talking to us; and to describe our accommodation as a flop-house did even that word an injustice.

About thirty long minutes later, a well-dressed, dignified gentleman came over to me. The first thing that struck me was his wide, intelligent eyes. He smiled with genuine warmth and asked in a deep, richly cultured Kenyan accent if he could join me.

'Of course,' I replied, intrigued at the prospect, and offered him a chair.

He put out his hand. 'My name is Professor Medo Misama. I'm a mediator for the peace talks.' He handed me his calling card.

That certainly caught my attention. If he was a mediator he must surely know the LRA delegation.

'If you will excuse my poor manners,' he said in the splendidly polite way Africans have with strangers, 'but I was wondering what a white man was doing sitting here so patiently. You have been here all day and I am afraid that some of the delegates have been asking questions.'

For 'delegates' read LRA, I thought.

'Some things are worth waiting for,' I said, smiling. 'And, strangely, I believe you may be the exact person I have been waiting for.'

'Well, that's most interesting,' he said, sitting forward, obviously curious at my reply. 'Please tell me how I can be of service?'

'I presume you must know the LRA delegation?'

'Well enough. I've been working with them daily since the start of the conference.'

'As a mediator, I assume you have their ear?'

He laughed. 'I believe I do,' he said. 'Why?'

I decided to play all my cards at once. Sometimes in life you need a bit of luck and I was not going to question it when it arrived and sat down next to me. So I told him who I was, where I came from, why I was here, and gave a detailed history of the northern white rhino and the current crisis in the Garamba park.

I described how the rhino were on the brink of extinction and that due to the presence of the LRA in Garamba the guards were too frightened to do their duties. The situation was desperate and unless I could do a deal with the LRA the rhino could go extinct. I told him I needed to persuade them to protect the rhino and not attack the guards or the main camp, something I believed could happen if the talks broke down.

'Despite everything else,' I said, closing my impromptu presentation, 'the LRA are Ugandans and the rhinos are their natural heritage.'

Professor Misama listened patiently, asking questions and making points here and there. He paused for a while, digesting all this information before he replied: 'This is certainly a most unique and unusual request. It's at odds with the purpose of the talks, but important nevertheless. I need to go back to the meeting, but please don't leave, and I'll see what I can do.'

He stood up and then hesitated briefly. 'I've had a sincere interest in nature since I was a child. I'm deeply concerned by what you have been telling me. I will do my best to represent you to the LRA.'

'Thank you,' I replied. 'I'll be here.'

It was late evening before Professor Misama reappeared with a smile on his face. 'Good news,' he said after I introduced him to Julie and Christopher. 'I met with the leader of the LRA delegation and he will speak with you now. Please follow me.'

Breakthrough at last!

He led me across to the same group who had previously ignored me and called one of them aside.

'May I facilitate introductions,' he said formally. 'This is Mr

Lawrence Anthony, the conservationist from South Africa I have been telling you about. Mr Anthony, please meet Mr Martin Ojul, the leader of the Lord's Resistance Army delegation to the Juba peace talks.'

We shook hands.

Martin Ojul was a shortish, heavy-set man with a round face, and despite his formal demeanour, it struck me that he looked more like someone's kind-hearted uncle than the political leader of a vicious rebel army. I later found out that Ojul, a Ugandan businessman who lived in Nairobi, had won the trust of the military wing and was appointed Chairman of the LRA delegation to the peace talks.

'Yes, I have heard about you,' said Ojul in a heavy Ugandan accent. 'You have an interest in rhinos?'

'That's correct,' I replied. 'I have a problem of international significance and I believe you can be of assistance.'

'What can we possibly do?'

'I would appreciate the opportunity of a brief presentation to your delegation, if that is possible. I believe it will be to your benefit to hear my proposal.'

'That's OK,' he said without hesitation. 'Be at the Juba Bridge Hotel tomorrow at ten a.m. and you can do your presentation.'

With that, he turned away and rejoined his group.

My heart jumped. Professor Misama had done his work well. I finally had the meeting that I had travelled all this way for.

Back at our table Frank, the reporter, was with Christopher and Julie. I introduced them to the professor and told them what had happened.

'That's great!' said Julie. 'We must film the meeting if we can.'

'I don't know if that will be possible,' said Professor Misama. 'Perhaps it would be better to achieve some progress first before asking to film anything. This is a very suspicious and distrustful organization.'

'No problem,' said Julie with a smile. 'Let's make friends with them first.'

'Friends?' said Frank, his eyes opening wide. 'You cannot make friends with the LRA. They trust no one. You must be very careful. Insist that the meeting takes place here at this hotel. You must not go to the Juba Bridge like they say. It's out of town and not safe.'

'But I am meeting the entire delegation,' I said. 'What can they possibly do?'

'What can they do? They can do anything – they're the LRA. Do you think their delegation is alone? Not at all. The whole town is swarming with their people, hard men from the bush right here in Juba operating undercover to protect the delegation and collect information. As a Westerner you are a prize. You could be kidnapped or killed and no one will even come looking for you. This is not South Africa.'

After more discussions about the potential risks, Professor Misama and Frank went back to the talks, which would continue late into the night.

Julie and I looked at each other.

'This is a one-off chance. If we try and change the venue we may not get the meeting,' I said. 'I have to go.'

'I agree,' said Julie. 'I'm in.'

CHAPTER EIGHTEEN

The next morning, high on anticipation and concern about our safety, Julie, Christopher and I took a taxi to the Juba Bridge Hotel. It was a spread-out, roadhouse-type establishment on the edge of town, but apart from the odd staff member, there was no one there. The place appeared to be empty.

After a brief and unsuccessful search for the delegation, we walked down past some prefabricated rooms and suddenly found ourselves staring at a mile-wide river. I was momentarily taken aback, until I realized that we were standing right on the banks of the Nile.

It was an absolutely beautiful sight and for the moment the LRA was forgotten. The great river was right at our feet, sweeping past us strong and deep. There were several islands in the middle, some no more than sand and reed banks, the river itself carrying huge rafts of reeds torn free by recent floods. Rust-brown bulrush bulbs growing like wild bottlebrushes on slender green stems flourished along the banks. It was such an iconic and ancient waterway that I felt privileged just to be able to stand on the banks. With a boat and provisions I could set off from where we stood and eventually arrive in Egypt and then the Mediterranean Sea, thousands of miles away.

I remember thinking that this was far too majestic a river to pass through such a decrepit city. That musing proved to be pro-phetic. A group of women was washing clothes on some rocks on the river's edge about fifty yards away. We walked up to them. I always try to speak to the locals wherever I go. It usually stands me in good stead.

Not this time. I was about twenty yards away when I called out a greeting. Without warning, one picked up a stone and hurled it at me. I ducked just in time. Then another grabbed a stone – this time bigger, more like a small rock – and soon there was a cluster of missiles coming at us. We dodged the first salvo and then ran back to the hotel. I don't believe in omens, but that certainly wasn't a good one.

Back at the hotel I walked down between the prefab rooms again looking for someone to speak to when I came across a woman sitting in an incongruous office chair on a dusty path reading some papers. She had on a smart blue blouse and a long white frock. Her hair was neatly parted in the middle and she had a dignified manner. I walked up to her.

'Excuse me, I wonder if you could help. I have a meeting with the Lord's Resistance Army delegation.'

She looked up sharply. 'Who are you?' The menace in her voice was palpable.

'My name is Lawrence Anthony. I am a South African here on a conservation mission.'

She stood up. Aggression steamed off her and anger now flared in her eyes as if a match had been lit.

'So you are the Anthony who is lying to the world that the LRA are slaughtering the rhino! And you dare to come here to tell us about it!'

That certainly put me on the back foot. This was not exactly the reception I was expecting.

'There seems to be some mistake,' I said as politely as I could, denying that I was accusing anyone. I just wanted to talk to them about what was happening in Garamba.

She stared at me. The anger felt as intense as if I was standing next to a furnace. I quickly continued telling my side of the story, how we needed to save the last surviving rhino in Garamba and how desperate the situation was. I stressed that I was here to ask the LRA to help, that if I was accusing them of global crimes the last thing I would be doing would be blatantly confronting them on their home turf. I also stressed I had no political axe to grind. I was merely a conservationist.

Eventually she relented and heard me out.

'We've been expecting you and I will now clear you for the meeting. Be at the Acholi mango tree next to the river in an hour's time.'

She then introduced herself as Josephine Apira, the deputy leader of the LRA peace delegation. I later found out she was a refugee from Museveni's regime, and living in London as part of the international diaspora of intellectuals and other Ugandans persecuted by the Ugandan leader.

I really needed to consolidate this piece of luck. However, I wasn't quite sure what she meant by the Acholi mango tree, but as there was only one mango tree that dominated the landscape on the banks of the Nile, I presumed that to be the one. Acholi was the tribe of the LRA; the tribe of Joseph Kony and Vincent Otti.

The delegation arrived an hour later, seven of them led by Martin Ojul. Their body language was not negative, apprehensive perhaps, but certainly not hostile. However, I did notice that Josephine's mood had softened somewhat and it appeared that she had spent time talking with them before the meeting.

Professor Medo Misama arrived to join us, and we all sat down. After introductions by Professor Misama I outlined why I was here and why I had flown all the way from South Africa to tell them about the last rhinos. I gave them all the information I had, step by step, but didn't get too dramatic because as far as I was concerned the facts spoke for themselves. I said the LRA soldiers in the Garamba park were the major factor affecting the rhinos' chances of survival and the entire species was about to go belly-up unless they helped.

As I finished one of the delegates said, 'We are surprised at what you are telling us. We understand that there are lots of rhinos around. They are everywhere.'

I replied instantly. 'I am afraid that is no longer true. In fact there are almost none.'

'What do you mean? We have rhino in Uganda in our parks.'

'You are referring to the southern white rhino, which were brought into Uganda to replace the northern whites that were wiped out during Idi Amin's time. In fact, we think that there are only fifteen northern whites left in the world. Just fifteen – at the most – and they are all in Garamba.'

I searched for a comparison. 'There are more people sitting around two tables in this hotel than all the northern white rhinos in the world.'

There was silence for a moment. 'How can we know this is true?' asked one.

'Because I have no reason to lie to you. It's also common knowledge. It's on the Internet. It's everywhere. That's all that's left.'

They spoke for a moment in Acholi. I could see – or hoped – that I had touched a chord.

'They're finished,' I added to drive the point home one more time. 'The fate of the rhino is now in your hands. Unless you help us, they will be gone for ever.'

They continued speaking to one another, which included much head-shaking, before Martin Ojul turned to me.

'The rhino is a sacred totem among some of the Acholi people. We do not eat rhino and we have no use for the horn. We cannot see them just die out. But what can we do to help?'

'I have four requests for your consideration,' I replied. 'Firstly, your military wing pulls all men away from the main camp at Garamba. You have done reconnaissance and you will know it is only game rangers that are being trained there, not soldiers. These are not fighters so you have no concerns.

'Secondly, I ask that the LRA does not interfere with the rangers' patrols.

'Thirdly, I ask that you do not allow any rhinos to be killed by poachers in your area of operations. By that I mean I am asking you to start protecting the rhino wherever and whenever you see them.

'And lastly, I am asking that you help gather information on the rhinos; that your men in the bush keep a lookout for them and you report to me if you find them.'

I paused. 'If you will do this, you will help save this species from extinction.'

Notes were taken as I spoke. Then there were further discussions in Acholi. Finally, Ojul turned to me.

'We can see you are a man of the animals,' he said. The others all nodded. In the West that analogy may mean you're a bit different. But in Africa it is an interesting compliment. It means you are unlike others in a spiritual sense: that you are somehow part of the animal kingdom and not entirely of the world of humans. Importantly, it also meant that I had no financial, political or military agendas.

'We will speak to our commanders in the bush,' he continued. 'We will tell them what you have asked of us and will meet here tomorrow at the same time and report back. Thank you for coming.'

After the meeting ended some of the delegation stayed and chatted informally with us for a while. I met the competent and highly intelligent Godfrey Ayoo, head of public relations, who resided in Germany, and their lawyer, Crispus Ayena, a scholarly looking man with spectacles. Obonyo Olweny, a published author and spokesman for Kony who lived in Nairobi, was also present. Josephine joined us and I gave them photocopied pages from both the Earth Organization and Thula Thula websites, outlining my conservation work. I then told them about our rescue of the Baghdad Zoo during the invasion of Iraq and handed out copies of my book *Babylon's Ark* about that experience to stamp some authenticity on our project.

'I have been online to look at your websites,' said Godfrey Ayoo. 'There is another matter we wish to raise with you.'

'I'm happy to help in any way I can,' I replied. 'Would you like to discuss it now?'

'All in good time,' he replied, leaving me in a bit of suspense.

Christopher, Julie and I went back to our waiting taxi and took the slow drive back to our hotel, where we sat and discussed the day's events for hours. After a barely edible dinner, we spent a restless night on lumpy beds with bugs and mosquitoes everywhere. My air-conditioner was a noisy monster, way too big for the small room, so either I kept it on and froze under a thin blanket, or turned it off and died of heat. I wasn't sure whether opening a window in a strange city was a good idea. Remembering JP's malaria in Garamba, I also kept the mosquito net tight around my bed.

But despite all that, I was happy. It had been a fruitful day. Regardless of all the hassles we had faced, from getting stoned – literally – to a historic conservation meeting with the political wing of a terrorist army, we had made progress.

CHAPTER NINETEEN

The next morning we were told that the meeting with the LRA had been cancelled.

The message was delivered to our hotel by a rough-looking man with bad manners who looked like he would be far happier in the bush with an AK-47 on his shoulder than pretending to be a courier. One of the LRA undercover troops, I thought. We had deliberately not told them where we were staying, but they knew.

With nothing better to do, we went across to the Juba Raha Hotel, hoping to find the delegation and ask what was going on. They were nowhere to be seen.

I went for a walk and near the hotel entrance bumped into two unkempt soldiers keeping guard while slouched in cheap plastic chairs.

'Give cigarette,' said one, beckoning to me rudely with an outreached arm.

'Sure,' I said, walking across and smiling. I took one from my packet, lit it for him and then handed him three more. 'For later.'

'Thank you.'

'How is the conference going?' I asked, trying to get some small talk going.

'The LRA are here,' he said with a grimace, drawing hard on the scrounged cigarette.

'Will the meeting bring peace?' I asked.

'With the LRA, never,' he said. 'The LRA do not understand peace.'

'But their leaders are here,' I said. 'They are talking.'

'These are not LRA leaders,' he said with a mirthless laugh. 'Joseph Kony is not here, Vincent Otti is not here. These people inside have no power, nothing. There will be no peace.'

We continued talking about Juba and he told me his family had had a miserable time during Southern Sudan's twenty-year civil war with the north. The army often didn't pay wages on time, causing enormous hardship at home.

Then the strangest thing happened. His AK-47, which he had been resting on his outstretched leg, slipped and fell to the ground, landing at my feet. He just left it there in the dust.

'Do you know this gun?' he said, gesturing disrespectfully at the fallen rifle.

'Yes,' I replied. I had been trained to use an AK by mercenaries during the rescue of the Baghdad Zoo, as at the time we were at risk of being attacked by insurgents.

'Then pick it up.'

I hesitated.

'Here,' he said, laughing, leaning over and picking it up himself, putting it into my reluctant hands. 'Check the rounds.'

'Are you sure?' I said, looking over my shoulder. I was very uncomfortable standing at the gate holding a soldier's AK-47 in this extremely volatile city.

'Check,' he insisted.

I quickly removed the magazine. It was empty. Then I cleared the breech. It too was empty.

'You see how they treat us?' he said, taking the rifle back and reinserting the empty magazine. 'They forgot to give me bullets this morning. To hell with them.'

I was absolutely stunned. This vital conference, with a terrorist army in the area, was guarded by a soldier with no bullets in his rifle. What a crazy place this was!

A few hours later, an LRA messenger found us in the terrace garden and told us to be at the Juba Bridge Hotel at 3 p.m.

We hailed a taxi and suddenly my high hopes from the night before were punctured by a deep foreboding. I was now desperately worried that Ojul's call to shadowy guerillas on a satellite phone somewhere in the bush would be rejected. What the guard without bullets had said was true; no matter what this delegation did, if Kony and Otti said no, then it was all over for the rescue mission and for the rhino.

The LRA delegation was waiting at a table under the Acholi mango tree and I was immediately heartened by the jovial welcome they gave us. My dejection evaporated. This had to be good news, I thought.

It certainly was.

Martin Ojul said that he had contacted General Otti last night and discussed the matter with him at length. This morning he received a call back from Otti, confirming that Kony and the military high command had agreed to all my requests. They would protect the rhino. Just like that.

They all stood up, beaming. Everybody shook hands and there were congratulations all round. It was certainly a massive turn-up for the books. But not only that – the delegation wanted to submit this historic treaty as a formal document to the peace talks. Their lawyer, Crispus Ayena, would draw up the agreement.

He stepped forward. 'Please come with me, Mr Anthony,' he said. 'We will sit separately and record the points of agreement.'

In essence, the treaty – possibly the first of its kind ever to be drawn up during a war – stipulated that the LRA would protect the northern white rhino and would not harm or interfere with the Garamba rangers and staff.

I wanted to be sure that it also included a clause that the LRA would withdraw from the area around the Garamba camp. Crispus Ayena confirmed that this too had been agreed.

I then pushed long and hard to get a clause inserted that included the protection of elephants. 'Thousands have already died,' I said. 'These are intelligent animals; we have to at least let them breed up again.'

'No,' he said, 'that was not discussed. We have no authority for it.'

I then asked about the pygmy Congo giraffe, which I quickly explained was also critically endangered.

'The Congo giraffe is agreed to,' he said, and then quite unexpectedly added that they would also include the okapi.

That certainly took me by surprise. The okapi, a beautiful, charismatic creature that looks like a cross between a giraffe and a zebra, did not exist in Garamba. But the LRA operated over three countries and perhaps they had encountered them elsewhere. Who knows?

'What about all the other animals in the park?' I asked, realizing that I may never get another opportunity to push my luck like this again.

No. They would pledge only to protect those three species. And that was that.

Despite the fact that other extremely vulnerable species were not on the protection list, including – to my great despair – the elephant, I decided to go with what I could get. I was dealing with the reality on the ground rather than wishful thinking. In any event, we were creating a historic document that the LRA had already stipulated would be included in any peace treaty with the Ugandan government. If, of course, that happened.

I returned to the main table while Crispus Ayena went off to draft the agreement.

Then Godfrey Ayoo, head of LRA communications, spoke

up. 'We have been studying your activities on the Internet and checking up on you. I'm sure you will understand that we had to know more about you for security reasons.'

'I understand,' I replied.

'We are intrigued by your work in Baghdad during the Iraq war, particularly your proposal to the Iraqi government to create a Truth and Reconciliation Commission after Saddam Hussein had been deposed.'

I sat forward. This was going in an unusual direction. When apartheid collapsed in South Africa, a Truth and Reconciliation Commission (TRC) was set up as a platform to confess offences committed in the name of either apartheid or liberation. The way it worked was anyone who truthfully acknowledged their crimes, and then apologized to the country, would be exonerated. The proceedings, carried live on national television and chaired by Archbishop Desmond Tutu, were extremely successful in defusing tensions between blacks and whites and setting the country on the road to real peace. At a conference in Baghdad I had given an in-depth presentation on the TRC at the invitation of the Iraqi interim government. This is what Godfrey had picked up on the Internet.

He pointed to print-outs of some website pages lying on the table in front of him. 'We need your Truth and Reconciliation Commission to heal the wounds in our country. But we don't trust Museveni' – that elicited a round of mirthless laughter – 'and we don't trust the Sudanese. We are assisting you with your rhino. Will you assist us with this, a quid pro quo, if you please?'

I had been impressed by Godfrey's obvious intellect in all the discussions we had had so far. This was a strategic move on the part of the LRA, as a TRC would compel both their leaders and Museveni to confess publicly to all crimes. With each side accusing the other of atrocities, such revelations would be earth-shattering. In fact, they would radically change the political landscape in Uganda.

So now I knew. This is what they wanted in exchange for helping me to protect the rhino.

'I will be happy to help if I can,' I said. 'I have detailed information on the TRC on file, which I'll send to you as soon as I get back home. I also have some high-level contacts in the South African government and will advise them of your request.'

'The South Africans have influence in Africa . . . they have the power,' said Godfrey. 'If they help with a TRC, this stalemate can be broken.'

The following morning, 21 August, we met at the Acholi mango tree again. Crispus Ayena handed out copies of the agreement and we went through it point by point.

'Elephants,' I said once again when we were finished reading. 'Gentlemen, please can we add elephants to the protected list? Too many have already died. They need your help.'

The response was that they had not discussed elephants with the leaders in the bush and going back to them now would delay matters. They suggested that I should rather accept what had been agreed upon and save further requests for later.

The agreement was signed. Julie had permission to film the proceedings and Christopher took photographs of us and the LRA delegation on the banks of the Nile, treaty in hand. I had signed what was possibly the most significant document of my life, an agreement with a warring party to protect an endangered species in a combat zone. I was subsequently told that this had never happened before.

However, I still chuckle at the chaotically random sequence of events that had culminated in this historic signing. From deciding out of the blue to go and find the world's most notorious terrorist organization, talking our way onto planes, bribing our way into Juba to being stoned at the Nile and chatting to a soldier with no bullets in his AK-47 . . . well, you couldn't make it up.

However, this was the first time since we had taken on the project that I felt we had made significant progress. Obviously, the signed deal with the LRA was not enforceable by law; it was the equivalent of a handshake with an illegal terrorist organization.

But it was a lot better than nothing.

CHAPTER TWENTY

Professor Medo Misama, who had been at our first meeting with the delegation, arrived at our hotel just as we were leaving for the airport. 'How did it finish?' he asked.

'Surprisingly well,' I replied. 'They signed the agreement to protect rhino and, more importantly, not to harm the game rangers or disturb the administration of the park.'

The Kenyan academic was impressed. 'Now that is something. How on earth did you do that?'

'It seems the rhino is a spiritual totem – an icon – for some of the Acholi people and so they contacted the leaders in the bush for instructions. They gave me an answer the next day. The orders to assist me come from Vincent Otti himself.'

The professor's eyes widened. 'Otti! That is incredible. You don't get much higher than that. This is a major breakthrough. Major!'

He looked at me for a moment, as if thinking carefully about what he was going to say next. 'I am not sure you realize what you have achieved. This is the first time that the LRA, and by that I mean the military wing, Kony and Otti, have made deals with a complete outsider. The first ever. The biggest problem they have is that they trust no one, no one trusts them, and everyone is too scared or too horrified to have anything to do with them. But if no one listens to them, if they have no one to talk to, we will never have peace here and the suffering will continue.

Out in the Landy at Thula Thula, with two of our
rhinos grazing happily alongside.

Françoise with George the bushbaby, a frequent
guest at the bar and quite a character.

Our beautiful Heidi, who was orphaned at
an early age and befriended by our herd of
wildebeest, one of which is in the background.

Above We have been protecting a herd of elephants for fourteen years. Here Mandla is browsing on an acacia tree. *Below* Me, Jason, a member of Garamba security and JP with the plane that flew us to the Democratic Republic of the Congo.

Christopher Laurenz took this photograph of me on the banks of the Nile at Juba with the LRA delegation and Frank Nyakairu, the reporter.

Above After Juba, I was invited to meet the LRA generals in their secret jungle camp. From left to right: General Okot Odhiambo, General Vincent Otti and Brigadier Bok Abudema.

Tough LRA soldiers in well-worn uniforms patrolled Vincent Otti's camp.

Sitting outside my shelter with Godfrey Ayoo and a relaxed Vincent Otti who was pleased to have news in the jungle.

There were many women and children throughout the LRA camps, which had a village atmosphere.

Frankie on duty protecting the herd.

Our brutally murdered Heidi, with our game ranger Promise. She was the most gentle of giants, killed for her horn.

We brought in a new senior bull, Gobisa – who almost immediately escaped. We caught up with him eventually and darted him. Here he is being winched unconscious off a ravine. Today he offers a calming influence on the young bulls at Thula Thula.

Shaking hands with Chief Biyela and his brother who are leading efforts to protect the rhino.

Our hope for the future – baby rhinos Thabo and Nthombi who arrived at Thula Thula with their handler Alyson McPhee. They followed her everywhere.

Françoise with Nthombi.

Thabo and Nthombi sleeping on our bush airstrip.

It's not just the rhino we have to protect. Thula Thula's abundant wildlife includes zebra (*above left*) and serval (*above right*). And the Cape Buffalo (*below*) – regal, powerful, unpredictable and symbolizing all that is the very best of the African Bushveld.

'I and others are becoming concerned that Museveni does not really want peace; that he prefers to keep Kony out there as a bogeyman. The LRA is Museveni's ticket to all sorts of aid from the USA, Britain and other countries, and we fear he will once again break the ceasefire agreement and go back to war just to keep his meal ticket. The LRA's reputation is such that he will simply blame it on them again and everyone will believe him.'

'Again?' I asked.

'Yes,' said the professor. 'It's a little-known fact that the LRA have reached out for peace several times already. And it seems as if every time progress is made with talks, Museveni pulls out, or attacks. There is no trust any more. We need some other dynamic to help break the deadlock.'

He paused. 'It's early days, and I say this with a great deal of circumspection, but I have the sense that the LRA may be starting to trust you. It's your relationship with the animals that makes it so different. They say you talk with the elephants. If this is the case, it may put you in a truly unique position. You have to build on this. There is a lot at stake.'

I could see now that I was probably the first person to come to speak to the LRA without either a political axe to grind or recoiling with revulsion. To them it may have been bizarre that I was only interested in saving a handful of animals, but maybe that was the whole point. I was uniquely neutral, and far removed from the war or the politics and violence surrounding it. In fact, I had barely heard of the LRA before I went to Garamba. Maybe they thought it was fate that brought this strange white man to their doorstep. Suddenly I had become a possible conduit – through either sheer fluke or force of circumstances.

'Be prepared,' the professor said. 'They have been doing background checks on you, and you may well hear from them again. And by the way, in my opinion, they will honour their agreement with you for the rhino. You are potentially valuable to them, and while that lasts they will stay true to their word.'

I thanked him for his assistance and advice, and we parted. He was a fine human being, one of the precious few intellectuals involved in the peace talks, and his help had been invaluable.

Once I was back at Thula Thula, the LRA delegation stayed in contact with me as the professor had predicted, and held up their side of the bargain. Vincent Otti instructed LRA troops to pull away from the main camp at Garamba, not to engage the game rangers, and for LRA patrols to report any rhino sightings. I was elated. I also received two calls from them specifically advising me when LRA patrols would be moving close to the Garamba camp and I was able to phone African Parks and warn them. The LRA patrols came and went without incident.

From my side, I sent them detailed presentations on the TRC and how it functioned in South Africa, and answered their questions.

Life carried on at Thula Thula, and my negotiations with the local Zulu tribes to bring their land into conservation continued well, albeit slowly. Here too it was a matter of building trust, of growing to understand each other, of putting faith and goodwill ahead of apartheid-induced prejudice between blacks and whites. It was slow but it was working, and the direct beneficiary was our nation's wildlife heritage. Africa has its own pace and requires patience.

Then a few weeks later I received an unusual call. It was Martin Ojul. Joseph Kony had requested that a representative come out to South Africa to meet me as the LRA had 'an important matter' to discuss.

I was intrigued at the prospect, but there was an immediate problem as the LRA was defined as a terrorist organization and their members were in all likelihood banned from entering the country. I discussed it with Françoise and, despite the complications, I decided to go for it. More communication is always better than less, no matter with whom. Not only would a visit give me the opportunity to reinforce the rhino agreement, but I could again try to stop any killings of elephants in Garamba.

So I phoned a contact in the South African Department of International Relations and Cooperation who had helped me when I went into Baghdad during the Iraq invasion, and told him of the request. He listened to my argument and finally agreed that two members of the LRA peace team, not the LRA military, would be granted a one-week visa, on the strict condition that I was responsible for their whereabouts. The LRA nominated the head of their peace delegation, Martin Ojul, and head of public relations/communications Godfrey Ayoo, to make the journey. For obvious reasons I told nobody that they were coming except JP, Dr Ian Raper, and of course my sons, Jason and Dylan.

Martin Ojul and Godfrey Ayoo arrived at Thula Thula the following week and Ojul immediately placed a call to Joseph Kony somewhere in the Congo jungle to say they were here. As he did so, I reflected on how surreal my life had become. Just weeks ago the LRA was a horror story somewhere out in the bush. Now they were here staying with me at Thula Thula with the infamous Kony on the other end of the phone line.

'Before we start, we must be frank with you,' said Ojul as we sat down for the first meeting. 'The purpose of our visit is to complete our "audit" of you. We have done our background checks and now that we are here I am able to tell you we accept your credentials.'

'I understand,' I said. 'Thank you for being straightforward.'

We got to work immediately, starting with the Truth and Reconciliation Commission, how it functions, and how they could adapt it to work in Uganda as part of the peace talks. It was simple logic, I told them. A TRC is a proven system that would receive international support and could help end the war. A TRC would also compel Kony, Museveni and their respective generals and soldiers publicly to confess their crimes in order to obtain amnesty.

'But,' I asked, 'is it workable? It's really no good us talking about this unless Kony, Otti and the LRA military high command understands this and agrees to the public confessions.'

'We have discussed this with them at length,' said Ayoo. 'They understand the process and they have agreed.'

'What about the International Criminal Court, the ICC?' I asked. 'Kony, Otti and two other LRA generals are their most wanted men.'

'We are aware of this too,' said Ayoo. 'The ICC indictments are an obstacle to peace. The Acholi people of Northern Uganda do not support the ICC indictments. We are proposing traditional justice; let the Acholi, the victims of the LRA, decide on justice in the Acholi way.'

'Will this be enough to satisfy the ICC?' I ventured.

'The Acholi are a nation, a true nation with an age-old justice system. Who are Europeans to impose their justice on us? Westerners use punitive justice, based on ruthless punishment. In Africa we understand the values of confession, mercy and forgiveness. Westerners, however, do understand the TRC, which is very close to our traditional justice. That's why it will work.

'We are confident we can find a way through this problem,' he said, 'but this is enough talking for one day. Let's enjoy dinner and start again in the morning.'

The next morning they raised the matter of the camps in Northern Uganda where the majority of the Acholi people lived in such desperate conditions. I listened to their perspective patiently, always careful to assert my neutrality, being sure never to give any impression that I sided with them on their point of view.

Whether the camps housed refugees fleeing the LRA as the Ugandan government claimed, or were prison camps where Acholis were penned against their will as the LRA claimed, was by now a moot point. The more I'd looked into this, on returning from Juba, the more horrified I was. People were dying like flies, either from famine, disease or despair – and that's not counting war casualties. This was clearly a situation even worse than Darfur, which at the time was dominating headlines with the Sudanese 'Janjaweed' (militia) attacking defenceless black villages at will. Yet the world stood by. How could the world stand by when there were nearly two million people in these Ugandan camps calling either a rudimentary thatched structure or a plastic sheet their home; when clean water was but a trickle, and food provided by the UN was in such short supply that most inhabitants were either starving or seriously malnourished? The most vulnerable were the least likely to get fed. Many children had *kwashiorkor*, severe malnutrition caused by lack of protein. Young girls became prostitutes simply to survive.

Ugandan Anglican Bishop Ochola said that Northern Uganda is the worst place in the world for a child to be born and live. The bishop went on to state that a geocide was taking place. A slow genocide of the Acholi.

I tried to persuade Martin and Godfrey that any LRA attacks on the camps and villages were not helping matters; that they were their own worst enemies in this regard. They immediately denied such attacks were taking place, but pointed out that this was a matter that could only be discussed directly with Otti.

'Please let us not underestimate this,' I said. 'Nothing can be achieved if you are indeed attacking your own people and taking away their children. On the ground it is a humanitarian disaster, and for the LRA it is a PR disaster. If it is happening then it must stop and this must be conveyed to Otti. There is just nothing to be gained by it,' I added.

The more I talked to Martin and Godfrey, the more I realized that something imaginative had to be done to break this impasse. It was difficult to focus exclusively on saving rhino with such a horrible war going on and while people were living in such appalling conditions. The dreadful humanitarian and conservation situations in Central Africa are intimately entwined. Worse still, the peace talks were not going well at all. There was genuine fear of a surprise Ugandan attack on LRA camps and there was no trust whatsoever. If the talks broke down the dogs of war would be unleashed, and Museveni would once again have his reason to get more money from the major powers.

'Mr Anthony, we need your help,' said Ojul. 'Vincent Otti is pressing for peace, with Kony's blessing. These talks must not fail. Will you assist us?'

'If I can,' I said. 'But how?'

'We will let you know shortly. First we must go back and report to Kony and Otti on the outcome of this visit, and then we will contact you.'

'Thank you,' I said. 'But there is something I must be clear about. I will help, but I am afraid that I cannot support the LRA and do not want to be perceived to be supporting you politically or otherwise. This, I am afraid, is a non-negotiable precondition on my part. If you have something else in mind then I am afraid we must end the discussions. I will help where I can to find peace, but I must remain completely neutral.'

As I stopped speaking I realized that I had been very direct, perhaps too direct, and if they took exception to what I had said, or the way I had said it, then the rhino deal would also go out the window.

'We fully understand,' said Godfrey. 'With the LRA's reputation, we do not have many friends, but this is peace we are talking about, peace for the first time in twenty-two years.'

He paused and looked at Ojul. 'There is something else you

must know,' said Godfrey. 'Joseph Kony is a famous seer, a clairvoyant, if you will. He can predict the future.'

'I have heard of this,' I replied.

'During your visit to Juba, Kony called us to say that he had a vision that our salvation would come from out of South Africa. This is why we met with you in Juba and why we have come to see you here, and that is why we are protecting the rhino. He believes it is more than coincidence that brought you to us.'

I sat back. So that's what happened. Ancestral worship, black magic, spirits, demons and wizards are all an integral part of African tradition. Animism, the belief that individual spirits inhabit plants, animals, and even rocks and mountains, is deeply ingrained. Kony was a wizard and he had had a vision. In Africa this is serious stuff; the spirits had spoken to him and his predictions would come true, unless of course someone else countered with more powerful magic.

I didn't realize how quickly the counter-spell would materialize.

CHAPTER TWENTY-ONE

That afternoon, after a particularly long working session, I asked Godfrey and Martin if they would like to go on a game drive. They both jumped at the opportunity to relax a bit. Neither Godfrey nor Martin had ever seen an elephant or rhino before and I wanted to try out my brand-new Land Rover, so we went searching for them.

It was a magnificent evening and I pointed out various antelope species, mainly nyala, of which Thula Thula has some of the finest specimens in the world. I showed them the abundant bird life, warthogs, giraffes, zebra and buffalo. They were absolutely entranced.

We drove around a corner and there in the road right in front of us, staring malevolently, was my eldest elephant bull, Mnumzane, all six tons of him. I could see instantly that he was in musth, the condition in which elephant males come into heat, due to the oily secretion from his temporal glands and the uncontrolled urination that had blackened his legs. An elephant bull in musth is at his most unpredictable and can be very dangerous. Their testosterone levels go through the roof and they are best avoided, no matter how well you know them. In the old days, when herds were large, there was always at least one female in oestrus at the time to remedy the situation. But on smaller reserves today this is not always the case.

The fact that he was in musth was not an immediate problem,

but he didn't know my new vehicle, and so to be safe I slammed the Landy into reverse and slowly eased backwards. Mnumzane's mother had been shot in front of him several years before, just before he came to Thula Thula, and he had always been a special case. Once they reach adolescence, male elephants are ostracized by their herd and so Mnumzane had fostered a relationship with me. Over the years we had spent many happy hours out in the bush together, but as he got older I put distance between us to let him grow up wild. However, even without being in musth, Mnumzane had been worrying me for months. His behaviour had become unpredictable and he had developed an unreasonably bad temper, and I was unable to work out why.

As far as he was concerned, he was now the biggest gun in town and he had developed a loutish swagger. He disappeared off to our left and suddenly surprised us by appearing out of the thick bush, right at the front passenger window. Worse, he was standing in a belligerent pose and swinging his trunk – always a bad sign with a bull elephant. Both Godfrey and Martin started shouting, 'Elephant! Elephant!', agitating him even more. The golden rule when you have an aggressive elephant right on top of you is to do everything silently and slowly – unless, of course, it's mock-charging, when you use noise to try and distract it – so I tried to get them to quieten down while I eased the vehicle backwards very gently. Mnumzane took a step closer and put his tusk to the window, and as I looked it started buckling under the pressure.

Dear God, I thought, he's coming through, and in that split second I realized that if his tusk burst through the window it would pierce Godfrey. I abandoned caution and floored the accelerator, and as the Land Rover lurched backwards Mnumzane's tusk slid along the window and hit the supporting strut.

He made a noise that sounded more like an almighty shriek

than a trumpet, and with that I knew we were in desperate trouble. I revved the engine to a screaming pitch with my hand on the hooter to try and give him a fright and grant us just a few precious seconds to get away, but it was too late. He swung to the front of the Landy, dropped his head and charged, and with a sickening crunch he hit the bull bar so hard my head smashed into the windscreen. For a few dazed seconds all I was dimly aware of was this enraged six-ton monster filling my windscreen, driving the Landy violently backwards into the bush as if it was a dinky toy. The noise of branches and trees snapping and breaking under the impact roared in my ears for an eternity, until we hit a huge tree and came to a crashing stop. How we didn't roll over I still don't know. But that was the least of my concerns. There was a deathly silence as Mnumzane broke off. Walking sideways, his angry eyes never leaving the vehicle, he moved off to the left. I knew with a terrible certainty that all he was doing was giving himself room to build up another vicious charge. And this time he was going to do the job properly.

Then Martin yelled something that intrigued me despite all the mayhem: 'It's Museveni, he's trying to kill us,' and for the briefest moment time stood still. In Martin's mind this was all witchcraft, pure and simple. These things in Africa run deep indeed.

Once again I desperately revved the engine, until it shrieked in protest, at the same time pressing hard on the hooter, making as much noise as possible to try and confuse him, and then released the clutch, desperately trying to get out of the way of the coming charge. Too late. Just as we started moving, I felt an earth-shattering impact and all of a sudden I was staring through the windscreen, not at the road ahead, but at the ground below, and we went over sideways violently and slammed into the ground on our side. But Mnumzane was not finished, not by a long shot. I heard him roar as he hit us again on the underside of the vehicle, and then again, smashing the two-ton Landy chaotically into a grove of trees.

Then silence.

Surprised at how lucid I was, I frantically assessed the situation. We were over on our right side, the doors and roof were caved in and the windscreen and all the windows smashed. Godfrey was lying on top of me and Martin was in a heap in the back. Miraculously, no one was injured, but Mnumzane was still out there stomping around in anger and we were dangerously exposed. I somehow managed to twist around and draw my tiny .635 pistol, a pea-shooter against an elephant. Being careful not to hit Mnumzane and anger him further, I quickly fired four shots through the open windscreen into the air. I knew that elephants who have heard shots before will sometimes freeze at the sound of a gun. Either that or they go berserk. Firing the shots was a huge gamble, but there was no time to think about it. If he came at us again it would be the end.

Thankfully he froze, and I quickly called out to him, again and again, letting him hear my voice, speaking in a tone he would recognize from his youth. If the worst came to the worst, I would put the remaining four bullets into his foot in a last-ditch attempt to immobilize him. Perhaps that would give us a few precious seconds to escape. It would be the absolute last resort. I would only fire at him if the situation was completely lost.

He stared at me. His eyes were glazed. Elephants can only think of one coherent thing when in musth, and that's females.

'Mnumzane, my big boy!' I called again. 'It's me! You have scared the hell out of me and we are in big danger. Back off, back off.'

He spread his huge ears as he heard my voice, then he lifted his trunk and aimed it towards me like a massive elastic wand, looking for my scent. After a few seconds he slowly walked across and gently started pulling out the broken windscreen with his trunk. He was right on top of us, his huge foot inches from my head. All he had to do was lift his foot onto the cab and we would be crushed. I could see the end of his trunk twitching, moist and bristly as it snaked into the vehicle. All the while I kept talking to him in a soothing voice, reassuring him of my presence, trying to keep him calm. Most importantly, I could see that the glaze had gone from his eyes, and then he very gently put the end of his trunk right on top of my head and slowly moved it all over my body, smelling me. There was a peace about the vehicle now and it was almost as if he was checking if I was OK. Satisfied, he eventually walked off a few yards and then, as if unsure of what to do, stood there silently looking at us for a few minutes before moving away completely.

Both my passengers were bug-eyed with adrenalin, wide-mouthed but barely breathing. They couldn't believe what had just happened. Nor could I. It was an astonishing experience.

'He listened to you!' said Godfrey. 'He listened to you and he spared our lives.'

Martin was more direct. 'We're alive.' He didn't sound totally convinced.

I said nothing. It had been a close call.

Back at the lodge, Françoise rushed over and put her arms around me. Godfrey, a lifelong teetotaller, ordered three of the biggest whiskies the barman could pour.

I then asked Martin exactly why he had shouted 'It's Museveni' when Mnumzane had charged. He suddenly became extremely animated. So did Godfrey. They leaned close towards me.

'It was because the spirit of Museveni was in the elephant,' Martin explained. 'Museveni was trying to stop us talking to you because he knows the truth will come out about his lies and what he is doing to the Acholi. Museveni doesn't want peace, he is scared of peace. He wants to destroy us. He was right there in the heart of that elephant.'

'Yes,' said Godfrey, chipping in, 'I was talking to the elephant in my head all the time, I told him directly with my thoughts, I said, I have no fight with you, and Museveni should not influence you against us.'

Many Africans are deeply spiritual people and believe that nothing happens by chance. If you are bitten by a snake, it means either the gods or your ancestors are angry with you. If you lose your job, or your wife, it is due to black magic. If you are charged by a bull elephant, it is not because the animal is in musth. It's something mystical. I knew nothing that I could say would change Godfrey and Martin's opinion: that during those enraged few seconds Mnumzane was in fact Museveni. I didn't even try.

They left for Southern Sudan the next day, saying they would be in touch. Things were getting interesting, I thought.

I had no idea.

CHAPTER TWENTY-TWO

It was only a few days later when the call came in from Martin Ojul. I was sitting with Françoise in the lounge of our small bush cottage.

'Mr Anthony,' said Martin formally. 'I am in the forest with our leaders. We will call you in one hour for an important discussion. The call must be kept short to avoid anyone tracking our position. Can you be available?'

'Yes,' I replied. 'I'll keep the line clear for you.'

Every communication from the LRA peace team was important; every call another opportunity to strengthen the agreement to protect the rhino and keep Garamba safe. This time it was different, as Martin was actually in the bush with the military leaders. I was intrigued to find out what was coming next.

Exactly an hour later the phone rang.

'Is that you, Mr Anthony?' Martin said.

'Yes, it is.'

'Please hold on for General Vincent Otti.'

The statement took me completely by surprise. Otti was the second most wanted man on planet earth, at least as far as the International Criminal Court was concerned. As I mentioned earlier, the ICC issued arrest warrants in 2005 against Joseph Kony, his deputy Vincent Otti, and LRA commanders Raska Lukwiya, Okot Odhiambo and Dominic Ongwen – the first international warrants ever issued from the court's headquarters in The Hague. Lukwiya had since been killed in a fight with the Ugandan army in August 2006. Now Otti was coming to the phone, wanting to talk to me in my home. I was staggered at the implication and knew in that instant that Pandora's box was being opened, and that whatever happened thereafter, things would never be the same again. I focused hard.

'Good morning, Mr Anthony, this is General Vincent Otti of the Lord's Resistance Army. How do you do?'

The softly spoken voice intruded into the sanctity of Thula Thula and into my life.

'I am fine, thank you,' I replied mechanically, wrestling with the dilemma of actually speaking with the notorious Otti, purported to be one of the world's most hard-bitten mass murderers.

'I am pleased to meet you,' he said, and then dispensing with formalities continued straight on. 'My people tell me that you are a man I can deal with. I request your support with the South African government.'

'In what way would that be?' I replied, conscious of Martin's warning that the call may be tracked through the satellite signal; that the discussion would not last long.

'We have reliable information that Museveni will violate the peace accord and attack our positions. I cannot allow this to happen. Our urgent request is that you ask your government to intervene and to change the venue for the peace talks from Juba to Kenya or South Africa. People will listen to the South Africans,' he concluded.

As a precondition for the Juba peace talks, the LRA and Ugandan government had agreed to a cessation of hostilities. The main body of the LRA troops, some say several thousand men, were situated in a safe zone in assembly areas hidden in the far north of the Garamba game reserve in the Congo and this is where they anticipated the attack.

'We do not trust the situation here,' Otti continued. 'We are picking up troop and aircraft movements. They will attack shortly. Unless you can help us, and the talks are moved away from Sudan, we will be forced to withdraw from the assembly areas. We will go back to the bush and back to war and this is exactly what Museveni wants – to end the talks.'

'I understand,' I replied. 'I will speak to my contacts in the South African government.'

'I will call you back in two days,' he said. 'We do not have time.'

'Thank you for your assistance with the rhino,' I squeezed the words in.

'It is important,' he replied, and with that satellite line went dead.

I closed my cellphone, aghast at the immensity of the request. By coming directly to me, Otti had bypassed the UN-sponsored peace talks entirely.

'Who was that?' said Françoise, who had overheard the conversation from the couch where she was sitting.

'Vincent Otti of the Lord's Resistance Army just called me,' I said. 'I can't believe he phoned me here.'

Her eyes opened wide. 'What did he want?' she asked, standing up and walking over to me.

'He doesn't trust the venue for the peace talks. He wants them moved to Kenya or South Africa. He thinks Museveni is planning an attack. He wants me to get my government contacts to intervene, otherwise he is pulling out of the peace talks.'

'So why is he talking to you about it? The whole world is following these talks. You are not a diplomat.'

'God only knows,' I said. 'Somehow he believes I can help. I'm not sure if I can.'

She looked at me for a long time. 'You can,' she said eventually, 'and you must.'

The words surprised me. We had been together for twenty years and incredibly, she supported all my somewhat risky adventures, never critical, always reassuring. But encouraging me to intervene with a group like the LRA was very different.

She continued, 'You must help, this time not only because of animals but because of the human suffering caused by this horrible endless war. I have been studying it on the Internet and it's the most shocking thing I have ever read. The child soldiers, the atrocities, the horror – it defies belief.'

She held my gaze. 'This LRA, they don't know anybody. They have no contact with the outside world, and now they have found you. They have been in the jungle fighting for over twenty years, and let me tell you as a woman, their soldiers are tired of it. No one can willingly go on that long. Whatever they have done, whatever they have become, they also have mothers, fathers and families they would like to see again. Remember that once upon a time they were all children themselves, children stolen from loving families and loving homes and forced into the LRA. Despite the degradations, despite what they have become, I promise you that there is nothing they want more than to just go back home. I don't know a lot about politics and war, but I know about families. I came to South Africa so long ago to be with you and I have never been happier, but I still think of my home, my culture, my old friends – and I can still go back when I need to. Imagine what it's like for them. No cause is worth that sacrifice.'

She sighed. 'It's such madness. Child soldiers being kidnapped by those who were once child soldiers themselves; how crazy. But at the bottom of it all, they are still human beings. The contact you have with them, the trust they have in you, must be taken advantage of – very carefully. But you can do much good. This is a door you must walk through, this time not only for animals, but for the sake of people.'

Talk about a life-changing lecture.

'You know, of course, that whatever I do will be heavily criticized, by both sides,' I said. 'This issue is just too hot; actually, it's way beyond hot, it's inflamed.'

'It's already started,' Françoise said. 'I saw on the Internet that you've been attacked by the ICCN and another conservation group in Kenya for even meeting the LRA peace team in Juba.'

'I know and I am afraid that this is something we are just going to have to get used to.'

We chatted for a while longer before I finally took the decision, picked up the phone, and called Dr Ben Ngubane in Tokyo. Ben was an old friend, an elder African statesman who was the South African ambassador to Japan. He was highly respected internationally and very well connected in high places. If anyone could help with this, he could.

'Do you know of the Lord's Resistance Army?' I asked when I finally got past his secretary.

'Joseph Kony, Museveni's arch enemy,' he replied. 'Who doesn't?'

'Then you are not going to believe what I have to tell you,' I said.

'Whew,' said Ben once I was finished explaining. 'This is most unusual. I thought you were a conservationist?' He laughed. 'Leave it with me and I will make enquiries. I'll have to get back to you.'

He phoned me the next day.

'I have spoken with Foreign Affairs, but they have some difficulty believing that anyone has close contact with Vincent Otti, of all people. But I am working on it; please keep me informed of any further developments on your side.'

The following afternoon I received the expected call from Otti. I recognized the soft voice immediately and reminded myself that the conversation would of necessity be very short.

'I have spoken with my contacts in government,' I replied to his question about progress. 'These are senior people who can influence decisions, and they are interested, but I am afraid there is a question of credibility. They are having difficulty believing that I am in direct contact with you, that you are bypassing the peace talks and dealing with someone like me.'

There was a brief silence.

'Then please tell them this. We want genuine, lasting peace. The time for fighting is over. But several of my soldiers have just been killed by Ugandan forces and this is unacceptable. Museveni has violated the ceasefire and we believe an attack on our positions is imminent. If I do not get a positive response within three days, we will be forced to go back to the bush. We will abandon the talks.'

'I will do so,' I replied, appalled by the implications of what I was hearing.

'Thank you,' he said. 'I will contact you again shortly.'

It is fair to say that at the time both sides accused the other of breaking the ceasefire and I had no way of knowing what was really happening on the ground. I passed the contents of the call on to Ben in Tokyo, and then, beset by the small problem of a war starting if I failed in my task, drove out into the reserve looking for the natural antidote to all problems – the elephants.

It is interesting, I thought as I searched the open bush for the herd: if elephants are just great big pieces of ambient meat, why does one feel so good in their presence? Why would I be seeking them out for my own benefit, for my own well-being? I have spoken to so many people about this over the years, and all agree that time spent around elephants in the wild precipitates a sense that all is well with the world.

And all was not well in my world. The UN-sponsored peace talks between the Ugandan government and the LRA were on the verge of collapse. Thousands of vicious LRA soldiers were going to be let loose and the oldest and ugliest civil war in Africa was about to restart, unless I could somehow help find a solution.

How on earth did I get myself into this situation? As with so many other conservation activities, one had to resolve human problems before you could help the affected animals, but this time it was right off the scale. This started with rhinos and come hell or high water it will end with rhinos, I vowed to myself.

I found the herd grazing on the rich green grasses surrounding Croc Pools, a beautiful open wetland near the Nseleni River. As I got closer I picked out Nana standing off a little to the side of the herd. As was her habit at this time of the morning, she was reading the newspaper.

She stood there unmoving, her trunk carefully positioned just off the ground hoovering the passing air for tell-tale scents and odours. Her huge ears spread slightly into the breeze were deftly picking up every sound for miles around. Apart from small flicks of the ears and movements of the trunk, she was absolutely motionless, focused on the task at hand.

As always in the bush, one reads the obituaries first.

The longest, biggest nose in the animal kingdom could detect scent particles in one part per hundred million, so Nana could easily detect the tiniest whiff of blood coming in on the breeze from afar. She had heard the hunt the night before and the scent now confirmed it was successful. Her incredible elephantine memory would remind her which animals lived where, and she would know exactly which herd had experienced the death. She may even be able to ascertain which individual had died.

Then she tuned in to the funerals. The distant smell of putrefaction and the scent of hyena, jackals and vultures, wafting in from over the hills, told her that the final remains of a dead body had been consumed. For in the bush nothing is buried, everything is eaten.

The births column was next. The odour of afterbirth was

distinctive in the morning air. This scent also attracted predators and was the reason baby animals could stand up and run, sometimes within minutes. Nana had noticed the pregnant zebra when the herd moved into the area the day before, and now had olfactory confirmation that a new baby had arrived. Perhaps she silently congratulated the mother, who knows.

The weather report was not as good as she was hoping for. Water molecules on the gentle breeze brought news that just a little rain might fall in the next day or two. It had been hot and dry for a long time, for years in fact, and Nana needed the heavy rain for her family, but it was not to be, not this time.

She could easily discern the strong smell of a large bull in musth approaching. It was Mabula coming over a distant hill to check if any of the females were going to be receptive to his overtures. But as Nana already knew, none of the females in the herd was in oestrus. He was going to be out of luck this time.

Her incredible ears, also the biggest in the animal kingdom, were edging back and forth picking up and interpreting every sound for miles around, and all of this information was being uploaded into the biggest brain in the animal kingdom on land, and cross-referenced with the scents and smells.

And that was not all, not by a long way.

Elephants have their own private wavelength which they use for elephant-to-elephant communication. It's called infrasound. These incredibly low-pitched rumbles are barely audible to humans, but they travel over vast distances, some say hundreds of square miles. Nana could feel the thudding rumbles coming in from a herd in the nearby Umfolozi game reserve with the news of the day. Not only could she hear it, but she could also pick up the vibration through her feet. Replicas of the airborne rumbles were coming through the ground as well. Incredibly, elephants are able to use seismic vibrations at infrasound frequencies to communicate.

I watched her for a while, understanding only the concept of what she was busy doing. With my pitifully inadequate human senses I could only try and imagine the vastness of information she was gathering and analysing, all of which was unavailable to me.

If one adds to all of this the sophisticated emotions and awareness that elephants so readily display, one must be left with a sense of wonderment at this incredible creature that we slaughter with such gay abandon for its two front teeth.

Nana picked out the sound of my new vehicle long before I got there and raised her trunk. She had always quickly been able to recognize the sound of my vehicle from others of the same make and model. As soon as I stopped, she put the newspaper aside and casually led the herd over. I hadn't been with her for a while.

After elephantine greetings which included Nana's trunk coming into the driver's window and covering me in slime, they simply hung out, grazing near the vehicle for hours. Some of the youngsters and babies who didn't know me held back, watching warily, but they were orderly and well mannered, following the adults' lead in my presence.

It's just not possible to fixate on one's own problems when you are surrounded by a herd of elephants oozing contentment. That they are so huge and imposing creates just enough concern for safety to keep you on edge. But as you get used to it and relax, you find there is no elixir quite like it.

I thought back to how unhappy and dangerous they were when they first arrived, and how Nana eventually reached out to me, and taught me so much about herself and her kind. Against the odds she had somehow managed to keep her family safe through dire circumstances – by befriending a human. They were now fat, happy and breeding at Thula Thula. How content they looked painted against that verdant marshland.

Reluctantly, I took leave of the herd and drove home, taking the long route around to give myself a bit of time to think.

As I walked into our cottage, Ben was on the phone from Tokyo talking to Françoise. He didn't have good news.

'I am afraid,' said Ben as I took the phone, 'that the LRA proposal for the venue to be moved to Kenya or South Africa has already been tabled at the Juba peace talks and rejected. No one believes your warning that the LRA are going to pull their army out and abandon the talks. They say they've heard it all before.'

I was stunned.

'But what happens if he means it?'

'Well, there is nothing much we can do in three days,' said Ben. 'The ball is in Otti's court.'

CHAPTER TWENTY-THREE

Three days later the call came in from Vincent Otti on a satellite phone somewhere deep in the jungles of the Congo.

'Mr Anthony, the situation is bad. Regrettably, I must advise you that we are pulling out of the talks. We're going back to the bush. Did you tell your people that this would happen?'

'I did exactly as you asked,' I replied, 'but it was not believed. There is unfortunately still a credibility problem.'

He went silent for a moment or two and I was afraid the connection had been lost. Then his voice came through again.

'Now you have credibility, your predictions have taken place, and they will believe you,' he responded. 'We are out of options; I want you to please continue your work for peace. Goodbye.'

I put a call through to Tokyo right away.

'Hi, Ben. Otti's just phoned me. The LRA are pulling out; the army is going back to the bush.'

'So you were right,' he said.

'It's small comfort that a war has to start up again to prove me right,' I said. 'This is a nasty situation.'

'You have Otti's ear. This is unique and we must build on it. I will be travelling back to South Africa. We must act.'

A week later Ben was back in South Africa trawling the corridors of power, trying to find solutions. It took a perilously long time before there was a breakthrough and Ben was already back in Japan before we received some positive feedback. It was not what we wanted, but it did offer a solution. The venue could not be changed, that was final, but South Africa would appoint a monitor to the talks, as would Kenya and Mozambique. The monitors would oversee order and security and interact with the delegates on all matters.

'This proposal is yet to go to the LRA formally,' said Ben when he called again. 'But there is concern that it may not be well received. Your role will be to present it to Otti and to get the LRA's agreement. A lot depends on your success, because if they reject it . . . well, there just isn't another plan.'

I put the phone down and got straight on to Martin Ojul.

'Martin,' I said, 'this has taken a lot longer than I thought, but we may have a solution. It is not something we can discuss on the telephone. Are you and Godfrey able to come back to South Africa?'

'We will need clearance from Kony and Otti,' he replied, 'and you will need to get us new visas.'

So I forked out for their airfares, arranged special visas again and they were here within days.

'Gentlemen,' I said once they had arrived and settled in. 'Let me be direct. Despite all our efforts, it has become clear that there is no support for a change of venue from Juba to Kenya or South Africa. Neither government will agree.'

'We have heard rumours about this,' said Martin. 'But Juba remains completely unacceptable to us. Another venue must be found.'

Godfrey nodded in agreement.

'The problem,' I said, 'is that Kenya and South Africa are both leading members of the Organization of African Unity, and as both countries have said no, it is highly unlikely that any other African country can or will override the decision.'

'This is a problem,' said Godfrey. 'There are too many out-side influences and cabals destabilizing the talks and Juba is unsafe for our delegates. There has already been an attack on our troops and we have concerns that if our soldiers go back to the assembly area it will be a trap. It's becoming more and more clear to us that Museveni doesn't want peace.'

'There is a proposal that will soon be put to your delegation formally,' I said. 'But I felt it important that we discuss it between ourselves first, so we can brief General Otti in advance.'

Godfrey and Martin frowned and looked at each other and I felt my stomach tighten. This was a chance to get the LRA army back to the assembly areas (the huge tracts of jungle where the LRA remained hidden during negotiations) and restart the peace talks. Martin and Godfrey said they genuinely wanted peace. Otti had told me he wanted peace, but it was difficult to judge. I had no formal training in diplomacy or politics and was relying on common sense to guide me through some very unfamiliar territory.

I found it curious that the LRA said they had tried several times previously to achieve peace. Could it be true that the most violent terrorist army on earth was genuine about wanting real peace, that they had simply had enough? Were people right in saying it was Museveni who didn't want peace? I just didn't know.

What I did know was that the proposal I was about to present was all that stood in the way of resumption of war. The LRA army was already out in the field and on full alert for an attack. Tensions were high and everybody was nervous. It would take just one incident, one careless shot, one mistake, and all hell could break loose. We were sitting on the edge of the abyss. People throughout Central Africa were horrified at what was happening. The story of the LRA abandoning the assembly areas and the talks was all over the media, locally and internationally, and panic was spreading.

'Let us hear what they have to say, then,' said Martin. 'We are intrigued.'

'Please correct me if I am wrong,' I said, 'but you told me, when we met in Juba, that you didn't trust Museveni or the Sudanese. As I understand it, the LRA believes the Juba talks to be incestuous, that there is a covert relationship between Southern Sudan and Uganda. Is this why you want the talks moved?'

'Betrayal at the talks is just one of our reasons,' said Godfrey. 'A Ugandan attack is also a constant concern.'

'As well as the personal safety of our delegation in Juba if something goes wrong,' said Martin, 'the Southern Sudan army, the SPLA, is no friend of ours. We do not have diplomatic immunity.'

'Well,' I said, 'the refusal to change venue makes options very limited, so if we cannot take Mohammed to the mountain, then we must try and bring the mountain to Mohammed.'

'In what way?' asked Godfrey.

Here goes, I thought.

'Monitors at the talks,' I replied. 'Monitors from neutral African countries who are well briefed on the dynamics of the situation and who will help supervise the talks and defuse tensions. The monitors will have carte blanche to attend meetings, travel, investigate complaints, make input and see fair play.'

I looked carefully for any sign of how this was being received by Martin and Godfrey, but they both sat stone-faced, completely unmoved.

'The governments of South Africa, Kenya and Mozambique will each appoint a monitor. They will report to their governments on all matters, and carry recommendations back to the talks and to the negotiating parties.'

'Continue,' said Martin.

'Most importantly, this proposal plugs these three governments into the talks, meaning their interest and involvement will be substantially increased. This will help close the door on irregular activities and drive the process forward.'

That was the pitch. It was short and it was not at all what they wanted to hear, but it was workable.

Martin spoke first.

'Is there a possibility the talks can be shifted elsewhere, perhaps overseas?' he asked.

'I highly doubt it,' I replied. 'Any government will refer back to the OAU. This is an African matter.'

He fell silent. Martin was a politician always looking at the angles and opportunities, of which there were precious few in my words.

Godfrey was an intellectual who took a measured, thoughtful approach to matters. He was in my opinion a huge asset to the peace talks, someone who could genuinely help end the war if he wasn't sidelined by the arrogance of the not-quite-so-bright, of which there were too many examples in the diplomatic mess that was Juba.

'Will Uganda accept the monitors?' he said.

'I believe they will,' I replied.

'Then the choice for us appears to be quite simple. If we don't accept the monitors, the war will continue.'

'It appears so,' I said. 'But let's relook at it. It's not a perfect solution, but it is a workable solution. I want to emphasize the word "workable".'

Martin and Godfrey spoke to each other at length in Acholi, obviously debating and discussing the proposal.

Then Martin spoke again in English. 'Mr Anthony, this is not our decision to make. We need to take this to General Otti. Will you please excuse us?'

They left the table, walked out of earshot and placed a call to the jungle.

'The matter requires a meeting of the leadership,' said Godfrey when they returned. 'We have been recalled. There are more questions and points we need to cover, but we must leave the day after tomorrow.'

'There is one thing that stands in the way of any further progress,' said Martin sombrely. 'Our military leadership need assurances that MONUC, the UN in the Congo, will not make another attack on our positions during the talks.'

'I have some contacts,' I replied, amazed at the confidence they had in my ability to achieve the impossible.

'This is non-negotiable,' he continued, 'we have a ceasefire with Museveni; we must also have a ceasefire with MONUC otherwise we cannot continue with the talks.

'I understand,' I said. 'I will do my best.'

'Excellent.'

'Now I must make arrangements to get you to the airport,' I replied.

'And we would like to thank you, Mr Anthony, for all you have done in the name of peace. One day the Acholi people will thank you.'

This sounds like good news, I thought. Surely they would have said something if the answer was no.

'There is one last thing,' said Martin. 'Joseph Kony and Vincent Otti want to meet you.'

I stared at him in complete and utter disbelief.

Chapter Twenty-four

Joseph Kony and Vincent Otti wanted to meet me! That meant going alone into their secret camps in the Congo jungle. I was in way over my head, and it was all happening so fast.

All I wanted to do was step back and leave this convoluted, dangerous mess for someone else to deal with, and I was sure nobody would blame me.

But then again, in two decades of war nobody had ever been able to deal with it, and I actually was in a position to help. The leaders of both the political and military wings of the LRA were dealing with me directly and showing high levels of trust. They were of course continuing down other formal and informal routes, but it had become clear they had no confidence in those forums.

What do I do?

Then I thought back to what Professor Medo Misama had said to me as I left Juba: that the LRA were starting to trust me, and that this put me in a unique position to help countless people affected by this never-ending war.

My thoughts then went to the thousands of children who had already been taken by the LRA over the years. Innocent children, kidnapped from loving homes and families and taken away with no return ticket. Then there were the internally displaced persons (IDP) camps in Northern Uganda, where nearly two million people had been rounded up and forced to live, if you can even call it that, in what many call a man-made purgatory.

Imagine going out and rounding up two million people. It defied belief. Refugees are not rounded up; they flee danger and arrive at places of safety of their own free will, they don't get put there by force. I was to meet many people who had visited or lived in these camps where 500 children died each week and life expectancy was less than forty years. I did not believe Museveni's PR that they were refugee camps, or for that matter the counterclaims that they were concentration camps. They were something in between, a bit of both, appalling, terrible places nevertheless, where no one should ever be forced to stay.

And what of the night walkers, the thousands of children who left each afternoon out of blind fear of being taken by the LRA, because Museveni couldn't or didn't protect them. What would happen to them if I backed out? And what of the countless people who had been displaced and uprooted across the entire region in this horrible, horrible war, where atrocities, mutilations and rape were weapons of choice?

Since they had downed MONUC's two attack helicopters in January, the LRA had feared reprisals. Now Kony and Otti wanted me to get the UN to agree not to attack the LRA camps, before they in return would accept the idea of monitors. I looked up the number of MONUC, the United Nations branch in the DRC, and made the call. They're not going to bite me, I thought. They can only say no.

'The man you need to speak to is Mr Mujahid Alam,' the girl on the switchboard said. 'He is in charge of all these matters. I will put you through.'

'Mr Alam,' I said when she patched me through. 'Thank you for taking my call. You don't know me,' I added, giving my name. 'But I have something unusual to ask of you.'

'I believe I do know you,' he replied before I could continue. 'We supported your efforts to try and prevent the extinction of the northern white rhino in Garamba National Park with aircraft and equipment. How can I be of assistance?'

So I gave him the outline.

The very next morning I made the five-hour flight to Kinshasa, and early that evening chose a table by the swimming pool at the Grand Hotel. It was a Sunday night, and I was pleased the terrace wasn't busy and we would be able to talk privately. In Kinshasa you never knew who could be listening.

Mujahid Alam, whose impressive official title was Principal Adviser to Special Representative of the Secretary-General of the United Nations, arrived on time and we introduced ourselves. Alam was Pakistani, urbane and sophisticated in both dress and conversation. His ready smile and open demeanour took the edge off the meeting, and after some small talk I was able to engage him on the history of my unusual involvement with the LRA and their important request.

'At the end of it all,' I said, 'the issue is that the LRA believe, correctly or incorrectly, that Museveni is endeavouring to get MONUC to attack them again, and this is standing in the way of the resumption of the Juba talks.'

'I understand,' he said thoughtfully when I finished speaking. 'Mr Anthony, I can assure you that MONUC fully supports the Juba peace talks, and we have no plans to engage the LRA militarily at this time. Provided, of course, the LRA are in the assembly areas, and pose no immediate risk to citizens in this country.'

'Well, this news will go a long way to getting them back into the assembly areas,' I said. 'And it will certainly go a long way to help restart the peace talks.'

We talked for another hour or so over dinner, analysing the situation in depth and giving me the opportunity to learn a lot more about the history of Museveni and why Kony took up arms against him. Alam certainly knew the ins and outs of

African politics very well. He wasn't telling me anything about MONUC's military capability, that was for sure, but what was also sure was that unless the LRA did something tactless, they need not fear an attack from the MONUC. I was most heartened by the conversation.

The important thing, he told me, was that the Juba peace talks were bereft of credibility, and that my involvement, if I continued, could help open reliable communication lines to the LRA military leaders for the very first time.

'This is a critical juncture in our search for solutions,' he said, using diplomatic language. 'The Juba talks are all that stand in the way of war, and I ask that we please stay in close contact, and that you update me on progress.'

'That I will gladly do,' I replied. 'And I ask in turn that you let me know if anything fundamental changes.'

'And that I will do,' he replied. 'And for the sake of your own security, we must keep details of our discussion private.'

'Thank you,' I said. 'I appreciate your interest and concern.'

We exchanged contact details, and the next afternoon I was back in South Africa, where I placed a call to Godfrey and told him of the visit to Kinshasa and the outcome of my discussions.

'I must reiterate,' I said to him, 'that these undertakings not to attack come with the specific provisos that your troops are in the assembly areas and you are engaged in the peace talks.'

'This is very important information,' said Godfrey. 'Martin and I will update Kony and Otti immediately. Thank you for what you are doing. We will contact you again shortly.'

The next day I was out in the veldt with David, catching up on my much-neglected bush work, when the radio came alive.

'Code red, code red! Anybody, anybody, come in.'

I braked the Land Rover hard and grabbed for the mouthpiece. David beat me to it.

'Standing by.'

'Help me, help me, please; it's trying to kill me. The buffalo is trying to kill me.' The guttural Afrikaans voice was stilted and heavy with distress.

'Where are you exactly?' asked David, glancing at me as he did so, worry creasing his brow.

'I'm in a tree near Shaka River crossing. Come quickly, it's bad, man.'

'OK, we are on our way. Just hold on.'

'Quickly, please. He really wants to kill me.'

I plotted the shortest possible route, swung the Land Rover off the dirt track into the open bush and floored the accelerator. As I did so, David reached for the rifle standing on the floor between us, expertly removed the magazine and checked the rounds.

On the radio had been our young new ranger, Pieter. It sounded like he had got himself into a lot of trouble.

The Cape buffalo is one of my favourite African animals. Regal, powerful and unpredictable, it symbolizes all that is the very best of the African Bushveld. It is also one of Africa's most dangerous creatures. Lone bulls, dagga boys as they are called by some, black death by others, are a ton-and-a-half of bad temper best left well alone. Pieter must have walked into one near the river, and had somehow, thankfully, made it to a tree.

I called him back, holding the radio's mouthpiece in one hand and the bucking steering wheel in the other.

'Pieter! Come in, Pieter.'

'*Ja*, I'm here.'

'What happened?'

'The bull was sleeping in the reeds covered in mud and I didn't see him. Man, I very nearly walked right into him.'

He paused, catching his breath.

'He came at me and I ran like hell and managed to find a tree.

I am OK now, he can't reach me, but he won't leave. He's waiting underneath. He wants to kill me.'

'You'll be fine,' said David, taking the radio mouthpiece, trying to calm him down. 'Hang on and don't worry. We will be there very soon.'

'It's not just the buffalo, it's the thorns,' he said. 'They're stuck in me all over my body.'

I could just imagine the panicked scenario: Pieter's adrenalin-charged run for his life had ended with him scrambling up the first available tree. Unfortunately for him, his arboreal sanctuary happened to be the namesake of his nemesis: the legendary buffalo thorn tree, legendary not only because of its Zulu connection to the spiritual world, but because it harbours thousands of vicious, hooked thorns.

'Use your Leatherman,' I replied, referring to his combination knife, pliers and screwdriver, the obligatory accessory of every ranger. 'Cut the thorns off.'

'I can't.'

'Why not?'

'Because I threw the buffalo with my Leatherman.'

'You mean you threw your Leatherman at the buffalo,' I replied, smiling to myself and imagining both the buffalo and the Leatherman flying through the air.

'Yes, he wouldn't go so I threw him with it.'

'Well, you are lucky you didn't throw him with your radio,' I said. 'Otherwise we wouldn't be having this conversation.'

Ten minutes later we arrived and, just as he had said, he was clinging on for dear life up a tree with the massive mud-covered bovine on the ground below him. Dozens of intractable thorns hooked through his clothes, stabbing wickedly into his body.

By the simple expedience of hooting, shouting and banging the outside of the doors with our hands, David and I managed to get the bull to move off far enough for us to get out and help Pieter down.

David looked up at the forlorn ranger, laughed, and then retrieved his Leatherman off the ground and passed it back up to him.

'Next time, watch where you are walking,' he said firmly, oblivious to the young ranger's discomfort as he started cutting the sharp thorns from his body. 'This is not a sheep farm. And get those thorn punctures treated before they get infected.'

Every over-confident young ranger has to go through some form of bush initiation to attune him to the real dangers of the wild. Pieter had just had his – and survived. He would be all right.

The buffalo reminded me of Garamba, and my thoughts turned to the LRA and the failed peace talks. There had been a lot of hubbub in the media, but the good news was that despite accusation and counter-accusation there were no military incidents. The tenuous peace was holding.

A few weeks later I received two telephone calls, first from Martin and then from Godfrey, with the best possible news. The LRA had agreed to accept the monitors and return to the talks. Their army would stand down and go back to the assembly areas. I phoned Ben in Tokyo and told him. If we were closer, we would have met and shared a bottle of champagne.

I then phoned Mujahid Alam and gave him the update.

'The LRA are going back to the talks,' I said.

'This is excellent news,' said Mujahid.

'Yes, it is,' I replied. 'Your assurances played a big role in this. They are a very suspicious group and have feared reprisal attacks by MONUC for a long time now. The information from our meeting has reassured the LRA, and will allow them to focus on getting back to the peace talks.'

*

About a month later, in April 2007, when the monitors started attending, the peace talks resumed.

On the rhino front the agreement was holding. The LRA were avoiding the Garamba guards and camp and they were still looking for rhino on their patrols in the north of the park, though by now I had little real hope they'd find them.

With the talks progressing, I had the opportunity to concentrate on my somewhat neglected work with the chiefs around Thula Thula. Several months later, after many meetings we finally signed the agreement to bring the first piece of their land into conservation. It was an existing KZN Wildlife reserve situated on their traditional land which was returned to the tribes and put into a joint venture with Thula Thula for its upkeep and development.

We moved onto the neglected land, and with an excited sense of purpose set about repairing fences, cutting roads, building dams and doing all the things needed to create a superb game reserve. Once we dropped the fences into Thula Thula game started migrating into the new areas and we were soon getting sightings of buffalo, zebra, kudu and all the other indigenous species.

The strangest thing, though, was that Nana and Frankie refused to lead the herd into the new reserve. They would stand where the fence used to be, looking over into the new area, but would not take even one step inside. One day I decided to intervene. I went across the boundary into the new area and called them. They both recognized my voice immediately and came forward, but then stopped on the old fence line.

'It's OK, Nana,' I said to her comfortingly as she stood there undecided about what to do, 'you can come over, it's safe. The new area is for you.' Still she didn't move.

'Frankie,' I said calling out to her, 'come across, there is a huge new area waiting for you and your families. This is all part of Thula Thula now.' Still no response.

They were all still standing about sixty-five feet inside Thula Thula, so I got out of my Land Rover, walked towards them, then turned around and walked back into the new area, talking to them all the while.

It took some cajoling to get them to come forward, I can tell you. Frankie was the first to react and took a few hesitant steps towards me, then a few more, then strode across the boundary and walked a hundred metres into the new reserve. The whole herd followed except Nana, who stood fast. Frankie stopped and turned back to face Nana and waited. Eventually she joined them and they all disappeared into the beautiful thick virgin bush which had not seen an elephant for a hundred years.

The next day was a Sunday, and family and friends with children, grandchildren, and an assortment of domestic dogs were running around playing as we had a bush braai (barbeque) next to a damn on the Ntambanana River. I watched out of the corner of my eye as David, Jason and Dylan walked to the edge of the river, clapping their hands and shooing away what I thought was a dog. At second glance I realized they were in fact shooing away a young croc who had taken an interest in proceedings and come to the river bank. I kept an eye on the spot and a few minutes later the croc was joined by another. Crocs love eating dogs, and it was the barking as the dogs ran around with the kids which was pulling them in.

David and Dylan chased them off again, but as the boys turned their backs, both crocs immediately returned to the river bank. A third, much bigger one came up from the depths of the river and surfaced between them.

'Watch out guys, these crocs are ganging up on us,' I called out, 'I think we must move the braai, we don't want to lose a child, or a dog.'

'Don't worry,' said David, as the men threw an old tennis ball at the crocs, briefly routing them. 'We're covered. It's policy that the head ranger must immediately replace any child that is lost on the reserve. And we are the head rangers,' he added, putting his arms around Jason and Dylan and smiling broadly. A moment later they all had to duck as Dylan's wife's shoe came flying past their heads. The look they got from her could have killed at fifty paces.

The girls, though, are tough in rural Zululand. A few months earlier, Phiwe, one of our young trainee chefs, was pregnant for the first time when the baby decided to arrive early. There was panic as two rangers were woken and given my Landy to rush her to hospital, and then more panic as the Landy broke down half way to town, and then complete terror in the ranks as Phiwe started giving birth on the back seat. The first tough ranger took one look and ran off retching, while the other actually managed to be of some help by shouting encouragement and then cutting the umbilical cord with the only tools he had – a machete and a stone.

The tired mother happily gathered the perfectly formed baby in her arms, as the rangers managed to get the car started and set off once again for the clinic.

'Where are you going?' called Phiwe from the back seat.

'To the clinic,' replied the driver.

'Why?' asked Phiwe. 'I have already had the baby.'

'But you must go to the doctor.'

'No, what for?'

'Where do you want to go then?'

'Back to my room,' Phiwe insisted. 'I am very tired.'

And so they turned around and drove back to Thula Thula. There they were met by a couple of Phiwe's young friends, who helped Phiwe and the baby through the night. She never did see a doctor and we had to stop her coming back to work with the baby on her back a week later.

During this time, I was continuously in touch with Otti,

Godrey and Martin. Then, one day in September, Martin phoned me again.

'Good morning, Mr Anthony. Things are happening fast. Are you available to travel to Nairobi?'

'Yes, I am,' I replied.

'Excellent. Godfrey and I will meet you at the airport, and then we will travel on to Juba together.'

'And the purpose of the trip?' I asked.

'You have an invitation from Joseph Kony and Vincent Otti to stay with them as their guest. We are going to go to the jungle,' he replied.

Even though I was expecting it, the statement threw me.

'Why?' I answered reflexively, forgetting my manners.

'Your news from the UN in the Congo was well received. The military high command wants to thank you personally for your role in helping the talks, and they want to enlist your assistance to ensure the peace talks do not fail again. This is important. Godfrey and I will accompany you. Your safety will be guaranteed by the LRA.'

'How will we get there?'

'We will drive from Juba.'

'Drive!' From the little I knew of the area, Garamba would be a two- or three-day drive from Juba through bandit territory, across Southern Sudan and then down into no-man's-land in the Congo. Just getting there would be a nightmare.

My head was spinning. I was being invited to travel 3,000 miles to stay with some of the world's most dangerous men in their secret jungle camps. On the positive side, my safety would be guaranteed by the most notorious terrorist army on earth. Absurdity didn't even begin to describe it all.

Strangely enough, to have my safety guaranteed by the LRA actually gave me the best possible security. The only way I could die, I reasoned, was if the instruction to kill me came from Kony or Otti themselves, which appeared unlikely. Unless, of course, there was an attack by the Ugandans or by the Southern Sudanese army, the SPLA, who hated the LRA, or an internal revolt, or disease I had never heard of, or of course rebels or bandits along the way – I had forgotten about them. Things were looking bright.

I have always trusted my gut feelings. You do or you don't. Too much thinking can complicate things, especially with big decisions.

'Martin,' I said, 'if they genuinely want my help, if they are serious about peace, then I will accept. But first I have to know that the agenda is open, that I can raise any matter.'

'What are you thinking about?' he asked.

'The LRA is defined in the minds of the world by the issue of child soldiers. If they genuinely want peace, this has to be on the agenda. I need to hear from them on this.'

'It is already done,' he replied. 'We briefed Otti about this matter after our last visit to Thula Thula. They are prepared.'

'Then there is the matter of the attacks on the IDP camps, and on the Acholi in Northern Uganda, which we discussed when you were first here. These attacks are not helping matters, and if we are to make any progress at all they must be brought to an end. I need to hear from them on this as well, if they want my help.'

'Your sentiments on this matter have already been taken to our leadership. The subject is open.'

'Then please thank them for me and tell them I agree,' I said, more confidently than I felt.

At long last, I thought, I will be able to speak to the senior LRA leaders face to face about the rhinos, the reason this all started in the first place.

'When do you want me to be in Nairobi?'

'In exactly one week on Saturday,' Martin replied. 'You must bring your own sleeping bag, medicines and any special food you need. I am afraid there are no shops where we are going.

'And please,' he concluded, 'do not tell anyone. It will complicate security if the wrong people find out when and where we are going.'

Now that was a real confidence booster.

Despite the obvious risks, this really was a unique opportunity. According to reports, no outsider had ever stayed in the secret LRA camps – voluntarily, that is.

I then phoned JP to ask him to join me.

'I'm in,' he said immediately. 'When are you planning to go?'

'I must leave shortly, within ten days,' I replied.

'But I am in Europe, I have just arrived. I have meetings that cannot be cancelled. Can you delay it?'

'I am sorry, JP, but I can't,' I said, and proceeded to explain to him why and what was happening.

'I am so sorry,' he said eventually. 'But I just cannot get back in time.'

'I am sorry, too,' I replied.

'Go well and stay safe, my friend,' he said, 'and give the LRA my love.' He chuckled.

This was not something I could hide from Françoise. I didn't like to involve her unnecessarily, but in this case she would have to know.

Given that she was French and could put on a show in the very best Gallic tradition if she wanted to, I braced myself for a dose of common sense.

Her reply was unusually calm and considered.

'This is what you do best,' she said once I had explained the situation. 'They have no credibility whatsoever, and they need your voice and your connection to the outside world to achieve peace.'

In my heart I agreed with her. Realistically, any danger could only come from those who wanted the talks to fail. Peace would bring Kony, Otti and the others out of exile and into the international spotlight, and they would start talking. There would be a lot to tell after two decades of war and atrocities, and it takes two to tango. The LRA was guilty as sin, everybody knew that; but what about the other side? Someone once told me that the only difference between a rat and a hamster is PR.

I would have to watch my back.

CHAPTER TWENTY-FIVE

The following Saturday afternoon I landed in Nairobi as arranged. Martin and Godfrey were waiting, and we travelled on to Juba, where we were met at the airport by a driver and bodyguards, and taken to the Juba Bridge Hotel.

I put my bag in a little prefab room, walked down past the Acholi mango tree where the rhino agreement was signed, and stood again on the banks of the magnificent Nile River, revelling in its majesty. The thick reed banks were healthy and in ten minutes I watched as a local fisherman pulled out two good-sized Nile perch.

'We leave tomorrow morning at four a.m.,' said Martin over supper. 'The journey will be made in two four-by-four Land Cruisers. We are not allowed to travel alone, so we will be accompanied by soldiers of the Southern Sudan army, the SPLA.'

'Do you have money for petrol?' He looked at me expectantly.

'I do,' I said, feeling the comforting US dollars between my toes.

'Good, we are always short of money for our work.'

'Exactly where are we going and how long will it take?' I asked.

'The drop-off zone is on the border of Southern Sudan and the Congo, at a place called Ri-Kwangba. It's not on any maps,' he said. 'If we are not held up too much, we should do it in two days.'

'What about security?'

'They know we are coming and it's taken care of. The closer we get to where we are going, the safer we will be,' replied Godfrey.

I finally bid them good night and went back to my room as I still had one important thing to take care of. Going into remote areas with malaria hidden in your body is a death sentence, and the only way to ensure you are completely free of the disease just before an expedition is to do the so-called 'self-pregnancy test'. This is administered by drinking two quick tots of alcohol and waiting for the effect. Malaria incubates in the liver and if the disease is lurking, dizziness and biliousness will shortly follow the drink. Thankfully I was malaria free and the expedition was on.

The next morning at 3.30 a.m. we were standing in a dark, dusty street somewhere in Juba loading the vehicles. I was in one cruiser with Godfrey and two SPLA soldiers, one of whom was driving. Both carried AK-47s. We had one other man, a civilian, as a passenger. Martin was in the other cruiser with a similar accompaniment.

'Who are these guys?' I whispered to Godfrey, referring to the civilians.

He glanced at the SPLA soldiers and put his finger to his lips. 'Later,' he said.

By dawn we were well on our way. This is going to be a long trip, I thought after the first few hours of bone-jarring corrugations on the poor roads.

We took the road south-west to Yei, then turned north-east to Faraxica, the crossroads, and then bore west, on towards Maridi. It was an uneventful journey until we got to the first minefields. There were a set of tracks on the road ahead created by the mine-clearing vehicle and we were instructed not to veer from the tracks. Do not pull over for any reason, even for the toilet, they said; and we didn't, as we drove very carefully, keeping our wheels firmly in the tracks. There was only one set of tracks and I wondered what would happen if we met a vehicle coming in the opposite direction. Luckily, we didn't.

The SPLA soldiers in our 4x4 were sloppy and ill disciplined, always complaining and always asking for a cigarette or something to eat. Their AKs lay neglected and were being kicked around on the floor. Our passenger, on the other hand, stayed silent and alert, watching everything, accepting what was given without a murmur.

Some way after the minefield we stopped for a break and I returned to my question for Godfrey.

'Who are these guys, Godfrey, do you know them?'

'These are our men,' he replied. 'They are here to protect us.'

'But they don't have weapons. What's the plan if we are attacked?'

'Don't worry,' he replied. 'It's arranged, but there's no danger in this area.'

We arrived in Maridi in the late afternoon. It was a dirty, dilapidated town in the middle of nowhere.

'We will sleep here,' said Martin as we pulled up to a ramshackle flophouse that hadn't seen a lick of paint in a decade. 'It's not too bad.'

The hotel was owned by a friendly woman who put us up two to a rustic room. I shared with Godfrey. We were handed a pair of brightly coloured rubber sandals and a towel, and I was able to find a working shower and get the dirt off my body. Then we went across the road for warm beers and a very simple supper consisting of cornmeal with a bit of meat and gravy before I took a walk.

Maridi was really out on the edge of the universe. There were no police, I was told by a friendly resident I met on the side of the road who was interested in what a white man was doing there. I questioned the absence of any form of police. Vigilante justice ruled the day, he told me in broken English. Trials would be held in the main street with even the most severe sentences passed and carried out immediately by the crowd. It was like stepping back 200 years.

I did notice as I walked around that I was being discreetly tailed – by the LRA, I hoped – and then caught the incongruity of the thought. I must be the only man anywhere who hoped he was being tailed by the LRA.

We slept well and the next morning we were on the road very early.

If the first part of the journey had been uneventful, this was not. The road narrowed, the topography changed and, as we progressed, the vegetation thickened, with huge trees eventually canopying the road. The defining features were water and mud, and lots of them. The rains had come, and every stream and rivulet was swollen into formidable barriers that assailed the roads and strained the 4x4s to their limits. The road was little more than a muddy wallow, and river crossings were heart-stopping. Without exhaust snorkels we wouldn't have gone five miles – our bonnets were perpetually underwater as we forded watercourse after watercourse. Several times the wheels slipped during the bigger crossings and I feared we could be carried away by the river. The driving was alternately reckless and over-cautious. My pleas to be allowed to take the wheel were ignored.

'This is a military vehicle,' the driver said firmly, waving away my request with his hand, 'and you are a civilian. You can't drive.'

I rolled down my window to create an escape hatch in case we went into the drink.

We passed broken-down trucks dominating the centre of the road, blocking our passage, seized down to their axles by the intractable mire that in the rainy season passed for a road. In one case the entire upper body of a truck had been stripped from the chassis, which remained fixed in the mud. Fires had been lit around the chassis to try and dry the mud enough to get it out. They were going to be there a long time, I thought.

And then I started to get worried. We passed one burned-out truck, and then another. Both had copious bullet holes. This is recent, I realized, and with that I called a halt to the expedition and we got out.

The driver was unfazed.

'Rebels,' he said, looking accusingly at Godfrey and Martin, who had come across to join us. 'But they are gone now. We have military clearance to use the road.'

The four SPLA drivers and soldiers formed one group, Godfrey, Martin and our two passengers another. The divide was clear.

'What is the plan if we are attacked?' I put the question quietly to our group. 'We are not armed; I don't like this at all.'

Silence.

'Guys, I need to know. There has been fighting going on here. What's plan B?'

Silence.

Then one of the LRA cadres spoke quietly.

'We will kill the soldiers quickly and take their weapons,' he said in good English. 'These men,' he nodded at the SPLA group, 'are useless.'

Well, everything is just fine then, I thought. It was so silly for me to have been worried. These gentlemen have everything under perfect control. My head was spinning. He meant every word, and I suddenly understood that we had passed the last of civilization on the road somewhere before lawless Maridi, and with that everything changed for me.

I glanced across at the SPLA group; they too were talking, assessing the situation. But the man was right, I thought in my new frame of mind; they were very sloppy, they had left their

AKs lying on the floor in the vehicles. What would happen if someone came out of the bush at us right now?

My attention was distracted by a huge column of *siafu* ants that poured out of the thick vegetation and started crossing the road behind the cars. In the normal world I would have been excited, but I was too distracted even to pay attention to them. The conversation had taken me to a new dimension, and every nerve in my body was now on full alert.

We got back into the vehicles and drove on.

But it was different now; there was tension between the groups.

We continued on through the mud, streams and rivers, hour after hour, fighting the elements, pushing the vehicles to their limits; the evidence of previous battles littered the road, a continual reminder of where we were.

We passed through the little town of Eidi, and some time after lunch the driver called out, 'Nabanga in front.' It was with some relief that twenty minutes later we arrived in the very rural village.

'There is an SPLA base here,' said Godfrey quietly. 'We must stop for fuel, but I don't like it at all. Stay close to the car.'

'I have got to find a toilet,' I said as we arrived at the tented military installation, and was given directions. It was a long drop surrounded by a small wooded hut. Nobody warned me that I was about to enter the most vile latrine in the world. I closed the door, lifted the toilet seat, and recoiled as a swarming plague of trapped blue-green flies poured out of the bowels of the earth in their zillions, filling every inch of the air space in that tiny little room. That combined with the unearthly smell rising from the long drop had me gagging, and with my hands over my mouth and nose I leapfrogged out of hell's cistern, my trousers around my ankles, and fell over onto the grass outside.

There was nothing for it but to squat and go right there out in the open with passing soldiers pointing and laughing. Thankfully, experience had taught me to keep a roll of toilet paper for the journey.

Back at the vehicle things were not going well at all. Nabanga was the last outpost of the SPLA before LRA territory. The assembly areas started about twenty miles away. Nabanga was the military base set up as a bulwark against the LRA if anything went wrong with the talks.

Word had got out that LRA were in the vehicles, and insults started flying. More and more angry soldiers started arriving as the news spread, gathering around our 4x4s, gesticulating and brandishing their AK-47s. This was not good at all, I thought, as I ran up and climbed in. The drivers were standing around confused, still waiting for the barrels of diesel to arrive.

'Leave the fuel,' someone shouted at them. 'Go!'

They got the message, and just as I thought we might be forcibly hauled from the vehicles if we stayed much longer, the engines started and we accelerated off as fast as we could go, some of the soldiers running after us in their anger.

'That was not good,' I said to Godfrey. 'Not nice at all.'

'These people are arrogant,' he said calmly, gesticulating at the soldiers still standing on the road behind us. 'They are conscripts, regular army, and they are over-confident. They think they can defeat the LRA, but have no idea what's waiting for them in the jungle. We do not want to fight any more, we want the peace talks to work, but if they are stupid enough to attack the LRA positions they will all die.'

His words were to prove prophetic.

The last twenty miles was the worst piece of road I have ever been on. In the dry season it was passable, but this was just ridiculous. We literally slipped and slid sideways, one way and then the other, for the entire distance, praying that we didn't bog down, hoping we didn't get stuck and have to meet up with the Nabanga soldiers again. I felt completely cut off from the life I knew. My best option now was to get to Ri-Kwangba and the safety of the LRA. How crazy was that?

Nothing in my wildest imagination could have prepared me for what was happening, and I suddenly became very irritated and angry at the bureaucracy at the rhino meeting in Kinshasa. It was insane that I had to put myself through all this for the rhino, when it could all have been done with the simple stroke of a pen at that meeting.

Then without signpost or warning the bush broke open and we drove into a grassy clearing. 'We have arrived,' said Godfrey. 'This is Ri-Kwangba.'

My heart jumped.

The drivers pulled over and quickly helped with the luggage, obviously in a hurry to get us out and get going. We were right on the edge of LRA territory and they didn't like it at all. A few minutes later they bid us an overly quick farewell, and I watched as the two mud-covered 4x4s that had brought us so far drove back up the muddy track and disappeared from view. I looked around. Ri-Kwangba was no more than a simple clearing, totally surrounded by a thick, high, deeply shaded forest. A water tank stood forlornly on one side. A few benches hewn out of forest logs had been placed in a circle; there was not a soul in sight.

And then it came to me that the vehicles had completely abandoned us in the middle of absolutely nowhere. The clearing was unimposing, a nothing place, lost in an eternity of tall trees and tangled undergrowth. I was standing on the very edge of civilization, beyond which 'there be dragons'. All we could do now was to wait for the most feared rebels in the world to arrive, and to go into the dark jungle with them to their lair. If they hadn't forgotten to come and get us, that is.

'Now what?' I asked.

'We wait,' came Martin's reply as he walked over. 'Our men are here,' he said, sweeping his arm across the forest, 'but they will first check that our vehicles are the only ones.'

It wasn't long before a small movement caught my eye, and a few seconds later a man appeared from the jungle and stepped out into the far side of the clearing. He called out something in Acholi.

Martin called back, and the man came forward. As he did so, five more men also emerged from the trees and started walking towards us in single file, weapons at the ready. It was the first time I had ever seen the infamous LRA soldiers and I was spellbound. They were dressed in ageing military uniforms of some kind. Four were carrying AK-47s and two were holding 20mm machine guns. They were all in their early twenties.

They reached us and Martin shook hands with one and pointed at me, saying something in Acholi. They nodded, picked up our baggage and without further ado turned back to the jungle. Three took up the lead ahead of us, while the other three fell in behind.

'Now we walk,' said Martin, smiling at me.

And walk we did.

We strode on for a long time in single file down narrow jungle paths. Visibility into the undergrowth was practically nil; you couldn't see ten yards. How anybody believed they could take on the LRA in this dense bush and win was beyond me. I thought back to the over-confident Nabanga soldiers. They were going to be in for a swift, savage surprise if they let their bravado get the better of them.

At some point Godfrey pointed out a large tree and told me that this was the border; we had just crossed from the Sudan into the Congo. I realized I was back in Garamba National Park, this time in the north, in a World Heritage Site with an entire rebel army camped inside it. Conservation in Africa was a dangerous business.

Strangely, despite my precarious situation, I felt completely relaxed, and after being cooped up in the 4x4s for so long I was enjoying being out. I had given up on worrying any more, there was just no point. I was where I was, and there was no possible way out. Behind me there were three armed LRA cadres, and behind them a hostile SPLA garrison, and then a two-day drive to Juba, and I didn't have a vehicle. I hope to hell someone knows how we are getting back, I thought.

A tiny unnatural movement just off the path ahead caught my attention. I looked carefully. An animal of some kind, I thought, and I waited for it to run as it must. But it didn't move again. I knew no wild animal would ever let us get that close, and I suddenly realized it had to be men; LRA soldiers, sitting silently in ambush positions, waiting to see if we were being followed. They were certainly taking no chances.

The paths were getting narrower and less used, and I was sure we had doubled back on ourselves once or twice, when we approached a small clearing. Up ahead I could see some small thatched huts and then a tent.

'We are here,' said Martin. 'This is General Vincent Otti's camp.'

CHAPTER TWENTY-SIX

One of the men in front called a halt and we lost sight of him in the foliage as he went forward into the camp alone. A few minutes later he came back out and beckoned to us.

We entered the clearing, and about thirty yards away there was a group of soldiers coming towards us. Leading the retinue was a tall, thinnish man of about sixty years old dressed in a light-coloured safari suit.

Then the most bizarre thing happened. A soldier came up to me from behind, tapped me on the shoulder and, as I turned, he tried to hand me a baby baboon of all things. I couldn't believe my eyes, but there he was with the baboon in his outstretched arms. My attention was on Vincent Otti, whom I was about to meet for the first time, and I tried to shrug him off, but the baboon made a little jump, clasped itself firmly onto my chest, and buried its face into my collar. Martin and Godfrey were still laughing when the entourage arrived. The man in the safari suit put out his hand.

'Good afternoon, Mr Anthony,' he said, smiling at my predicament. 'I am General Vincent Otti. Welcome to my home.'

There is nothing quite like being introduced to the International Criminal Court's second most wanted man while holding a baboon.

I shook his hand. 'Pleased to meet you,' I replied, feeling like a complete idiot. This was like something out of a bloody Monty Python movie. But it certainly broke the ice.

'I see you are a friend of the animals,' he said.

'It is my life's work,' I replied, peering past the agitated baboon.

'I have heard this,' he said, before pointing at a rough pole-and-thatch lean-to on the side of the clearing, outside of which my bags had been deposited. 'This is your accommodation while you are with us. I am sorry it is not more comfortable, but it is difficult in the forest.'

'It is fine,' I said. 'Thank you.'

'We have prepared food for you. Please eat and relax after your long journey, and we will meet when you are ready.' He then turned and took a pile of local newspapers from Martin, sat down on a plastic chair outside my shelter and started reading them avidly.

I looked around, taking in my surroundings. In the centre of the clearing was a fireplace surrounded by long wooden benches, all freshly hewn from trees from the canopied forest, which formed a deep, impenetrable boundary around the camp. There was a main group of huts where Otti obviously lived, outside of which some young children were playing. Near the fireplace was a larger building that looked like it could be a kitchen and storage area. On the other side of the clearing stood two small tents where Martin and Godfrey were unpacking.

I went across to my shelter and inspected the baboon, which had remained tightly clasped around my neck. It was just a few months old and without injury, but the poor little thing was clearly malnourished.

'Where is its mother?' I asked the owner, who was standing off to the side waiting, a well-oiled AK-47 hanging loosely by his side.

'I don't know. The soldiers say they found it alone in the forest.'

'What do you feed it?' I said.

'We give it water and berries.'

'It needs milk.'

'There is no milk here.'

'Not even powdered milk?' I asked.

'No, the little we have is given to the generals.'

'Does it have a name?'

'No.'

'Everything must have a name. We will name it Mfeni,' I said, giving it the Zulu name for baboon.

'I will tell the others,' he said. 'They want it to live. They hope you can help.'

'I will do my best,' I said as I handed Mfeni back to him. 'Do you have contact with a nearby village?'

'Yes, we go there sometimes.'

'Then get some cow's milk or goat's milk as soon as you can.'

It wasn't lost on me that these hard-bitten killers, accused of the most appalling crimes, actually cared for this poor little baboon. What a strange world.

After I settled my bags I was shown to a bush toilet enclosed with reed and grass walls. It was a simple squat hole in the ground but it was scrupulously clean, as was the rest of the camp, I realized. There was no litter anywhere and everything was orderly.

Martin and Godfrey came across and we shared a simple but tasty meal of beans, cornmeal and gravy in the African style, with the pots on the floor between us, helping ourselves to the sticky cornmeal with our fingers and dipping into the gravy.

When we had finished, the 'silent' LRA soldiers we had travelled with came forward and introduced themselves properly for the first time. 'I am Vincent Otti's son,' said one. 'Welcome, we will stay with you while you are here. This is my father's camp.'

So they were to be my bodyguards – and watchers, no doubt. They were both smiling broadly, the first time I had seen them do so. They were obviously pleased that we had arrived and that they had done their job, delivering me safely to Otti.

Soldiers dressed in well-worn military uniforms came and went across the clearing, all carrying AK-47s or heavier weapons. Two cadres carried 20mm machine guns, their shoulders laden with heavy bullet belts; these weapons would shear down trees in a firefight. Another toted a 50mm, capable of cutting a house in half with automatic fire. I whistled silently. Weapons like that are usually mounted; this was serious firepower to be lugging around by hand. The guns were all in good order, I noticed, well oiled and well used, but clean and in good condition. Then a soldier came over carrying something unusual: a short, black, modern assault rifle. I couldn't place the make, but it was new.

Now how did they get those? I wondered. Then I remembered the UN attack a little while before. It had to have been taken from a dead UN soldier in the failed Special Forces raid on the LRA.

Otti, who was still reading nearby, called out to one of the soldiers. The man ran over, came to attention, received orders and then went off in a hurry to do Otti's bidding. I was genuinely surprised at that level of discipline. This was not at all what I thought I would find. I had expected a rag-tag, ill-disciplined group of mercenaries, which was not the case at all.

Martin, Godfrey and I chatted for a while before a soldier called us across to join Otti.

'Mr Anthony,' said Otti after we pulled up some small plastic chairs and sat down. 'We want to thank you for your assistance with the peace talks, and for coming so far to see us. I know this has been difficult for you.'

'Thank you,' I replied simply, intensely focused on the discussion.

'I have arranged a meeting this evening with the full military high command of the LRA. I want you please to explain to the generals and senior officers why and how we can achieve peace. It will be good for all of us to hear from a neutral person from the outside.'

'Will Joseph Kony be in attendance?' I asked.

'No,' replied Godfrey. 'Unfortunately, with all the rain he is unable to cross the river to get here, but he will be here tomorrow, or after tomorrow. The generals and officers are all in the area waiting for you, and we must not lose the opportunity to speak with them before they disperse.'

'I understand,' I replied, my mind racing at the prospect of being invited to address the military high command of the LRA, known inside the organization as the Control Altar.

'No outsider has ever addressed a full meeting of the military high command before,' said Godfrey. 'Not even the members of the delegation. It is a great honour for you.'

Otti nodded as he spoke.

'Thank you, I will do the best I can,' I replied. 'What are the key issues that will be covered?'

'Please start by confirming to the generals that you have negotiated an agreement with the United Nations in Kinshasa not to attack us,' said Godfrey.

'Yes, that is important,' said Otti. 'We have been waiting for another attack ever since they were defeated by some of our men. Museveni is trying to mobilize them again.'

'And also please give the reasons why the talks venue was not moved, and why mediators were appointed,' said Martin.

'I will do so.'

'There will be many questions,' said Otti, 'and you will be given a full opportunity to raise your matters. This is an important meeting. There is much distrust surrounding the talks.'

'Thank you, I will do what I can.'

'It is I who must thank you,' Otti replied. He paused for a

while before continuing. Godfrey and Martin sat in silent anticipation.

'There have been many things said about us,' he continued,
almost reflectively. 'It has been a long war. Some of what is said
is true; a lot of it is lies. We do not own a government radio and
television or newspapers to tell the world lies like Museveni. We
have nothing.

'But you must remember, Mr Anthony, that we are the ones
who called for these peace talks, not Museveni. We called for
peace. Museveni has been forced into the peace talks by his
American and British allies, but we came willingly. You will see
this for yourself at the meeting tonight; that is why I brought
you here. So you can hear for yourself what is said and go and
tell the South Africans, and the Americans, and the British.

'They do not believe us, but they will believe you.'

A call came from out of the bush, off to our left.

'They are arriving; we will meet again tomorrow,' said Otti,
bringing the discussion to a close.

'A bath has been made for you,' said Godfrey, pointing at two
men placing a zinc tub near my shelter as Otti walked away.
'And do not worry; tomorrow we will discuss progress with
your rhinos.'

Bath time in the bush was light relief. I had thought I would
freshen up in one of the many nearby streams, but no, I had my
own tub full of fresh, clean water.

The two men who carried the bath stood very close by, intensely interested in the procedure, watching me undress and
taking my clothes from me as I climbed into the tub.

'It is good to be clean,' said one wisely. 'There is disease in the
forest, everybody must wash.'

'And you must brush your teeth,' said the other, taking my
toothbrush out of my vanity bag and mimicking a good tooth-
brushing. 'There are no dentists in the forest.'

I leaned forward and took the bag from him and pulled out three or four sticks of mosquito repellent, told them what it was and handed it over, showing them how to apply it. Their eyes lit up.

'This is good. Malaria is bad, I have had it ten times,' one man said, holding up all his fingers. 'But now not sick, now only headaches.'

I got out of the tub, dried off and dressed, then took out a stick of roll-on deodorant and applied it under my arms.

'Mosquito bite you here?' he said, pointing to his underarm.

'How long have you been in the forest?' I asked them, ignoring the question.

They both thought it was more than ten years, but couldn't be sure.

'How old are you?' I asked.

Again they were not sure, but they thought around twenty-three.

They had been taken when they were barely thirteen. And they didn't even know what a stick of deodorant was.

CHAPTER TWENTY-SEVEN

I watched as the generals and commanders arrived from out of the thick forest accompanied by soldiers and bodyguards. From their photos, I recognized heavyweights Okot Odhiambo and Dominic Ongwen, who along with Kony and Otti were wanted by the International Criminal Court at The Hague. Godfrey pointed out six or seven others. All were in freshly pressed military fatigues. In Africa one can still buy an iron that you fill with hot coals, and it does the job perfectly if you know how to use it.

I sat down in front of the high-profile gathering with Godfrey and Martin. Otti sat off to our left. The generals were sitting in a semicircle facing us. Armed soldiers stood guard all around the perimeter of the camp, and I had no doubt there would be plenty more positioned out in the forest. The entire LRA military high command was a valuable target and nobody was taking any chances.

Otti gave an opening address in Acholi in which I heard my name mentioned a couple of times. 'He is introducing you, and reminding them of the background and the reason for your visit,' whispered Godfrey.

'Thank you for being with us here,' said Otti, turning to face me, now speaking English. 'This is the high command of the Lord's Resistance Army.' He made a respectful gesture to the seated group. 'Joseph Kony sends his apologies. He will meet you as soon as he arrives.'

He then proceeded to introduce me to the delegates, each of whom acknowledged the recognition with a nod or a wave of the hand. Otti was about to begin the meeting when one of the generals spoke out in Acholi.

'Mr Anthony,' said Otti as soon as the man finished. 'Before we start, there is a question: did you bring our money, the five hundred thousand US dollars, did you bring it with you?'

As the question registered, everything went into slow motion for me. I recognized the feeling well because it had happened to me before, when I was charged by elephants and was in great danger. I couldn't believe what I was hearing. There was some other agenda that I was not aware of, and it had to do with me having half a million dollars of their money. I was supposed to have brought it here into the jungle with me, and they wanted it.

I desperately wanted to ask Martin what was going on, but that would have been the worst possible thing to do, because it might imply that I was involved with him in something.

I had to reply, and just as a wild animal does when it is threatened, I stood up straight, drew myself up to my full height, and tried to speak out loudly and confidently.

'Mr Chairman,' I said, 'I came here at your invitation. Everybody knows I am a conservationist, a man of the animals. I am not part of the world of money. I have a few dollars in my suitcase for travelling. I know nothing of what you speak.'

That's enough, I thought, suppressing the urge to continue. If you go on it will sound like you are making excuses. I forced myself to sit down, the timeless feeling I had earlier now drowned out by the immensely loud beating of my heart. What if they didn't believe me? These guys made the Mafia look like a bunch of wimps. They could have had me put against a tree and shot and then continued chatting as if nothing had happened. I listened as several questions were directed to and answered by Martin Ojul in Acholi. The tone of the discussion, though, was not hostile, and it gave me back some confidence. Otti then turned to me with a big broad smile.

'Thank you, Mr Anthony, and please forgive us for the question, but we are always looking for money for supplies. The matter is closed.'

To my great relief I saw the generals smiling as well.

Shit, I thought, what the hell was that all about?

'We will continue,' said Otti. 'The first matter is the position of the United Nations military in the Congo, MONUC. Mr Anthony, will you please tell us what you know of this?'

I stood up again and, taking care not to mention names, explained the nature of my private meeting in Kinshasa in some detail.

'The position of the UN forces in the Congo is clear,' I concluded. 'They will not upset the Juba peace talks with military action, provided that LRA troops are in the assembly areas, and provided there are no attacks against citizens in the Congo.'

My assurances created a brief hubbub among the delegates, followed by protracted discussions in Acholi; this was clearly more important to them than I thought.

'How can we trust what they say?' said one of the generals once they had settled down.

'In this world it is difficult to trust anyone,' I replied, mimicking their inherent distrust of anyone, or anything, anywhere. 'But the United Nations is formally committed to the Juba talks from the top down to the bottom of the organization. They have given me their word and I believe them, or I would not be here.'

'This is important information,' said Otti. 'Thank you for telling us.'

'Please will you thank your United Nations contact,' said a delegate, 'and tell them that we will respect their terms, but we remain prepared, and any attack on us will be returned with full force.'

'I will do so when I return,' I replied. 'They have also said they are willing for me to act as your direct contact with the UN in the Congo. This can help eliminate confusion and mistakes. Do I have your authority to do so?'

'You do,' replied Otti after a brief conversation with some of the generals. 'This will be good.'

'Museveni wants to attack and he will blame us for starting it,' said another delegate to a murmur of assent. 'If this happens, it will finish the Juba peace talks. Why did the talks not go to South Africa, why did we only get monitors?'

'Monitors are not what you wanted, but it's a lot better than what you had,' I replied. 'The monitors bring the international community into the talks and they will be active. If the talks are moved far away they will be difficult for you to control, and you will still be here in the assembly areas, where no one is watching, and anything can happen. With monitors you will bring the world closer, the monitors will be in Juba, listening and watching, and reporting to the world.'

This too prompted discussion, but as they had already returned to the talks it was not a serious matter.

These were military men speaking, and as the evening went on I realized they had very little confidence in the Juba talks ever achieving anything. The consensus seemed to be that Museveni had been forced into the talks unwillingly by his American and European allies, and all that was needed to start the war again was a covert attack by Museveni, which would then be blamed on them. They did not trust the Ugandan delegation, and they did not even trust all the members in their own delegation.

I was under no illusions about where I was and whom I was dealing with, but as the night went on in that faraway jungle camp, I discovered that I was being shown generous respect, and that my opinions were being heard. I eventually settled into the discussions comfortably, almost as if I was at a rural tribal meeting in Zululand. One thing about Africans is that they have a culture of patient listening, and I found that I was entitled to speak my mind freely.

The subject was peace and how to achieve it. These were men who had been in the jungles fighting all their lives, and the concept that peace could actually be achieved was foreign to them. It became more and more obvious to me as the meeting went on that they really did want to end it all and go home, but did not know how.

The agenda came to the IDP camps in Northern Uganda, which generated heated discussion. The absolute hatred of these camps, and the hatred towards Museveni for creating them, seared through the delegates like a naked flame.

'Gentlemen,' I said, 'you have invited me here for my advice, and I thank you for allowing me to speak freely. If I am to help, then there are certain matters we must discuss openly. The first is the attacks on the camps and the second is child soldiers.'

That certainly got everyone's attention.

'I am told that these camps, which you hate so much, are being attacked by LRA troops. You have your reasons, but I must advise you that each attack makes your enemies smile in satisfaction. The outside world is shocked by the attacks. Children in the camps are scared, and thousands walk to towns for shelter at night in fear of LRA attacks. This is on TV and newspapers in Europe and America and in South Africa. It is creating enemies for you all over the world.

'Whatever the reasons, I ask that you reconsider this strategy and halt attacks permanently. This is an important part of the road to peace.'

'It is because of Museveni's propaganda that we are feared by our own nation,' said Otti, standing up. 'Only our enemies fear us. We have fought for our people for many years and when we return home to Northern Uganda our people will welcome us and thank us.' He paused and deliberated over his next words. 'But we cannot always control our men, and we cannot run away from the responsibility of what happened in the war. There must be accountability, not just for us; for Museveni as well.'

It was worth all the travel and risk just to hear those words. The tone had shifted from blame to accountability. It was a huge change in attitude.

'Mr Godfrey Ayoo and Mr Anthony worked together to study the Truth and Reconciliation Commission in South Africa,' he continued, addressing the generals directly. 'The TRC is the basis of our delegation's submission for the Agreement of Accountability and Reconciliation, which we signed at the peace talks in Juba.

'There must be accountability,' he said again.

I was elated.

'Thank you, General Otti,' I said after he sat down. 'You say that your people in the IDP camps in Northern Uganda want to go home, that they are tired of the war, but' – I paused for emphasis – 'there are those who say that even though the Acholi were originally forced into the camps, they are now being compelled to stay there because of the LRA attacks. So, with your permission, I propose that such attacks are abandoned as a military strategy.'

I knew my proposal and the reasons behind it had already been conveyed to the LRA through Martin and Godfrey and had long been discussed, so I sat down and waited for the response.

Otti stood up again and was silent for a moment or two while some of the generals spoke among each other.

'We agree,' he said finally. 'There is already a cessation of hostilities agreement in place with Museveni. There will never be any more attacks on the camps or on the Acholi in Northern Uganda. You can take this to your people, Mr Anthony, and

Mr Godfrey Ayoo, our head of public relations, will carry this to our people. I will speak to the radio station and tell them it is over; the people must leave the camps and go home. They are safe to do so.'

This vital resolution had carried and I was absolutely elated. Godfrey and Martin had wide smiles on their faces. The effect of those words in Northern Uganda would be immense. If this was true, if the deeds matched the words, then the horror could now start to end.

'Are you now satisfied, Mr Anthony?' said Godfrey privately, with Martin listening.

'I am indeed; this could well be a historic meeting,' I replied. 'And thank you, both of you, for everything you have done. It would not have been possible without you.'

I made to stand up in order to push forward on the subject of child soldiers, but felt Godfrey's hand on my arm restraining me. Otti had leaned across, wanting to speak to us privately.

'The Acholi do not eat rhinos, Mr Anthony,' said Otti. 'We have no use for their horns and we do not take elephants for ivory. We have never done these things. I am sorry, but our patrols have not found any of your rhinos. We were told that hunters, Arabs, used to come from Sudan with horses and camels to kill elephants and rhinos, but they haven't been seen for a long time. Our patrols have asked the villagers living in the northern areas to tell everyone that the LRA will not permit anyone to come here and kill rhino or elephant.'

'And if they come in?' I ventured.

'They have been warned, and if they still come they will be asked to leave, but if they attack us we will finish them.'

Sitting in an office in a Western country, this might sound completely off the wall, but one has to understand what rangers have to deal with in these parts of Africa. The park had been abandoned by the authorities for years because of the violence.

Rhino and elephant poachers were hardcore professionals, who used AK-47 assault rifles with abandon and would shoot dead any park ranger who got in their way. They had already killed who knows how many thousands of elephants over the decades, and they had driven the rhino to the very brink of extinction. They were not going to give it all up just because someone asked them nicely. As far as I was concerned, if Otti wanted to keep them out then I was not going to stop him, and good luck to the poachers. If they were stupid enough to fire on an LRA patrol they would get a full dose of their own medicine.

It was already after 10 p.m. and all in all the meeting had gone on for nearly five hours without a break. Otti and the generals were engaged in another long discussion in Acholi, when I whispered to Godfrey that I wanted to continue with the important issue of child soldiers.

'No,' he replied, 'not now. The meeting is ending. You have done well and there is an important announcement coming. But do not worry, the generals are all coming back tomorrow morning to continue, and it is on the agenda.'

Eventually the conversation subsided and Otti stood up to close the meeting. 'We have come far together since you met our delegation in Juba,' he said, addressing me directly. 'And we have learned to trust each other. We have taken a decision to ask you to be our Godfather, and ask that you continue to help us and guide us home.'

'I beg your pardon,' I replied, completely staggered by the implications of what Otti had just said. I could see some of the generals leaning forward expectantly.

'We are asking you to be our Godfather, the Godfather of the LRA,' he repeated, smiling.

Godfather to the LRA? I have been surprised at a great many things in my life, but this really took the cake. My mind was racing. How on earth do I deal with this? From their point of view they were being sincere and bestowing a great honour on me, but this was not a parent-teacher association, this was the LRA, for goodness sake, and to be known as Godfather to one of the most vicious guerilla armies in the world was impossible for me even to consider. I desperately needed time to think.

'Thank you, General Otti, may I consult with Godfrey Ayoo and Martin Ojul to gain a better understanding?'

'Of course.'

'This means they trust you and they are giving you power,' said Godfrey, leaning over and whispering loudly. He was an intellectual, a logical and highly intelligent man, who had never fired a shot for the LRA and who desperately wanted peace. 'This is what we need, this is real power; you can now deal directly with the high command on all matters. This is how we will achieve peace. You must accept; you must reply.'

'Does Joseph Kony know about this?' I said to him.

'Nothing happens without Kony's approval,' he replied. 'You have seen what is happening in Juba. With all the corruption, lying and double-dealing, it is impossible for the two delegations ever to find peace. Our generals do not even trust some of our own delegation. You have been offered a unique opportunity to influence the talks for the LRA. No outsider before you has ever gained the trust of the Control Altar, the high command. For the first time the outside world can speak directly to the real leaders of the LRA through you. This will change everything. We can have peace.'

Martin nodded as Godfrey spoke. 'You must accept,' he said.

I had started off trying to save a species from extinction, and quite unbelievably I was now somehow being offered a critical role in an attempt to end the longest civil war in Africa. I thought of the people in the camps, and of the children, and all the innocent victims of the evil that had impacted this part of the world so savagely. What would they say?

I decided what I had to do and stood up. 'Gentlemen, I thank you for the trust you place in me and I accept. But I ask that I be known not as Godfather, but Godfather for Peace.'

'Then it is agreed,' said Otti. 'You are our Godfather for Peace.' And with that the generals began clapping.

'There is one more matter,' he said when the clapping subsided. 'We request that one of our senior generals comes to South Africa and stays with you. Then we will be able to work with you and strategize carefully how to end a war that Museveni does not want to end.'

'I will need to inform the South African government and speak to them about special visas,' I replied.

'We understand.'

He then stood up and led the way to the fireplace for dinner.

The meal stretched out until midnight, giving me the opportunity to get to know all of the generals and officers in a more relaxed environment. There was no doubt that they were all solidly behind the day's resolutions. I couldn't wait for the word to go out that as far as the LRA were concerned the war in the north of Uganda was over; the people held in the camps, pretty much the entire Acholi nation, could now go home.

I went to bed that night in my little reed shelter with my two armed guards, satisfied that this notorious army actually wanted peace, that they too wanted to go home, and that they were prepared to go the extra mile to try and achieve it.

All I had to do now was find a way to change the dynamics of the talks, and somehow get Museveni to agree to real peace, before a skirmish or some other altercation blew the lid off the talks. Realistically, only the Americans or the British had enough influence with Museveni to do this. I had some contacts in Congress and in London whom I would be speaking to.

Then there was still the *small* matter of the child soldiers and International Criminal Court warrants of arrest for my dinner partners. I put it out of my mind. Tomorrow would be a big day and I needed some rest.

That night I dreamed vividly of Thula Thula and my elephants, of Nana, Frankie and the herd. I dreamed that I was among them and that they were here in the jungle with me. I was on the edge of the known world, a long, long way from my home.

CHAPTER TWENTY-EIGHT

I was up early the next morning with my two minders just as the heavily armed night patrols came in. A half-dozen or so soldiers hung around, so I went over to them and asked if they knew where the owner of the baby baboon was. One went off to call him, and while I was waiting I found that they were happy to chat and answer my questions. I learned that the barracks for Otti's personal soldiers, although hidden by the forest, was only about 160 feet away, and that about thirty soldiers lived there.

'How do you get food?' I asked.

'Sometimes we go and collect supplies from the trucks at Ri-Kwangba, the place where you arrived,' said one. 'We also hunt, but the rivers have good fish. The fish is dried and stored. We have plenty of food and give some to the villages nearby to help them; they are our friends.'

'Our fishermen are good fighters,' said another, laughing. 'They are young but they fought the UN soldiers and killed many before they retreated.'

'Did your army fight the UN soldiers?'

'No, not our army, it was just the young soldiers who were fishing. They saw the helicopters coming and they shot them down and killed the soldiers.'

As improbable as it sounded, what they were saying was that a bunch of kids out fishing had defeated the UN Special Forces raid on the LRA.

'I guard the fields where the women work,' said another man, carrying a wicked-looking machine gun.

'Fields,' I said in surprise. 'You are farming.'

'All of the camps farm,' he replied. 'The soil is good and the women and children look after the crops.'

'How many women are there?'

'Many,' replied another. 'We have wives.'

'And children.'

'Yes, there are many children.'

'Are these the children who come back with the soldiers, the ones taken from villages?' I asked, expecting resistance to the question.

'No.' He laughed. 'These are our children; many of our soldiers have their own children.'

I did a swift calculation. If there were thirty soldiers at the camp and each had a wife, that meant thirty women, and if only half of the women had one child each, that meant there were forty-five women and children in the camp community, more in fact than the soldiers. Fishing, farming, women, children, pets – this was a village, I suddenly realized; the LRA camps were a series of villages, not barracks.

The patrol walked off as Mfeni's owner arrived with a few well-armed friends. I took the little baboon from him and looked it over carefully.

'Is it eating?' I asked.

'Yes, a little,' he said. 'He ate some fruit. Today I can get cow's milk from the village and he will be stronger, but the villagers want something.'

I reached into my pocket.

'Here is twenty dollars,' I said, pressing money into his hand. 'This is for Mfeni's milk, and here is twenty dollars for you if you promise to look after him well.'

'Thank you, but I have no use for money,' he said, staring at the unfamiliar dollar bills. 'I will get milk for Mfeni.'

'Where are you from?' I asked.

'We are all from Uganda.'

'And where are your families?'

'Our villages are gone; my family was put in the camps.'

'How long have you been with the LRA?'

'I think about six years or more,' Mfeni's owner replied. The others gave different answers varying from two to eight years.

'How is army life?'

'We are treated well; we are the best soldiers.'

'Do you sometimes go back home?'

'No, it is far, but General Otti will take us back home when Museveni stops fighting. That is why you are here; to help us go home. This is what the men are saying.'

'I am trying,' I said. 'I will do my best.'

We continued chatting about the war and some of their experiences, and once again I was surprised at the level of discipline and the air of raw professionalism among the men. They were loyal to the LRA, no doubt, and very confident in their fighting ability. These were some of the toughest, hardest soldiers I have ever met, and I have met a few over the years. I would hate to have to come up against them in battle. On their home turf in the jungle they would be formidable. On even terms, probably unbeatable.

'Have you seen rhinos?' I asked Mfeni's owner, making the shape of a rhino horn in front of my face. 'I am trying to find rhinos.'

'There are none in the forest,' he said. 'The patrols are always looking for rhino for you, but they have found none.'

A military shout came from the direction of the barracks. He took Mfeni back, adjusted his AK-47 and walked off, smiling back at me with the little baboon hanging onto his neck.

I went across to Godfrey and Martin, who were standing outside their tents talking.

'You are one of us,' said Martin, beaming. 'Yesterday was good.'

The statement jarred me, and it needed to be dealt with immediately.

'Please remember our agreement at Thula Thula,' I said. 'The condition of my involvement is that I remain completely neutral, and that will never change. I will act as an honest broker, not with one side or the other, but doing my best to help end the war. I must ask for my neutrality to be respected and reinforced, or the wrong message will go out and I will not be able to continue. I ask for your support with this.'

'We understand,' said Martin. 'We are working together for the same goal.'

'This issue is important for credibility,' said Godfrey. 'And we have already made sure that all the delegates to yesterday's meeting understand this.'

'Thank you.'

We chatted while waiting for a meeting with Otti, and as we stood there I noticed three women enter the clearing.

'Who are they?' I asked Godfrey and Martin.

'Two of them are Otti's wives, and the other must surely be the wife of a soldier,' said Godfrey.

'Please ask them to wait,' I said as I hurried over to my shelter.

Françoise, ever thoughtful, had handed me a large bag of toiletries as I was leaving for the airport. 'There will be women in the bush where you are going who will appreciate these,' she had said.

I came back, and after introductions to the very reserved women, I gave them the bag, which they opened cautiously, but when they saw what it contained their faces lit up. Creams, lipstick, make-up and all sorts of other things a man would never think of. I certainly made some new friends that morning, and thereafter they would smile and call out or wave whenever I passed by.

A little later Otti came out followed by two men carrying plastic chairs, and after morning greetings we all sat down.

'The generals will be here shortly,' he said. 'There are important things still to be discussed.'

'Thank you,' I replied.

'I believe there are some matters that you want to raise with me beforehand.'

'Yes, there are,' I said. 'I believe it is important for us to open discussions on two issues that stand in the way of progress: the International Criminal Court warrants against LRA leaders and the child soldiers.'

'Let us go forward then,' he said.

'The ICC warrants of arrest against four of our leaders are a big problem,' intervened Godfrey. 'The only way out of this war is the African way – with traditional justice.'

'How will traditional justice satisfy the world?' I asked.

'Let me explain,' Godfrey said. 'Just bear with me while I go over it all again.'

'Absolutely,' I replied. I had done some more study on the subject and was interested to hear what he was going to say.

'Museveni grew up with traditional African justice, the justice of his people and the justice of his ancestors. He knows that confession, forgiveness and penance have been the basis of his society for hundreds of years. He also knows full well that most of the people of Northern Uganda, the Acholi, fully support the LRA coming home to traditional justice, the name of which, by the way, is *Mato Oput*. *Mato Oput* means to drink a bitter brew and the words are symbolic of penance. *Mato Oput* is family- and community-based mediation that can bring healing in a way that Western justice can never hope to do. It is the ancient way of our people.'

Godfrey glanced at Otti, who motioned for him to continue.

'European justice is designed to punish offenders harshly. American culture demands a "High Noon" resolution of disputes where the one who is left standing is the winner. This is foreign to us here in Africa. It is not in our philosophy of life. We have learned the hard way that in our culture, confession, penance and forgiveness are the only way to bring violence and killing to a lasting end.

'So we have these two things in conflict: punitive Western justice, which is what the ICC wants, and reconciliatory African justice, which is what our people want.

'Let's look at the recent Rwanda genocide, where eight hundred thousand people died in an orgy of violence at the hands of their own countrymen. It happened not far from here. How are they dealing with the tens of thousands of killers? They are using traditional justice. In towns and villages all over the country the killers are facing the victims' families and communities seeking forgiveness and understanding, and it is working. In America they would have to hang ten thousand people.'

'So why, then, did Museveni take the LRA to the International Criminal Court in Europe, instead of using traditional justice?' I asked.

'I will tell you why,' Otti replied, giving me an explanation clearly influenced by his hatred of the Ugandan leader. 'The LRA have been isolated in the jungles for decades with no contact with the outside world, and Museveni wants it to stay that way. If the LRA leaders come home they will have a lot to say, and the world will find out what really happened in this war. We have enough information to completely destroy him and he knows it. So the last thing he wants is for us to come home and for the truth to come out.

'Believe me or not, everything he accuses the LRA of, he has also done himself, and worse. He came into power in a bloody coup on the backs of child soldiers, the International Court of Justice has found his government guilty of war crimes, he has nearly two million of our people locked up in camps where they get beaten, raped and killed, and die like flies. It is claimed many more people have died in those camps than in the actual war.

'He has created rebel groups who commit crimes in our name. The infamous 105 Battalion was created for this purpose, with ex-LRA soldiers who are encouraged to kill indiscriminately so we can be blamed. The Ugandan and Sudanese governments know that there are other copycat groups in our operational areas, but they still accuse us. We have the proof of this and all will be revealed when the time is right. But I can say this for now. Everyone knows LRA troops wear their hair in dreadlocks. We realized that attacks were taking place which were not done by us, so we ordered all our men to cut off their signature dreadlocks. Sure enough, the attacks by men in dreadlocks continued, and we were blamed for them. We captured some of them; we know who they are.'

I had no way of knowing whether Otti's interpretation of these events was correct or not, but Godfrey nodded in agreement.

'So, in order to stop the LRA leaders coming home to bear witness against him,' Godfrey continued, 'Museveni very cleverly asked the ICC to take them far, far away where no one will believe anything they say.

'The problem is that the LRA leaders would rather die than go to the ICC, and Museveni knows that too. So the war will just continue, and the deaths and suffering will never end. Despite his empty claims of victory, Museveni has not defeated the LRA for twenty-two years, and he never will. We need to break this cycle, and today we are ready to work with you to do so. 'We can end this war in weeks with an agreement to use traditional justice, with *Mato Oput* and the TRC, and as I have said, our views in this are supported by the victims of the war, the Acholi people.'

Godfrey's argument was the LRA's position, and I would need to hear the other side of the story. But one thing was absolutely clear to me personally. This endless war with its manifold horrors could not be allowed to continue, just because the ICC wanted to put three LRA leaders in jail in Europe. If they could ever even catch them alive, that is. If the past was a guide to the future, thousands more people were going to die before that happened, if it ever did, and that was too high a price for the already tormented Acholi people to pay. Common sense dictated that the perpetrators of the violence and atrocities should face their victims' families, in their own communities, in respected, traditional ceremonies, and end it.

'I agree,' I said to Godfrey, Martin and Otti, who were waiting expectantly for my answer. 'In my opinion traditional justice must prevail, and I will try and sell it to the international community as a home-based Truth and Reconciliation Commission, where both sides must confess their crimes to obtain amnesty. It worked to heal apartheid wounds in South Africa and, provided the Acholi agree, it can work here.'

'Museveni may not agree,' said Otti.

'I must be both honest and direct,' I said. 'At the moment the international community thinks you are a very dangerous, over-armed, crazy group that cannot be trusted and is wasting everybody's time at the talks.'

Both Otti and Godfrey smiled at this.

'But when they understand that the LRA do genuinely want peace, they will find a way to make it happen. I will get this news to them through my contacts.'

'We thank you,' said Otti.

It was a lot to digest, and I was pleased when some tea arrived while Martin went off to do something.

'So, Mr Anthony,' said Otti. 'We understand your interest in rhinos, but Godfrey tells me you are also concerned about the gorillas in Virunga park in the Congo.'

'Very concerned,' I replied, intrigued by his statement. 'Militia recently entered the park again and killed seven more gorillas. There are not many left. They could be wiped out if this continues.'

'I understand,' said Otti. 'I am sorry for your gorillas.'

'They are not mine, they belong to the world, but nobody seems to be able to do anything about it.'

'These militias are not strong,' said Otti. 'There are two groups fighting the Congo army in that area, and they are both weak and corrupt. The Congo troops are worse; they are ill disciplined.'

We chatted a while about the gorillas while waiting for Martin, and then went back to our discussion without him.

'Let us continue; you wish to discuss the matter of child soldiers,' said Godfrey.

'I do, thank you. Gentlemen, this really is a crucial matter. If you want support from the international community for peace then you must find a way to start dealing with this.'

I took a deep breath.

'Forgive me,' I said. 'But you are hated for this; it's all anyone talks about. It blinds people to the truth of this war, and they support Museveni because of it. You need to build support at the peace talks, and you cannot do it while you are harbouring child soldiers, or while there is the perception that you are harbouring child soldiers.'

'We do not call them children, they are the youth,' said Otti. 'In our culture, a thirteen-year-old is considered a man, and the youth have always fought with their fathers. Children never fight and we do not take children. Sometimes children help carry, but they are treated well and they are always free to go.

You are from South Africa. Do you think your freedom fighters never used the youth when they were in exile fighting apartheid? Of course they did, and so did many other countries in Africa.'

It is true that youths were used by the Afrikaners in the Boer Wars, and by Americans in the War of Independence. Every resistance movement in Europe during the Second World War used their youth. Children have been fighting with adults for as long as there have been wars. Even so, the entire issue of child soldiers was anathema to me. Whether it was cultural or not to use children as soldiers, whether or not everyone else did it, and whether they were called youth instead of children was all beside the point. This was an unacceptable practice.

But there is a lot more to this than meets the eye. The LRA and their child soldiers were a unique problem, the moral implications of which required much deeper understanding. For who was the LRA, who were these people who would sink to stealing children?

The answer is truly Machiavellian; for the perpetrators, the LRA soldiers, were themselves once forcibly abducted from loving homes as children. They too were stolen. They are also victims; these merciless killers are all stolen children themselves, now stealing more children. The realization shocked me.

This has become a huge social and moral dilemma for the Acholi, because the distinctions between victims and perpetrators have become completely blurred. The hunters and the hunted have become one; they are both stolen children.

I tried to conceive what it would be like to be a parent in one of these villages. I imagined the horror of armed rebels bursting into my home and stealing my precious children, taking them away from me. I imagined the desperate search for them, and then the eventual hopelessness of giving up and believing they were dead. Then there would be the relief when I heard that they were still alive but with the LRA, and how desperately I would want to see them again, and want for them just to come home.

This is what had been happening in towns and villages all over Northern Uganda. Sadly, the LRA is no more than their own lost children. They are your kids, my kids, the neighbour's kids, the next village's kids. Their parents and their communities just want them back, all of them; they want them to come home where they can try to help them. The majority of the Acholi want traditional justice because they understand it, and because formal European justice is just not designed to deal with the moral complexities of this uniquely African issue. And I agree with them.

'We have no children here,' Otti was saying as I refocused on the meeting. 'We walked here from Uganda. Children cannot walk that far. Our own children were carried by their parents and helpers.'

'I understand,' I said. 'But how do we start addressing this?'

'If we can get the ICC to withdraw in favour of traditional justice, then everybody will go home anyway,' he said.

'I understand, but I think a generous gesture of good faith in this regard will assist me immensely.'

'What do you have in mind?' said Godfrey.

'I would like you to give me ten of the youth, perhaps women, to take back with me. This will reinforce both my and your credibility. It will tell the world that the LRA are serious about peace. Such an act will dominate the news in your favour.'

Otti was certainly not expecting such a request from me, and it showed.

'We will think about this,' he replied eventually. 'I will need to speak privately with the generals, and then with Joseph Kony. But you have no transport for them anyway. Even if we agree, you will have to come back and get them.'

'That can be arranged, but please do not underestimate the positive effect of this,' I said, pushing the point. 'It will change everything, not only for the international community, but for your own community in Northern Uganda.'

'Do you not understand the conditions in the camps?' said Otti. 'You are asking me to send these women to hell? Here they are well fed and cared for. They have husbands and children, they may refuse to go. They do not want to die in the camps or become prostitutes.'

That statement took me by surprise and for a moment it confused me. Otti truly believed, or was trying to sell to me, the idea that they would be happier staying with the LRA than in the camps.

'Will you contact me when you have decided?' I asked.

'I will,' he said.

'And I in turn will start the visa application for the officer whom you want to come and stay in South Africa,' I said, putting it in as an incentive.

'The generals are arriving,' said Godfrey, looking up.

And so they were.

Otti and I stood up and shook hands.

'Speak to your government about the matters we have discussed here, and I will speak with Kony about the women.'

'Thank you.'

This can work, I thought. Despite his vicious reputation, Otti was a man you could deal with, and if I could facilitate negotiations between him and influential international leaders, perhaps, just perhaps, this bloody war could be ended.

CHAPTER TWENTY-NINE

I was surprised, and told Godfrey so, for the generals and senior officers were turned out in full ceremonial dress uniform.

'This is in your honour,' he said. 'I have never seen them in dress uniform before. It is a good sign. They trust you.'

There was no formal meeting, and after greetings everybody stood around, like at a cocktail party but without cocktails, and I was able to move from one group and one individual to another, talking and being engaged in dialogue on many issues. I was told that Kony sent his greetings but could still not cross the river, and with nearby streams still running strongly from the rain I could understand why.

It truly was a surreal experience for me standing around and talking casually with all these infamous men, whom I had only ever read about in the newspaper associated with war, violence and child soldiers. I spent time with General Odhiambo, who was clearly the senior man after Otti. Odhiambo was friendly, answering my questions and explaining issues, always checking on my well-being, seeing if I wanted more water or something to eat. Several were very interested in my relationship with animals and all knew my concerns about the rhinos.

One thing was certain from my discussions: if we could resolve the matter of the ICC they would all stop fighting in a heartbeat and go home. But they also made it abundantly clear that they were ready to fight, for another two decades if necessary. The ball was now in the hands of the international community. Peace with traditional justice, or war with the ICC.

At one point Godfrey came over and pulled me aside. 'Otti wants to offer you a gift,' he said.

I thought about it for a moment and then, not wanting to be beholden to them, or have them feel that they had in any way bought me, replied to Godfrey that a gift was not necessary. That the only gift I wanted was peace.

Godfrey said he understood and left. A few minutes later a young officer came and said Otti wanted to see me. I went across to where he was standing.

Otti then told me that he could understand my reasons for not wanting to accept a gift, but that he still had something to offer. I wanted to say no, but good manners prevented me from uttering anything but thank you.

It was something I could never ever have anticipated and it changed my view of the challenges facing conservationists in that part of the world for ever. He offered to send emissaries to Virunga National Park, where seven gorillas had just been killed by insurgents, to warn the rebels to leave the gorillas alone. He said that there were two groups in the area and he had good contact with them. He told me that his firm personal request to these groups may help them find the killers and 'dissuade' them from further attacks on gorillas. Otti knew the dark underbelly of Africa like the back of his hand, and he knew better than anyone else that the only way to protect the gorillas in that violent landscape was warning backed up by the threat of force.

Whether or not his proposal could succeed was beside the point. No thought whatsoever was given to the governments or Parks authorities; by his very words he obviously considered them to be inconsequential.

I was gobsmacked. Is this really what conservation in Africa was coming to? It truly was bizarre. Game parks had become war zones, rendering conservation groups and Parks authorities helpless. Rebel armies and bandits were deciding who controlled game reserves and the future of iconic species.

Wildlife in war zones, I thought. What chance do we really have to protect nature's finest?

The gorillas desperately needed help, and if it worked they would be safe for a long time. I wished I could accept the offer, but of course it would be impossible for me to do so. I needed a way out.

'General Otti, I must thank you,' I said. 'The gorillas are very important, not only to me but to the world. I need to do some research when I get home, and we can discuss this further when we speak on the phone.'

Over Otti's shoulder I saw a group of soldiers enter the camp. One came over and waited patiently until we finished speaking, then spoke to Otti in Acholi.

When they finished Otti turned back to me.

'We have word that there is a UN helicopter an hour's drive away. Instead of leaving tomorrow as planned, if you leave now you can get a lift to Juba on the helicopter, and save yourself a two-day drive. The roads are still very bad, and the troops at Nabanga are badly behaved.'

'But I haven't met Kony yet,' I replied. 'It is important that I meet him.'

'Kony is fully briefed on your visit and you will return shortly to meet him. He is still unable to cross the river, and it is better that you return to South Africa with the information we have given you, and start the process with your contacts.'

'I agree,' said Godfrey. 'Not much more can happen if we stay, and we will save days.'

'OK, when do we leave, then?'

'Immediately,' said Otti. 'I will send word, and General Odhiambo and I will accompany you to Ri-Kwangba.'

So I went over and took my leave of the generals and officers, thanking each of them for their hospitality, and then went to my shelter to collect my luggage. On the way I saw Mfeni and his owner standing with a couple of soldiers, and stopped to say goodbye.

'I am leaving now,' I said, taking Mfeni from him.

'You are leaving,' said one of the men accompanying him.

'I am.'

'Please wait,' he said, and quickly walked away towards the barracks.

'Mfeni is good,' said his owner. 'He finished his milk and he is happy. I think he will live now.'

'Good. Every second day you must put an egg in, and see if he likes it,' I said, giving him back.

'I will do this,' he replied.

I rummaged through my bag, and as I was giving him all my toiletries and a couple more sticks of mosquito repellent I noticed a large group of soldiers coming over from the direction of the barracks. They arrived and surrounded me, then one reached out and handed me the tiniest piece of paper with a name on it.

I looked at him expectantly, this tough hard soldier who was about thirty years old and carrying a big 20mm machine gun. I was surprised to see that there were tears in his eyes.

'Please tell my mother and father I am alive,' he said.

'Do you know where they are?'

'No, I don't know,' he said, the tears rolling down his cheeks. 'In the camps.'

'I will do my best,' I replied. 'Do you want to leave?'

'No, this is my place until Museveni is gone; just tell them.'

And so the procession began. One after the other the soldiers stepped forward and gave me notes with just their names written on. There was obviously little paper in the bush because the notes were so tiny they could barely take the names. A few were choking back tears, and I realized I was their first real contact with the outside world for years.

It was a revelatory moment, one of the saddest and most confusing things I have ever seen, and I felt my own emotions well up. These heavily armed men standing in front of me were the infamous LRA soldiers, the merciless killers, the hated child abductors. And here they were remembering the homes and families that they themselves were once abducted from, and it was breaking them apart.

They left quickly and I walked to the path leading to the outside world. As I stood there looking back at the camp, I saw Otti's wives, who smiled and waved at me. They too would have homes and families waiting, but I didn't have their names, and now it was too late, for Otti and Odhiambo were walking towards me with Godfrey, Martin and a contingent of soldiers.

For some reason the trek back to Ri-Kwangba was shorter than the walk in, and we entered the clearing to find several large trucks carrying food. It was delivery day. As part of the peace talks the Danish government was providing food for the LRA. This was to prevent marauding during the negotiations. Parked off to one side I saw the two Land Cruisers that had brought us in.

'Mr Anthony,' called out Godfrey excitedly as he walked across from where he was standing with Otti and General Odhiambo. 'There has been a development. Joseph Kony has just crossed the river and he is asking that we return.'

'Excellent,' I replied, motivated by the prospect.

'Good, we have to alter the transport arrangements. We will ask the vehicles to come back in two days.'

Martin and Godfrey went across to the Land Cruisers and, after a lengthy discussion with the drivers that seemed to get more and more animated, they went across to Otti, then returned to me, shaking their heads.

'The drivers refuse to come back,' said Godfrey. 'They say

their orders are to collect us and take us to the helicopter. They say that if we want to change the schedule we must do it through their superiors in Juba.'

'So let's phone them,' I responded. 'They must come back. Tell them Kony wants to see me.'

'We have been trying,' he said. 'But there is no response from the Juba numbers and the drivers want to leave. They have seen Otti and Odhiambo and the LRA soldiers and don't like being here at all.'

'So what are our alternatives?'

'Well, either we take the helicopter, or we stay with no way of knowing how or when we are going to get back,' said Godfrey, obviously frustrated by the turn of events.

'What about the food trucks,' I said. 'How long will they be here? Will they wait for us?'

'They leave today and they will never carry LRA passengers for fear of attack.'

My heart sank.

'We have no choice,' said Godfrey. 'We must leave now or we are stuck. I do not trust the Southern Sudan army to ever come and get us.'

'So be it, then,' I replied, resigned to the circumstances. 'We will come back soon. Please give my apologies to Kony.'

'Otti will let him know,' Godfrey replied. 'It is a great pity.'

'That it is,' I said dejectedly.

The drivers started the vehicles and I went across to take leave of Otti and Odhiambo. We exchanged phone numbers, my cellphone and his satellite phone, and I then shook hands with him and Odhiambo.

'You are our Godfather for Peace,' said Otti. 'Please take our message to your people, that we are ready to end this war. They will not believe us, but they will believe you.'

'I certainly will,' I replied. 'I will do everything I can.'

'Thank you,' said Otti. He held my gaze, and I found myself looking straight into the eyes of this most notorious man, and believing that he and the generals meant every word they had said.

I didn't know that would be the last time I would ever see him.

CHAPTER THIRTY

The roads had dried out somewhat, and the trip back to Na-banga was uneventful. Thankfully we didn't go anywhere near the SPLA army base where the soldiers had been so hostile to us on our way in. The giant white Mi-8 Russian helicopter stood waiting in an open field, and a few hours later we landed at Juba Airport, where we were collected by Godfrey and Martin's LRA bodyguards and taken back to our hotel.

I walked out past the Acholi mango tree to the Nile River and stood on the banks, reflecting for a while on the experiences of the past few days. The magnificent watercourse had moved through history for a million years, uncaring of man's folly, and on its banks two new men were playing another bloody game that would one day too pass into antiquity.

We had an early dinner and I suddenly found myself ex-hausted and not keen to get into another long discussion about events. I took early leave of the table and thirty minutes later, despite hearing a few distant gunshots, I was fast asleep in my prefab room.

The hammering on the door thundered into my sleep, and I jumped up and stood in the corner of the room nearest the door trying to wake myself up as fast as possible. Someone hitting on your door in Juba at one o'clock in the morning can never be good news.

'Yes, who is it?' I called out.

'They are coming, you must go,' said a voice I recognized. I quickly opened the door. It was one of the LRA bodyguards.

'You must go out now,' he said. 'They are coming.'

'Who is coming?' I asked.

'Soldiers, go away from your room,' he replied before quickly moving off into the dark.

I did not question the warning and dressed in three seconds flat, amazed at how lucid I was. If they, whoever they were, are searching and find a used bed they will keep looking, I thought, so I very quickly made up the bed, tidied the room as best I could, then grabbed my baggage and ran out into the dark, still barefoot, heading for the only sanctuary I knew: the river.

Thankfully the outside lights were poor and the river edge was in complete darkness. I moved to the edge of the reeds, carefully shifted forward until I felt the water around my ankles, then stopped and turned to face the hotel rooms. I found that by squatting I was almost completely hidden by the reeds – unless they came down with torches, I thought, and then I would be completely buggered. The last thing on earth I wanted to do was have to go deeper into the reeds and get into the river, at night, in the dark with the crocodiles. The thought absolutely horrified me. There was a small boat moored about sixty feet from my hiding place, and as a last alternative I considered getting in and casting off into the strongly flowing waterway.

From the hotel I could hear banging and shouting, which went on for fifteen minutes or so, and then a little later I heard vehicles start up and leave. Then silence.

I waited for another ten minutes before I left my hiding place and went back to my room. Everything was as I had left it. I didn't know where Godfrey and Martin were staying, so there was nothing for it but to get into bed and go back to sleep – which took a while, I can tell you.

The next morning I was up at dawn searching for coffee, and found a lone staff member near the kitchen.

'What happened last night?' I asked.

'The town is locked down,' he replied. 'There was shooting last night, they were searching for some people; they do it all the time.'

He was a friendly guy, a Somali on a work contract. A highly educated man, but unable to get a job at home, he'd been reduced to travelling and working in restaurants. He was able to get me my much-needed coffee and we sat outside overlooking the river and chatted a while.

Eventually I told him what had happened, how I had hidden in the reeds, and he stared at me, shaking his head.

'The LRA are staying here,' he said in a loud whisper as if imparting a secret. 'It is not good. Here they can take people away for no reason. Juba is crazy.'

'What do you know of the LRA and their war with Museveni?' I asked.

'This is a violent war waged by violent men,' he replied. 'Neither Kony nor Museveni have the interest of their people at heart, it is all about them as individuals. They are truly cut from the same cloth those two, and their legacies will be defined by each other, by barbarism, slavery, and oppression.'

Later, I recounted the story to Godfrey at breakfast.

'They didn't wake me,' he said, laughing. 'I changed rooms so nobody knew where I was.'

I realized that I may have overreacted by going to the reeds the night before, but I was not sorry. The alternative if things had gone wrong could have been much worse.

The military roadblock at the end of the street meant we were unable to leave the hotel, and a couple of phone calls by Martin revealed that the town was indeed completely locked down and the airport closed.

We were stuck in our hotel, so spent the morning debating the significance of the visit to Otti's camp. That afternoon I taped some radio interviews with Godfrey. He spoke with Otti, who confirmed he had already made some calls, getting out the word that there would be no more LRA attacks in Northern Uganda, that the people in the camps should all go home. But words were one thing, and people would wait to see if the attacks actually stopped completely before they would move. This would take time.

I also thanked Godfrey for the LRA's continued commitment to the rhinos, which underlay all that had been achieved.

The next morning we were at the airport early and managed to book a flight to Nairobi.

While we were waiting for the plane I bumped into a conservationist from Sudan who told me an interesting story. He said that during the long war between North and South Sudan many elephants had migrated to Kenya and Uganda. What was unusual was that when the peace agreement was finally signed after decades of fighting, they immediately started migrating back again. The question is, how did they know that hundreds of miles away the war was over?

I checked into the Intercontinental Hotel in Nairobi, where I immediately phoned Ben Ngubane in Tokyo and Mujahid Alam in Kinshasa to update them on my visit to the LRA camps.

Godfrey and I spent the next few days strategizing the way forward, during which time I was able to brief some senior people in South Africa and in both England and the USA about the progress we had made. The response was positive and I informed Godfrey and Martin.

Otti remained in close contact and we had already planned a return visit to the camps when I flew out of Nairobi the next day, heading home.

CHAPTER THIRTY-ONE

The transformation – from the LRA jungle camp and hiding from SPLA soldiers at Juba in the middle of the night, to the tranquillity of Thula Thula – was as surreal as a mirage, but it came with the absolute relief that this was no hallucination.

It was great to be home. Françoise and I hugged as I told her of my adventures. Jeff the Labrador actually got up from his favourite spot at the pool and wandered over. Gypsy, our little black pavement special, followed me everywhere, jumping on my heels. Bijou, Françoise's Maltese and queen of all she surveyed, deigned to greet me briefly, but she went back to sleep immediately.

Françoise and I discussed my trip into the night, and as we went to bed it was still sinking in that I had been actually living with the LRA, and doing deals for peace and the release of child soldiers. When I thought of where I had gone to, and what I had been doing, I realized some guardian angel must have been working overtime.

I reflected on Kony's divination that the Acholi's salvation would come from South Africa, and on Africa's general preoccupation with matters spiritual. I remembered how Martin and Godfrey had told the LRA leadership that when Mnumzane charged us, the 'evil' spirit of Museveni had been in the elephant, and how just as Mnumzane was about to kill us, I spoke to him and he stopped. They were amazed at this, and so too was I, but for different reasons. They certainly believed that I had a mystical relationship with the animal kingdom, and there is no doubt that this was an entrance point to earning the trust of the LRA high command.

Such matters have greater significance than most Westerners can easily accept. For instance, it is quite obvious to Africa's indigenous peoples that the earth and its life forms are inhabited by spirits and supernatural beings, good and bad, and that their ancestors are everywhere busily influencing goings-on and interfering in people's lives. 'Witches' are very much alive and kicking all over the place, and unfortunately still put to death regularly in parts of Africa. Both black and white magic are still commonplace.

But Africa is not the only bastion of the spirit world.

A billion Indians worship the elephant-headed god Ganesha, and this in a country where all cows are sacred. In India you ridicule these things at your peril; wars have been fought over less. In Hong Kong there is a great big hole in one of the most prominent skyscrapers so that the mountain dragon spirits can pass through. Many Chinese are highly superstitious, and among other things have a strong belief in animal spirits. For them, foxes are the Chinese equivalent of werewolves, and they believe that dogs have the ability to see supernatural beings.

It has always interested me that people will spend more time practising a golf stroke than connecting with their own dogs or cats – and then say that communication with animals is all hocus pocus.

Closer to home in South Africa, the ancient San people, the Bushmen, have a saying about the evanescence of the material world: 'There is a dream dreaming us.'

One thing for certain was that the dream of Nana and the herd that had come to me in the hut while in the deepest jungle with the LRA had given me huge inspiration. Was some of

Africa's spiritual side rubbing off on me? The dream was more real than anything I could remember, and so I decided the next morning to go and see my elephants.

Vusi, my section ranger, said that the herd was just a couple of miles away, and I drove out to them. I remained in the Land Rover, watching as they leisurely browsed the surrounding bush. Although heavy with fresh dew, the vegetation was lifeless. We were very short of rain in the months before I left, and unless we had relief soon would be facing a drought that threatened to be of Old Testament proportions. But the sky remained clear and swollen purple rain clouds were a distant memory.

I took out the binoculars and focused on Nana. Her one eye was getting more opaque. It was obvious she would soon have little or no vision in it at all. This was confirmed by watching Frankie, who seemed to be in charge now. When she started to move off, the others instantly responded. She was the new matriarch and Nana, although deposed, would be a respected elder who would be loved and cherished until the day she died. That was the elephant way.

I started the engine and kept pace with them, staying about a hundred yards off. They were aware of my presence and occasionally would look in my direction. I drove a little closer, and then Nana broke away and started coming towards me. Frankie watched for a while and then followed. As soon as she turned the rest of the herd trailed her.

I remained in my car as Nana came right up to me. Her massive head loomed large in the windscreen, obliterating all else. She looked at me slightly askance to favour her good eye. When you get to know elephants, they have extraordinarily expressive faces, and sometimes you can tell just by looking at them what they are thinking. Right now, Nana was confused; why was I not getting out and greeting her? But the herd was on top of us, and being surrounded by fifteen elephants while on foot wasn't a good idea. After standing in front of the car for several minutes she seemed to shrug and then moved off.

I waited until the herd had been swallowed up by the bush, then drove away, the road veering sharply to the right. I turned – and then got the fright of my life. There was Nana directly in front, just yards away, almost as if she had been waiting for me. I braked hard, tyres struggling to grip on the dirt track, and twisted the steering wheel full lock. As soon as the vehicle stopped I quickly looked around for the rest of the herd. They were nowhere in sight.

Nana walked up to the car and poked her trunk inside, sniffing me and touching my face. I was instantly wrapped in that incredible bubble of contentment again, one of the finest sensations in the world.

I opened the door and got out, keeping a lookout for the rest of the herd. Not that I felt in any danger with them being around, but you always had to remember that these were wild elephants.

She stood next to me, towering and huge and exuding total tranquillity. 'Hello, my beautiful girl. I've missed you.'

Then I got it. The rest of the herd was not there because Nana had deliberately left them. Somehow she knew which route I would be taking and had doubled back to meet me. She had in effect given Frankie and the rest of the gang the slip to wait for me.

Or was that being too fanciful? Was I reading too much into the mind of an elephant? Believing just because I wanted to believe?

I didn't know, but the cloud of goodwill wrapped around me like a cosmic cloak. I didn't want to leave. For a moment I cared about nothing else. I understood – or thought I did – that she knew I was not getting out of the vehicle or talking to her when the rest of the herd was around. So to counter that, she simply left them. She and I would have our own little private chat.

After about ten minutes she turned around and wandered back into the bush. As she left, I started to have second thoughts about my theory that she was deliberately leaving the herd to come to me. Perhaps I was just being stupid in thinking that she sensed I was not approaching her because the others were around.

So the next day I set out to see if it was true.

I again drove close to the herd, and once I had made sure they all knew I was there, I slowly drove off. Sure enough, in my rear-view mirror I saw one of the elephants detach from the rest.

It was Nana. I shifted the gear lever to neutral and let her approach. When the herd was out of sight I got out of the vehicle and spoke to her. Just like the day before, we spent an incredible few minutes revelling in each other's company.

Then she moved off. I have never felt so gratified and humbled in my life. She had worked out that I would not come to her, so she would come to me. When I later told Françoise the story, I almost choked up.

On the way home, I heard a distinctive bark and was almost surprised when I saw an actual wildebeest and not Heidi. But a subtle movement some yards back caught my eye, and I saw that it was indeed Heidi, hanging out with the wildebeest gang like friends in a shopping mall.

I edged the vehicle over, directly opposite to where she was, behind an anthill. I knew the rangers got quite close to her in game drives, which is why she was such a favourite with the tourists, so she was not alarmed by vehicles. All the wildebeest by now had moved off, but Heidi carried on browsing the diminishing grasses, once sweet but now sparse and desiccated by the meagre rains. She knew I was there, but was not too worried by it.

I wondered abstractly if a human could get as close to a rhino as I had done with elephants. Maybe – but I think only if you had been with it since it was a baby. Elephants as a species are more socially interactive than rhino, and in my opinion far more intelligent and aware, so I suppose it's easier to form a bond with an elephant than a rhino. But Heidi was so good-natured that I felt anything was possible. This didn't mean you could treat her like a pet; on the contrary, Heidi would have ripped my Land Rover open like a sardine can in an instant if she felt threatened. She thankfully didn't feel threatened.

She had grown into a spectacular specimen, her armoured hide dull grey but heaving with rude good health, massive shoulders supporting her huge head and her yard-long horn protruding like Father Time's scythe. I immediately put that image out of my head. It was too much like the Grim Reaper. Heidi was a constant reminder of what we were up against in the north. To me, she was symbolic of what conservation stood for.

Once again I vowed that the demise of the rhino would not happen on my generation's watch if I could help it. But things didn't look too good at the moment. You only had to look out over the bush at night to know it was impossible to protect any animal in the impenetrable, never-ending darkness that is a game reserve.

That night I truly knew I was home when George the bush-baby and his girlfriend, or now wife, visited us at the lodge. His partner lacked the social skills that George had acquired as a barfly, and always kept in the shadows. Sometimes we didn't even know if she was there, or if George was reverting to his bachelor ways again.

The first dish on the menu was soup with a French name that only Françoise could pronounce properly. Just as the guests were 'oohing' and 'aahing' over the broth, George leapt onto the table and stuck his snout into one diner's plate.

The soup was, of course, piping hot. With a startled yell, George jumped back. You would have thought he had learned his lesson. But no. His athletic leap backwards landed him near another guest's bowl and, eyeing the aromatic liquid, he again

stuck his nose in for a slurp. It was a repeat of the first perform-
ance: a yowl of indignation, and then a jump that landed him
at the next guest's bowl. Before we could move, he ran down
the length of the table, putting his feet into every bowl along
the way, yelling with soup-rage as his toes got more and more
singed. Finally he vaulted off the table and, jabbering at his
spouse in bushbaby lingo something along the lines of 'Let's go –
the food here's on fire,' they headed for the trees.

Thanks to Françoise, we had plentiful supplies of soup – as
there are almost always demands for seconds – and so each bowl
was soon refilled.

David then told the guests they were lucky. George's singed
whiskers were just the floor show. In fact, it was nothing compared to what he had 'organized' a couple of nights before when
a mouse had landed on the table, tumbling from the thatched
roof above. Just as diners lurched back in surprise, it was followed by an *mfezi*, a Mozambican spitting cobra, which had
also launched itself from the roof. It pounced, all fangs and
hisses, before slithering off with the bush rodent in its mouth.
To say appetites were put on hold would be bland. We do not
kill anything on Thula Thula, and the snake was captured by
a ranger and released far away. But only after he had finished
eating his hard-won dinner, of course. Interrupting someone's
meal is just bad manners.

The next morning I watched as guests got into the Land
Rover for a game drive. I could have told them something that
may have surprised them even more than George's soup-tasting
foray. Barely a decade ago Françoise and I ploughed everything
we owned into buying Thula Thula, and were so broke that the
sheriff arrived one morning to repossess the Land Rover just as
the few loyal guests we had were getting into it to go on a game
drive. We had a quick cash collection among the guests to ap-
pease the sheriff's fiscal demand, and the game drive continued.

I then dashed into town to go down once more on my threadbare khaki-clad knees to my thankfully understanding bank manager.

The reason for our penury was that when Nana and the herd first arrived they were too rogue to let guests onto the reserve. For two years we had absolutely no income, as I worked to pacify the troubled elephants while still having to pay staff salaries and the never-ending repair bills. Somehow we persevered, and I occasionally tell that story to people who think running a game reserve is all ponies and rainbows.

The irony is that today the elephants are one of the best viewing herds around, and Nana is now the reserve's prime attraction, with people coming from all over the world to see her. I never looked at her as an investment – you cannot do that to a soul mate – but her repayment to Thula Thula and our conservation activities has been immeasurable.

Sadly, she is now going completely blind in her right eye. I could bring her in and let her live out her days in luxury and be with her every day. Or I could leave her where she is, with her family. The choice is obvious. But what to me is infinitely gratifying is that she's given me total visitation rights. All I have to do is drive up to the herd and she will sneak off to see me. Just the two of us and no one else. Ironically, as she wasn't the leader any more, this became easier, because if she had been the matriarch the rest of the herd would have followed her. Although I've noticed that sometimes she does still step into the lead – perhaps old habits die hard.

Something else happened at this time that also affected me profoundly. I discovered Nana was pregnant. The father could only have been Mnumzane. She would later give birth to a creation that combined my two most favourite non-humans. He had other progeny, but this was to be his last one – and with Nana.

She is a truly magnificent creature. I cannot believe my good fortune in just knowing her. Just being with her.

CHAPTER THIRTY-TWO

Less than a week after leaving the camp, my cellphone rang as I was driving down to Thula Thula's lodge. It was Godfrey in Nairobi.

'I am afraid something is wrong,' he said.

I waited; he was struggling with his words.

'There is a rumour Otti may be dead.'

'What? But that's completely impossible,' I said, staggered at what I was hearing. 'Are you sure?'

'We don't know if it's true. A call came through to someone we know in Nairobi saying Kony killed him. We can't verify it; all the satellite phones in the bush are off. I can't raise anyone.'

'It's just not possible,' I said anxiously. 'Kony and Otti are best friends, they have been in the bush together for over two decades. We have just spent two days with him and all the generals. This has to be mischief.'

'I hope so, but we should talk. I will come to South Africa and see you.'

'I agree. I will arrange the special visa.'

'I will find out when I can get there and let you know.'

A few days later Godfrey arrived alone. He looked drawn when I collected him from the airport, and I knew immediately that he didn't have good news.

'There is no formal confirmation,' he said as we sat down at the lodge. 'Until I have all the facts, as head of public relations for the LRA, I must deny the rumours of Otti's death. But from the information coming in, it is true.'

'What the hell happened?' I asked, shocked to my core.

'We don't know for sure, but it appears that just days after we left the camp something occurred, and he was arrested and shot almost immediately.'

'But why, for what reason? What could possibly make Kony kill his best friend?'

'That's what we don't know yet. The rumours are flying,' said Godfrey. 'My phone just doesn't stop ringing. One story is that Kony suspected Otti of a plot to kill him. Another is that Otti had received a large amount of money, which he didn't disclose to Kony, and yet another is that he was sidelining Kony, usurping his power, taking major decisions without him.'

It was a lot to digest, and I was struggling to come to terms with it, when I recalled that Kony had phoned as we were leaving Ri-Kwangba, asking me to stay to see him. If I had done so I would have been in Otti's camp alone and cut off from the rest of the world when my host was arrested and executed. The thought gave me a chill. Suddenly I remembered the first question I was asked at the meeting with the generals. 'Mr Anthony,' Otti had said. 'Before we start, there is a question: did you bring our money, the five hundred thousand US dollars, did you bring it with you?'

I never knew what he was talking about, and still don't, but it was certainly a most unusual question to ask a conservationist. Something else must have been going on, something that I was not privy to. Did this large amount of money have something to do with Otti's death? Was I at first perceived as being involved in something else that was going on? My suspicions were partly confirmed when I later heard a rumour that Kony and Otti had both been told before my visit to be careful because a mercenary named Orence [Lawrence] would be coming to see them.

'What will happen to the agreements I made with Otti? These are very important. Must I continue with my side?' I asked.

'Absolutely; that is why I came to see you. Nothing will change. The agreements were with the military high command, not with Otti as an individual. Kony was kept well informed during the process. He is the leader and everything was approved by him. We must go forward.

'Do not forget that it was Kony who invited you to the camps to thank you for helping us to try and achieve peace. Otti was just carrying out Kony's instructions.'

That was correct, and it made me feel a little bit better, but Otti's death had really come at the worst possible time. I had just made some real breakthroughs. We now had the first direct communication line between the LRA military leadership and the outside world. The LRA had agreed never to attack the Acholi in Northern Uganda again. This was incredible. The people could at last leave the hated camps and go home; the 'invisible children' could stop walking. They had agreed to public accountability for their actions, and in fact had already signed an agreement of accountability and reconciliation to this effect. They were busy considering my request for a symbolic, 'good faith' release of some of the captured women, which I believed would start the ball rolling for the release of them all. Most importantly, though, I believed they genuinely wanted to end the war. There had been hope.

And then Otti had died in the middle of it all.

Godfrey and I discussed the issues into the night, and on the next day he left. I could do nothing until there was a formal announcement of Otti's death and we found out exactly where we stood with Joseph Kony.

Several weeks later I was invited to Kinshasa for a meeting with the ICCN, African Parks and other rhino conservation groups. It was a huge disappointment.

I had long since given up hope that the DRC government, at the urging of Ambassador M'Poko, would intervene on our behalf and accept our original rescue plan. Despite this setback, we had removed the principal threat to the rhino by getting the LRA to agree not to attack the game rangers. The LRA had also agreed to withdraw from the area around Garamba's main camp, and they had been advising tribes around the far north of the park that they would not tolerate the killing of any more rhino.

At the meeting in Kinshasa we were told that the belated fixed-wing aerial survey had spotted only four rhino. I expected no less. The rivers had dropped, and as predicted the poachers would have been able to cross the rivers and get into the rhinos' last home range.

To say the outlook was bleak would be an exaggeration. It was far worse. African Parks officials now planned to go back and try and find them again to dart them. This time using a helicopter, something we had offered so many months ago. If they managed to find the last remaining rhino again, which was unlikely, the plan was to take them to Kenya. They will all be dead before then, I thought. The last realistic chance to save them had already passed. There were still a few northern whites in zoos, but they were not breeding, so in effect they were doomed.

I offered to help with some donor financing if they ever found them and then flew home, sick to my soul.

For a couple of days I wandered around Thula Thula listlessly. The fight for the rhino in Africa was being lost hand over fist. Not only was the northern white rhino to all intents and purposes now gone, but Africa's western black rhino, the last of which existed in northern Cameroon, had also just been poached to extinction, without a fuss in the media at all. People, it appeared, were more interested in the private lives of celebrities than in the desperate fight for survival by some of the earth's major life forms.

There were now only four sub-species of rhino left in Africa, three of them black and one white, most of which were in South Africa. The poaching syndicates knew this only too well, and they were already moving their lucrative operations south. The battle lines were being redrawn. The fight for Africa's last rhinos was about to begin, and a lot of people were going to get hurt before this battle was finally decided.

We desperately needed solutions, and somehow we had to take the fight not only to the poachers, but to the end users who were creating this insatiable demand. At the end of the day rhino horn was just plain old keratin. I sometimes wonder why we don't just send all our finger and toenail trimmings over to the East for them to chew on; it's the same thing.

Were there other ways to halt the systematic slaughter of rhino? I started asking around and found that there were indeed some radical ideas out there. One idea was to dehorn all the remaining rhino on the planet. There were two problems with this idea. First, in areas where rhino were few, poachers would kill the dehorned rhino anyway. Because they had spent so much tracking it, they would kill it so they didn't waste time tracking it again by mistake. And second, the horn was so valuable that poachers would sometimes shoot the dehorned rhino just to get the piece of horn remaining under the skin.

Even more extreme was the idea of injecting the horn with poison so anyone eating its horn could die. I checked this out with some top-class lawyers, who said that even if the rhino owner advertised that he had poisoned the horn, he could still be found guilty of manslaughter. There was also the potential problem of the poison slowly leaching out of the horn into the rhino's head.

So I consulted with toxicologists, poison experts, who suggested that if we infuse rhino horns, we do so with a human repellent rather than poison. For example, the purple colouring in methylated spirits is a repellent so people don't drink it. It won't kill you, but tastes awful. Perhaps that is the route to go. But then all medicine tastes awful, so how much would it help?

Then there were those who advocated legalizing the trade and flooding the market. That sounded logical at first, but my enquiries revealed that there were not even nearly enough rhino left to flood a market that size. The insatiable demand for horn in the East means that the legal supply from the few remaining rhinos wouldn't even begin to satisfy demand, and the poachers would just continue poaching until they were all gone. Then there was the idea of colouring the horn. Well poachers wouldn't see the colour of the horn at night, and would kill the rhino anyway. Things really did seem bleak. (There is, though, one idea that may just work which we are having investigated by top scientists in the UK. We will make the details known as soon as final tests are done.)

Sadly, there was little good news about the LRA on the international scene to counterbalance the bad news about the rhinos. In the aftermath of Otti's death Martin had disappeared into civilian life and Godfrey's influence seemed to wane. That was a great pity for all of the people involved in the peace process, Godfrey was the one man with the intellect to grasp the nuances, and the strength to plot a path towards real peace. He was a man who hated what was being done to his people, the Acholi, and he was doing whatever it took to try and help them.

Somehow the talks continued into 2008 and the ceasefire held, although the ICC arrest warrants remained a stumbling block for Kony. So what if the debates were going on endlessly, I thought, so what if the politicians spent every moment insulting one other? There was no more of that terrible war. Most significantly, the LRA generals kept their word and there were no more attacks in the camps or anywhere else in Northern Uganda. People started to go home at last.

Otti's death had been a huge blow to my efforts, and the reason for his death is still not clear, even today. All anyone knows is that he was called to Kony's camp one morning, and on arrival at his best friend's hut was instantly tied up and told he was to be executed. He asked to see his son, one of the young men who travelled to Ri-Kwangba with me, and was then bound to a tree and shot with a machine gun, all without trial or explanation.

Many around the world would have rejoiced, I am sure. I did not; for, despite his infamous reputation, I believed he was sincere in our dealings, and with him probably went the only real chance for peace.

Despite the deserved notoriety of the LRA, the paradox was that I saw much humanity in those jungle camps. It was like visiting a rural village, not a terrorist camp, and people were courteous, polite and respectful, not least the soldier caring for the baby baboon. They all seemed to be making the most of it and just getting on with their lives. There was a lot of laughter and playfulness, especially among the women and children. I say this not to give any credibility to the situation, but to give some measure of comfort to those families whose children are there, and who want to know how they are and how they live. The scene when hardcore LRA soldiers, the killers, who themselves had been abducted from their homes many years ago, gave me tiny scraps of paper with names on asking me to tell their parents they were still alive, will haunt me forever. I gave the names to a man in Nairobi who was going to the camps, but as he said to me, how do you find these parents among almost two million people, many with the same family name? Hopefully the pictures in this book will identify some of them.

The trip to Otti's mobile headquarters had also opened my eyes to the fact that there were many more women and children than fighting soldiers in these village camps. Bearing in mind that the women were abductees with parents and families waiting, to me any attack on these camps was inconceivable, as it could result in scores of innocents being slaughtered. This was a uniquely African problem that I believe can only be solved with African solutions: confession, forgiveness, atonement, and penance – what the Acholi call *Mato Oput*.

Is *Mato Oput* a perfect justice system? No. But that's not the question. Is it a workable system, will it help end the violence and suffering? Well, it's certainly what the Acholi respect and believe in. And who are we to tell this ancient nation that their own justice is rubbish; that only alien European justice will suffice for crimes committed on their soil, by their people. That *Mato Oput* could work was borne out when the LRA delegation led by Martin went on a conciliatory tour of the towns and villages of Northern Uganda.

'The delegation was sometimes harshly criticized,' Martin told me later, 'but the tour brought hope and despite the accusations we were welcomed back. There was dancing at some of the meetings.'

This is the soul of Africa that Westerners have difficulty understanding, and this is why traditional justice works.

I was told that Kony wanted to see me, and had asked me to continue the peace effort, so I returned to Nairobi several times. But for one reason or another, the journey back to the bush never took place. So I worked with others in or close to the LRA in a desperate effort to try and keep the talks going.

On the American side, I spoke with the Under-Secretary of State for Africa, Jendayi Frazer, and dealt with senior State Department official Tim Shortley, through whom I received US State Department clearance to continue dealing with the LRA. Kony was skittish and wary of traps and plots to kill him, and progress, if any, was very, very slow; but all the while there was peace, real peace. The hornet's nest that was the LRA was self-contained, farming and fishing.

Unfortunately this status quo was disturbed when SPLA soldiers stationed at Nabanga, the same ones who had long been spoiling for a fight, concocted a poorly planned attack on the LRA assembly areas in June 2008. The attack failed and the LRA struck back viciously, killing dozens of soldiers and civilians before burning Nabanga to the ground.

And then the war talk had started, and in late 2008 the unthinkable happened. Uganda, with the logistical support of the US, led a surprise attack on the peaceful LRA village camps using helicopter gunships and MiG fighter jets.

Let me put this into context.

For the first time in two decades the most vicious terrorist army in the world had laid down their arms and stopped fighting. Not just for a month or two; they had stopped fighting for two years. For the first time in twenty years there was no more fear or terror. Africa's longest-running civil war was to all intents and purposes over, and at last people were able to go back home, and were doing so by the hundreds of thousands. The LRA 'child soldiers', captors and captured alike, had created villages, and were living peacefully, farming and fishing. That's the fact of it. I was there. I saw it with my own eyes.

And the best solution they could come up with was to attack these peaceful village camps, teeming not only with abducted women and their children but with the child soldiers everybody was trying to get back to their parents. And they did it with MiG jet fighters and helicopter gunships.

Why? The ridiculous answer is that they didn't believe Kony really wanted peace because the talks were taking too long. Well surprise, surprise. Everybody knows that in Africa things take time, lots and lots of time. That's why they call it Africa time. And who cares how long it took, all it was costing was a monthly delivery of ridiculously simple food, the sort of thing the UN hands out to refugees all over the world, all the time, and there was no more war and no more terror for millions of people. What a deal.

Jan Egeland, the United Nations' Under-Secretary-General for Humanitarian Affairs, in his book *A Billion Lives* quotes Museveni as saying about the LRA, 'These talks are not to our benefit. Let me be categorical – there will only be a military solution to this problem.'

So were the LRA generals right when they told me that it was they who had been seeking peace all along, and not Museveni? As Godfrey had so patiently explained when I was in the camps, Museveni never wanted peace. 'He has been duping the Americans for years,' he later told me, 'and he suckered them into supporting the attack.'

The US-backed Ugandan attack on 14 December 2008, code-named operation Lightning Thunder, failed miserably.

The LRA shot down an attack helicopter and disappeared back into the jungle with minimal casualties.

Then they went back to war in the worst possible way. Deprived of their fields, fishing and food deliveries, they resumed their old ways, and launched a devastating series of attacks. Newspaper reports said that in the first attacks alone over 400 people were killed. Over the next few months, newspaper reports claimed the LRA killed some 3,000 people, and displaced 300,000 in the DRC alone. Hundreds of new boys and girls were abducted almost immediately, and continue to be abducted. Three years later, as I write this book, the region remains in turmoil, all as a direct result of that ill-conceived attack. And all because the International Criminal Court, something the American government doesn't recognize, and the Acholi nation probably never even heard of before, wanted to jail the three remaining LRA leaders in a foreign country.

Now how on earth does the violence and suffering that has caused compare to lasting peace using Acholi traditional justice? But then I am just a game ranger. What would I know?

Most unfortunately, JP's earlier prediction that the main camp at Garamba would be attacked if the peace talks broke down came starkly true. The attack happened in early January 2009. The guards defended courageously, and game rangers fighting against crack LRA troops somehow managed to repel the attack, but not without terrible losses. Eight brave rangers died, many were wounded and the camp was severely damaged. The attack rocked the conservation world.

Despite this catastrophe, the ICCN to their great credit rebuilt the camp and never abandoned the park again.

The only saving grace was the agreement made in Otti's camp with the LRA military high command, when they decided never again to attack the Acholi. Not a shot has been fired by the LRA in Northern Uganda since the day of our meeting over three years ago, and as a direct result nearly two million people have been able to leave the hated camps and go home. It has been claimed that it was Museveni's defeat of the LRA that did this. That is not true, simply because the LRA have still not been even nearly defeated, and have been out there creating mayhem across several countries including the Congo, Central African Republic and Southern Sudan.

The LRA know Northern Uganda like the back of their hand and have arms caches all over the place. Just one or two random attacks, by a few men, just as they have done for decades, would have kept fear locked in place, and no one would have dared to go home.

Interestingly, Kony has been calling for a ceasefire, incessantly, ever since operation Lightning Thunder. The response has been a deafening silence.

CHAPTER THIRTY-THREE

A few days after Otti's death I left home early with nothing planned except a bush walkabout to clear my mind. It's not just being 'out there' that is good for the soul, but every minute in the bush is an experience, often never to be repeated. Some sights you only get once in a lifetime, but you have to be out in the wild often to even those odds out.

I was walking along the river when something slightly irregular caught my eye. It was a large African rock python, a beautiful fifteen feet long, its dappled brown-gold coils blending perfectly into the landscape. I suddenly noticed that it was entwined around a young impala ram. The massive snake had unhinged its lower jaw from its skull to open its mouth wide enough to swallow the buck whole, horns and all.

I moved closer to get a better look, but unfortunately I made the slightest noise and the snake saw me, got a fright, regurgitated its meal and slowly slithered away.

The python, of which Thula Thula has plenty, could have been waiting for at least a week in ambush to make its kill. At first other animals know it's there and give it a wide berth. But after several days they get used to the python's presence, or simply get careless – and bang! The python has its prey. Now in just a few seconds I had ruined its meal. A python seldom returns to a kill once frightened off, which meant that it would not eat for several more weeks while it found another ambush spot and painstakingly laid in wait again. I regretted not being more careful.

Coincidentally, there had been another snake incident involving one of my rangers a few days earlier. I had recently removed three *mfezis* from under the decking of our storeroom and deposited them far away in the bush. A *mfezi,* a Mozambique spitting cobra, is a beautiful snake, metallic grey on top, with pink bars on its light-coloured stomach that only become visible when it rears. They are only about four feet long when fully grown, but they are formidable when trapped, and will bite and spit if you don't handle them correctly. However, we had a rather excitable ranger saying he had seen a fourth snake. You would have thought he had spotted the Loch Ness monster, he was so fired up.

He found the *mfezi* hiding behind a box and went to get a broom. All our rangers know how to catch these cobras. As it rears up, you gently slide the broom towards it, and when it collapses on the point where the handle fits into the broom it somehow always just stays there and you merely carry it away. Simple as that, but with one crucial proviso – you must wear glasses or some other form of eye protection. They're not called spitting cobras for nothing, and they are as accurate as a sniper.

The ranger was so excited about catching his first snake that he forgot to put on glasses, and as he gently slid the broom base under the snake it suddenly took fright. The snake spat and the fine spray caught the ranger directly in the eyes.

Realizing what had happened, he quickly washed out his eyes with milk and, feeling as though they were being scrubbed with sandpaper, he was taken straight to hospital and admitted to the emergency ward. Without prompt proper attention he could have gone blind.

It was a powerful and invaluable initiation to snakes. Like Pieter, who was put up a tree and 'threw the buffalo with a

Leatherman', as he put it in his Afrikaans way, he had survived a nasty shock. Next time he would remember to wear glasses when saying hello to Mr *Mfezi*.

I was walking away from the dead impala the python had left behind when suddenly I heard the unmistakable sound of a small helicopter approaching. I watched, a bit irritated, as it came in and flew very low across the reserve. Some pilots take chances, flying low and hoping to show their passengers some wildlife, so I radioed the rangers and told them to get the registration so I could report it.

A call soon came back. 'There is no registration number, Mkhulu. Over.'

'You mean there is no number on the chassis? Over.'

'Affirmative, there is no registration.'

I thumbed the radio's speak dial hard. 'There is a helicopter on the reserve with no registration, all rangers please get the make and colours.'

However, it was moving so quickly we could no longer see it in the sky. It had either disappeared or had landed. I hoped it was the former.

Forty minutes later I had begun to believe that the chopper had flown off, when we heard it again, and through binoculars we saw it flying low and fast, heading east towards the sea. Soon it was miles away, but something nagged at me. What was it doing here for so long?

I immediately phoned all the airports in the area giving the description and asking if anyone knew of a helicopter without registration, but to no avail.

It was exactly eleven o'clock the next morning when I got a very sombre radio call from Vusi, my section ranger.

'Mkhulu, Mkhulu, come in, over.'

'Standing by.'

'You must come here now.'

'Why?'

'I cannot tell you on the radio, please just come.'

Some Zulus hate being the bearer of bad news. I think it goes back to King Shaka's day, when messengers were sometimes killed for reporting what the monarch didn't want to hear. Something bad had happened and Vusi would rather I saw it for myself. He sounded very upset indeed, and from his voice I could tell that something dramatic had happened. My initial thought was that an elephant had died. Possibly even Nana or Frankie.

'Where are you?'

He gave his coordinates.

I saw the vultures circling long before I got there, and my dread intensified.

When I arrived Vusi was standing with two other rangers in the savannah. I could see the huge mound of grey carcass near him. The trees were heavy with vultures.

I got out of the car and looked at the dead animal.

It wasn't Nana or Frankie.

It was my beautiful Heidi, her face hacked open, her horns gone.

I turned away, fighting back tears of black rage and despair. Heidi, the most gentle of giants; Heidi, who would rather run away than hurt anyone; Heidi, who had brought so much joy to people's lives, people who had come from around the world to see her.

I couldn't bear to look at her. My big girl was gone.

Vusi was the first to speak. 'Look at the blood.'

It was like a swimming pool, purplish-red in the sun with scores of rivulets flowing into the cracked arid earth. Huge green-black flies were everywhere.

'They cut the horns off while she was still alive,' said Vusi sadly. 'While her heart was still pumping.'

It was then that I realized what the helicopter had been doing. The swines must have darted Heidi from the air with a sedative, then landed. The reason we didn't hear the shot is because with Heidi incapacitated by drugs, they could stand right over her and muffle the shot with something as mundane as a pillow. Then they quickly hacked the horns off with machetes or a chainsaw without even switching off the chopper's engine, and simply flew away. The whole operation could not have taken more than thirty minutes.

There was nothing we could do, no way to assuage the anger and frustration, and we just stood there looking at each other ineffectually. The poachers were gone and so was our beautiful Heidi.

I traipsed up to the house and told Françoise, who immediately burst into tears. Then I reported the matter to both the police and the Parks authorities.

'It's been a very bad month,' said the Parks ranger, the same man who had removed the other three rhinos after we had lost our first one – the death that had sparked the DRC rhino rescue mission. 'The three rhinos we took from you for safekeeping have also just been killed. We just couldn't protect them. This whole thing is way, way out of hand.'

Perhaps the same poachers had taken all four animals. Who knows? But what I did know was that there were no longer any safe havens.

Heidi's murder was reported in the press and was soon on the Internet. We got messages of condolence from people whose lives she had touched from around the world. Heidi's untimely and violent death affected many people. A pall of gloom descended on Thula Thula.

Coincidentally or not, rumours had recently circulated on the Internet about a Vietnamese government minister in Hanoi claiming that rhino horn had cured his cancer, which undoubtedly would lead to a soaring demand in his country. Also a Vietnamese diplomat was caught on camera taking delivery of contraband rhino horn outside her country's embassy in Pretoria. She bolted for home, claiming diplomatic immunity.

Then we heard some good news. A few days later KZN Wildlife, our Parks authority, captured a group of poachers with a rhino horn in their possession. The gang was as arrogant as hell, threatening revenge for their capture. To them, killing a rhino meant nothing but more dollars in their pockets.

From there, police traced the link to a syndicate in Johannesburg. These were the middlemen, but still pawns in the overall big picture. They too were arrogant, denying complicity even when the evidence was overwhelming, and showing no remorse for their crimes whatsoever.

The poachers were charged and went to court, and then to jail for fifteen years. No doubt their masters would just replace them and carry on as before. The price of rhino horn had gone through the roof and the trade had become way too lucrative to stop.

I began to realize that we probably would never get to the top men. Some were not only protected by their governments; in the Far East at least one government minister was by his own admission an end user. So we had to fight our way up from the bottom. And the bottom was rocky indeed.

But if that is what it took, that is what we would do. Along with many other game reserves all across South Africa, Thula Thula would have to start taking the fight to the poachers.

It was then I received the sad news that the search for Garamba's last four remaining northern white rhinos had failed. They were now extinct in the wild.

The next morning I went out alone and found a quiet spot on a hill at Thula Thula. I looked out over the African bush I loved so much and quietly and sadly paid my respects, bidding a personal goodbye to one of the most incredible creatures that has ever walked the earth.

If ever there was a time when I hit a personal low, that was it.

CHAPTER THIRTY-FOUR

The helicopter lifted into the English sky in the hands of an expert pilot out to practise manoeuvres. It was a beautifully clear day and, with the emerald-green countryside stretched out below him, the pilot adjusted the controls and put the aircraft onto its side in a steep bank. Suddenly at the critical point of the turn, the pilot realized that he had somehow lost all power.

When a helicopter loses power it is still possible to land safely. The blades keep turning and you have a windmill effect, which will bring you safely back to earth, provided that you have enough forward speed.

The pilot strained every sinew to screaming point, desperately trying to muscle the copter the right way round and land. But by the time he righted himself he was already too low, and too slow, and with wry chagrin he realized he was in the famous 'dead man's curve', from which there was no coming back. He was going down and there was nothing he could do about it.

The earth rushed up at him, and the next thing he knew it was much later and he was lying in an open field in the middle of nowhere. He looked across at the mangled wreck of the nearby helicopter, surprised that it wasn't on fire, and then realized that he must have gone right through the heavy perspex windscreen.

He tried to reach for the cellphone in his pocket, but couldn't do it because his hand wouldn't work. So he tried his other arm, but that wouldn't do what it was told either. His legs were the same. Although he didn't know it at the time, he had over a hundred fractures. His face and body had been smashed into pieces and he was surviving on adrenalin alone.

He decided he must try to get help or die where he lay. But to do so he had somehow to crawl on his stomach, his arms trailing uselessly by his side, and with pain searing through every tiny movement of his battered and broken body, he set out on the longest, loneliest journey of his life. For anyone else, even the thought of such an undertaking would have been impossible, but this man was not just anyone else. Inch by excruciating inch he squirmed and writhed, edging his way forward, each yard a triumph, shouting out in pain when he had to, with no one to hear and no one to help him. Driven by raw courage and a deep impulse to succeed against all odds, the same qualities that had made him one of England's most successful and charismatic businessmen, he somehow made it to a country lane and lay there, beyond exhaustion.

Falling in and out of consciousness, he became vaguely aware of people around him and that he was in a helicopter. What he didn't know was that he had already gone into shock and died. Somehow the paramedics pulled him back and got him to a hospital, where he promptly died again on the operating table. Once again an adrenalin injection to the heart brought him back from the dead.

Eight months later, after endless painful reconstructive surgery, he finally left hospital and, banned by his concerned and caring wife from ever flying a helicopter again, he immediately took up GT3 saloon-car racing and started flying around race tracks at 150 miles per hour in Ferraris and Porsches. The man was like someone from a Wilbur Smith novel. We met in London through my good friends Nick Thomas and David Bozas.

At forty-seven years old, Andy Ruhan was a proud Irishman who had created an international business empire from humble beginnings, and he wanted to give something back. We were polar opposites. He was a business tycoon with thousands of staff all over the world, and I was a non-profit conservationist. But that's where the dissimilarities ended. We got on well and Andy quickly grasped the perilous situation facing rhinos in particular, and wild places in general, and came on board with a vengeance.

Generous to a fault for the right cause, he started to plough expertise and funding into vital projects, especially those that involved and uplifted local Zulu communities living near game reserves, taking some of the load off my shoulders. And when he could get away from business, he would fly out from London and spend time at Thula Thula, where we quickly found he had no airs and graces, and was happiest out in the bush in an ancient Land Rover, or sitting around a fire with the staff, just being one of the boys.

He would have his hands full in our new conservation ventures, but that's exactly how he liked it.

Andy was the catalyst for the next stage of our fight for the rhino. He loved the land, he loved the animals and he had the guts and determination to make things happen.

CHAPTER THIRTY-FIVE

By 2009 our area of Zululand was in the grip of a devastating drought that had been slowly creeping up on us for years and was now unleashing its misery. The land came in any colour you wanted, as long as it was brown. From ochre to tan to terracotta or khaki, wherever you looked, it was some shade of bleak rust.

The savannah was as smooth as an old bar-room billiard table, dingy, torn and threadbare. The blades of grass that flourished up to knee-height in the initial spring rains had been chewed down to the roots. There had been no further summer rains to speak of and we had gone into winter with dry dams.

The trees were shorn of leaves as the browsers stretched up further and further, until only the tallest giraffes could reach the leaves. Hundreds of acacia trees were being pushed over by the elephants when they could extend their trunks no higher. Then the buck followed, gorging on the fallen booty until the branches were stripped naked as babies.

There had been no real rain to speak of for seven lean years – which had a stark biblical connotation. Thula Thula was dry and we started losing animals.

The reserve normally gets about thirty-two inches of rain a year, which is perfect for our type of vegetation and the key reason why we can support such large herds of healthy game. So when in one year we got significantly less rain, I didn't think much of it. The following year the rains were more irregular and we noticed the dam levels falling. Then the winters started to get longer, and each year the rain came later and later and when it did, it was less and less. A few meagre drizzles were the highlights of the summer, and it really was dry, but I reasoned that the animals had lived in this type of environment since time immemorial; although we might lose some among the young and the old, we would pull through. Then the underground water tables started to dry up as well, and the new boreholes were only producing trickles.

But it was not only we who were suffering. One morning, a group of Zulu cattle farmers whose scrawny cows had started dying came to the gate, begging me to allow them to graze inside the reserve itself. The fact that the cattle farmers, once extremely hostile to game reserves, had come to us for help and advice showed the special relationship that was starting to flourish between us. They were also our partners in building the Royal Zulu reserve and their requests had to be taken seriously. It showed how far we had come down the conservation road together and, significantly, there was no sense of entitlement in their request whatsoever.

My heart went out to them, these tough men of the outback. We were all in this together. I wished I could assist, but we too were in dire straits. I took them around Thula Thula to show first-hand that we were suffering as much as they were. We were also losing our livelihood. One grizzled and dignified *khehla*, an elder with the flinty sinews of a man who has lived a hard life, summed it up in four words: 'You have no grazing.'

However, I was shocked to see how scrawny the cattle were and we pulled out all the stops to help them. I hired machines to dig deep into the bone-dry riverbanks on their land to try and find some water, in many cases just oozing sand. In Africa, none survive alone.

A sad twist to this was that one cow somehow actually did

manage to break through the fences into the reserve and stagger to one of the last remaining holes of water in the river, where she just lay down and died. Unbeknown to the cow, we had one crocodile left in the reserve, the infamous Smiley. All other resident crocs, usually about twelve of them, had migrated downriver in search of water elsewhere, but Smiley held his patch of liquid turf. And that morning he couldn't believe his luck – 1,000 pounds of prime beef conveniently dropping right in front of him. Smiley was part of the furniture on Thula Thula, and even though several years ago he had killed my beautiful bull terrier, Penny, I hoped he too wouldn't have to leave us as the drought gripped us tighter.

The only creatures that fared well were the predators. Our hyenas had plenty of protein on tap and there were regular sightings of leopard. The smaller cats, the servals and caracals, were also thriving.

It's incredible how nature adapts. As the spring rains failed, pregnant impala ewes would hold in their babies, stretching the gestation period to the absolute limit as starving mothers tried to find food to manufacture enough milk. The browsers, nyala, bushbuck and, to a lesser extent, kudu, regarded the elephants as pied pipers, feeding on the fallen trees in their wake. The elephants fared best as they lived off the trees, and though it was tough for them, they could survive indefinitely as we had so much woodland. Also hanging in were the buffalo, one of Africa's hardiest creatures, although they too were becoming very thin.

Every day we watched as Africa's huge winged scavengers hovered in the thermals high overhead, picking out lunch with their binocular vision. White-backed and lappet-faced vultures and marabou storks became so commonplace feeding on the ground that we barely noticed them any more.

One of the few places where there was a smattering of water

was near the lodges. Skittish animals that would never normally go near people were now queuing up outside our little man-made pools. We have photos of guests actually stroking wild nyala bulls as the apathetic animals slaked their thirst at the waterholes we had built. We used whatever spare water we had to sprinkle the land around the lodges to get a touch of green, which was gobbled up instantly.

One bitingly cold night we lost an entire herd of wildebeest that were so debilitated they just gave up en masse. A major problem with drought is that without any clouds it gets frigid at night. The wildebeest had congregated on the riverbank, the lowest and coldest point on the reserve. When the temperature plummeted to below seven degrees Celsius – freezing by Zulu-land standards – they simply lay down and never stood up again, so weakened were their bodies from lack of food.

The Nseleni River that meanders through Thula Thula was now bone dry. Only a few deeper holes retained some water, one of which Smiley had made his home.

Despite his ever-shrinking domain, Smiley was . . . well, smil-ing as he patrolled the only viable waterhole on the reserve, pick-ing and choosing his dinner from the many visitors. Eventually he just couldn't eat any more and we had to pull some of the car-casses out of the water, which was going putrid because of them.

One of the other reserves nearby had only a single dam and it was completely dry, so we had sunk a borehole for their staff to fill a drinking trough for the animals. However, they didn't have a mobile pump to extract the underground water, so whenever their water ran low they would phone us and we would come and pump for them. But as there had been no requests for help for some weeks, we initially presumed they were all right.

One day I just had a gut feeling that something was not right at the reserve. I was sure they would be needing water by now, so I took a drive over to see what was going on.

When I arrived there were about twenty-five zebra standing listlessly around the front steps of the ranger's house. Others were lying on the barren ground. Elsewhere at least five lay dead.

Behind them were an equal number of wildebeest also not moving – just dazed, confused and dying. It was one of the most pitiful sights I have ever seen. They didn't even move as we walked between them to the front door.

The head ranger came out clutching a large bottle of water and took a long drink as he greeted me. I could not believe it; here was a game ranger, supposedly someone with empathy for the bush, seeing the dead animals and not even noticing them. To compound matters, he took another swig from his bottle.

'Are you thirsty?' I asked.

He nodded. 'It is hot. I'm very thirsty.'

'And the animals?' I asked. 'Are they not thirsty?'

He shrugged. 'This drought is very bad.'

That was it, I lost it. I grabbed him by the shirt, pushing him so hard that he lost his footing. 'You bloody bastard! The water is finished, your animals are dying, and you do nothing, and you stand here drinking in front of them! You useless bastard!'

He scrambled to his feet and it was all I could do not to beat the living daylights out of him and finish it there and then.

'What sort of human being are you?' I said, giving him another violent shove towards the dry, dusty drinking trough. 'Your animals are dying. Why didn't you ask us for water?'

He collapsed and lay there staring at the ground. 'You arsehole, you'd better not be here when I get back,' I shouted back at him as we jumped into the Land Rover, and sped back to Thula Thula to start the borehole pump. Then it was a race back to the ranger's house, and we watched with boiling anger as desperate zebra and wildebeest, now fearless of humans, jostled all around us to get to the liquid trickling agonizingly slowly into the trough. Sadly some were too weak to find the strength to get there. We scooped up water in whatever containers we could find and took it to them. Their tongues were as dry as sandpaper and so swollen that they could barely lap the liquid. Two more died still.

We then did a tour of the reserve and saw that their fence had been kicked down in several places on borders with tribal trust lands, where animals, crazed for water, had smashed their way free. These sections of fencing had not been repaired by the useless excuses for rangers and were now little more than an open invitation to poachers. But even worse, the animals that got out would have died in any event, as there was no water anywhere. I put in a scathing report on the ranger to the authorities and followed it up to make sure he never worked on a game reserve again.

I started to despair; would this drought ever end? The Zulu elders in the area, some in their late seventies, confirmed it was the worst they had ever experienced. No one talked of anything else.

At our luxury tented camp about two miles from our home, a bush pig – one of the most secretive animals in the African bush – started coming out into the open and scaring the hell out of the staff and guests.

A bush pig, or wild boar as it is known in Europe, weighs about 130 pounds, with razor-sharp lower tusks and a bunch of attitude. This one was raiding the refuse bins at night at the camp and claiming the area as its nocturnal territory. Anybody who came anywhere near got charged at. My previous dog, Max, a tough Staffordshire bull terrier, had once got into a fight with one and had been eviscerated within seconds. We managed to break up the fight and David scooped up Max and rushed him to the vet with his innards trailing. The vet just shovelled his stomach back in and sewed him up. It was touch and go whether he would survive. Fortunately, he did. Staffordshire bull terriers conduct themselves like big softies around humans and love children, but they are as tough as they come.

David and I drove down to the camp to find out what was going on.

It didn't take long to locate our answer. The sun had just set when a scream came from outside the kitchen and a staff member hurtled past us, heading for the hills. We bolted over and there was the huge pig, an old female, scoffing away at an upturned refuse bin. It took a cursory look to see what the problem was. A poacher's wire noose-snare had tightened around her body, eating its way deep into the shoulders and ribcage, opening huge suppurating wounds. The poor thing was in pain and couldn't even move her legs properly. She was starved as she couldn't forage properly for food in the wild.

David darted her with a sedative, cut off the wire and treated the wounds with gentian violet antiseptic. The next morning we had a great big purple bush pig ambling around the grounds, still refusing to leave, but no longer aggressive. She was old, so we took pity on her and built a shelter on the edge of the camp for her to sleep in and fed her leftovers from the kitchen. This normally very dangerous wild pig adopted us and lived around the camp for a year until she died peacefully of old age.

In another bizarre incident my mother's accountant, a man named Renier Botha who lives on a game reserve nearby, nearly lost his life trying to help the animals. At the height of the drought he started putting out bundles of alfalfa for a pod of starving hippos living in a small dam near his home. One afternoon the hippos started coming forward as he was emptying a bale of the feed. Watching these dangerous animals very carefully, he reached behind himself to grab another bundle of alfalfa when something pulled it from his hand. He looked around, startled, and standing right behind him was a huge buffalo bull, literally eating out of his hand. Even worse, barely a few yards behind the buffalo were the rest of its herd, completely cutting him off from his vehicle.

He was out in the open with six hippos in front of him and a herd of buffalo behind, completely trapped between two of the most dangerous animals in Africa. Somehow he was still alive, and, reasoning that if they were going to kill him they would have done it already, he kept his head and just kept laying out more alfalfa for the starving animals. Then, while they were busy eating, he casually walked right through the middle of the buffalo herd and somehow reached his vehicle. Drought does strange things to man and beast; it's as if all bets are off and the rule book goes out of the window. Under normal circumstances he would have been a dead man several times over.

Finally, the clouds started to stack up high in the sky. It was late September, spring in South Africa, and a front was moving in, but it had been seven long years and I was not building up hopes. The disappointment would be too bitter to bear.

Then in the afternoon I heard a clap of thunder. Then another. The skies turned dark as obsidian. The clouds banked higher and higher, like skyscrapers in the stratosphere. A jagged streak of lightning, neon in its intensity, was followed by a terrific thunderbolt that could have been heard across the equator. With that the clouds burst and water gushed from the heavens.

I went outside and got soaked to the skin in seconds, absolutely overjoyed. Françoise joined me, and the pulsing water slicked her blonde hair on her face as though she were a mermaid. It was a beautiful sight.

Soon every road, every track, every cranny was a foaming rivulet. The trees, shorn of leaves, first sagged under the deluge, and then started to spring to life. The grasses, chewed to the roots, received the life-giving liquid and started reviving.

For a week it rained on and off. But the earth was so dry it just soaked everything up like a sponge. No matter how much water pelted down, the earth gulped it in without a pause. The Nseleni River still didn't flow. The dams barely rose. The drought had penetrated so far beneath the crust that it seemed as if the water sank straight to the core of the earth.

The weather forecasts were good – more rain was on its way – but a brief respite of sunlight showed just how rapidly nature had repaired itself. The bush was thickening and the plains already showing a sprinkling of emerald. Wild flowers with radiant colours and rich fragrances sprouted everywhere. The animals that had been so listless just days before were gambolling in the savannah.

Eventually, like a great serpent stumbling out of hibernation, the Nseleni started to flow – brown, muddy, swirling with seven years of rotting drought debris – and absolutely magnificent. The dams also started to hold water. The wounds had finally healed.

But that is the wild. Every creature lives for the moment, and when you have survived deprivation that moment has to be savoured. Birds started to sing, antelope pranced in joyous abandon, cicadas chirruped and by the end of the year the land began to breathe again.

Nature had cleansed itself.

CHAPTER THIRTY-SIX

With the death of Mnumzane, whom we eventually and most reluctantly had to put down after he destroyed my Land Rover with the LRA officials aboard, Mabula was now the senior bull elephant on Thula Thula. We had to put Mnumzane down as he was becoming too aggressive, but we later discovered that a nerve in his tusk had been exposed. This had created a huge abscess, which must have been agony for him and was why he became so belligerent. Unfortunately it was not something we could have fixed with surgery. (A full account of Mnumzane's death is given in *The Elephant Whisperer*.)

Mabula was Frankie's son, and he had grown up while I was interacting with his mother and Nana, trying to pacify them during that hostile initial period when they first arrived at the reserve. He was big for his age, with strong developing tusks, but at eighteen years old he was just too young for the role of senior bull. A dominant bull is usually about thirty-five or older. Virtually overnight Mabula was the biggest dude in town by default, and he knew it; and, just as some humans can take a promotion at work too seriously, he started to become arrogant. Even his demeanour as he strolled across the reserve had a certain swagger.

We were waiting on our application to the Parks authorities to allow me to get a mature patriarch to teach these young guns some manners, but it was taking longer than we thought.

Matters came to a head when one of my senior rangers, Promise Dlamini, was taking a game drive with guests and they ran into a truculent Mabula in the middle of the road. Suddenly Mabula came forward at them – not a full-bodied charge, just a warning to get out of the way.

Promise is an experienced ranger and he did all the right things. He backed away slowly, revving the engine noisily and hammering the side of the vehicle, shouting at Mabula to move off. Usually this loud racket works, but not this time. Mabula came at them again, pulling up just in front of the vehicle, stopping short of actually hitting it.

A golden rule in taking game drives is that you watch your Zulu tracker. A tracker sits in a seat welded onto the car's bonnet and he is usually one of our more experienced men of the bush. In fact, most of our trackers have lived their entire lives in the wild. So when your tracker abandons his seat above the front left fender and scrambles over the bonnet to get into the front seat next to you, you know you're in trouble. And this is exactly what happened.

Promise did a magnificent job, calming the passengers, including a crying child, while keeping the vehicle in reverse, just easing out of Mabula's way. At the same time he asked his tracker what the hell he was doing sitting next to him in the vehicle. The tracker looked at him as if he was mad and pointed to Mabula looming massively in the windscreen. Promise had to concede that the tracker had a point.

Then once more Mabula came, but this time he was quicker and butted the vehicle with his tusks. It wasn't a full charge, but it was getting dangerous. At the same time Mabula backed off, surprise showing clearly on his face. He had never felt steel before and was confused by the strange sensation this hard cold substance had on his tusks. He paused to rub one tingling tip with his trunk and Promise saw that this was the fraction of a second he need to accelerate away, much to the relief of the guests, who now had a great yarn to tell the folks back home. Promise reacted magnificently, and the whole episode is on YouTube, filmed by one of the tourists.

Not long afterwards Mabula was involved in another charge, this time with a ranger doing his first game drive. Initially the ranger also did all the right things, reversing while shouting and banging the side of the vehicle in an attempt to shoo Mabula off. I just happened to be on foot about fifty yards away, watching with some concern as Mabula kept worrying the game drive vehicle. Suddenly there was a big problem. Just as Mabula was gaining momentum, the ranger stalled the Land Rover and the engine went silent. This changed the dynamics of the situation radically as now the ranger had no escape. Mabula wanted him to leave, to get out of his space, but he couldn't. I watched, horrified, as Mabula asserted his authority with a mock charge. If the Landy didn't get out of the way anything could happen next, but the ranger just couldn't get it started.

I ran towards them, calling him. Mabula, who must have recognized my voice from when he was much younger, stopped. By lifting his trunk and sniffing the air, he picked up my scent. His reaction showed that he had indeed recognized me, and he paused again as I shouted his name. Thankfully, he dropped his attitude and I managed to shepherd him away from the game drive vehicle simply by talking to him and chastising him gently. Even I was surprised at how well he remembered me after all these years.

He had now interfered with two vehicles, which was cause for concern. Young bulls are like boisterous young men, and they must have a proper role model, a patriarch, to settle them down. That's why shooting dominant bulls so often leads to rogue behaviour in younger bulls. You are removing figures of authority and stability. It was clear that we desperately needed a strong father figure on the reserve.

I again approached the authorities to speed up my permission to get a mature bull. They agreed – and it was not a moment too soon.

We had already put the word out that we were looking for a patriarch and we got a reply from a reserve in the far north of the country. He had a stable personality and would be perfect for us.

He was thirty-four years old and his name was Magobisa, which means 'the one that bends'. He broke a tusk in a fight many years ago, but instead of snapping off, the tusk had been bent upwards at an angle, hence the name. However, over the years the name was shortened to Gobisa, which means 'bend over' and does not have quite the same dignified connotation.

Gobisa was scheduled to arrive in a couple of weeks' time and we had a Herculean amount of work to do to make thousands of hectares of new area, which we had very recently acquired in partnership with the local chief and his tribe, elephant-proof. We needed not only to drop all the fences joining Thula Thula to the new land, but also to strengthen and electrify all of our extended boundaries. This was an enormous task and we had to work around the clock to get it done on time.

The situation was aggravated when much of our new electrified fence mysteriously disappeared, poles and all. One day there was a beautiful new electric fence and the next day it was completely gone. Ngwenya was in charge of security and he said he would deal with it. And deal with matters of security he could. I once found him with a poacher he had just arrested. The poacher's eye was swollen shut and his lip was twice its normal size.

'Did you hit him?' I asked Ngwenya.

'No,' came the implausible reply. 'I found him like that.'

This time, though, the thefts were repeated several times. Then suddenly Ngwenya disappeared.

I knew Ngwenya well. I knew he was not the thief, as it would have been too alien to his character. But where had he gone?

I asked around and fellow rangers told me Ngwenya had left because he believed he had failed us. The thefts had happened on his watch and despite his best efforts he had been unable to prevent it. I managed to contact him, told him it wasn't his fault and asked him to please come back to work. He politely refused. The shame of failure in his mind was too much. It was the Zulu equivalent of the ancient Samurai code. There was nothing I could do to entice Ngwenya, one of my most trusted men, to return. We still stay in contact and I'm hoping one day he will come back to where he belongs. Honour is something you cannot buy.

We never caught the thieves, and we finished replacing the stolen fences in the nick of time.

Then the big day came. Andy Ruhan flew out for the occasion and Gobisa eventually arrived at midnight in a huge truck. He had travelled over 500 miles to his new home.

CHAPTER THIRTY-SEVEN

Gobisa emerged from the transport truck and stepped confidently into the *boma*, a 300 square foot corral surrounded by poles nearly 10 feet high and electrified wire running at 8,000 volts. He would stay in the *boma* perhaps only a day, to settle him in and let the travel sedatives wear off. Then he would be released into the wider reserve.

He was a magnificent specimen – huge, powerful, imposing and regal, just perfect for what we needed, and everybody was excited to see him. Our problems with Mabula's bullying were soon going to be over. They would meet, Gobisa would size him up and demand respect, and if he didn't get it, Mabula would be hammered into submission. If after defeat he still resisted, he could even be killed, for among males in the elephant world, there can be only one leader. We all hoped Mabula would submit without getting seriously injured, and thereafter lead a life of subservience to his new patriarch and become one of the *askaris* – one of the younger bulls who traditionally accompany a dominant bull.

The first thing the giant Gobisa did after his fourteen-hour journey was shake his massive head, sniff the alien surroundings and stagger over to the water trough, where he noisily slurped down nearly a hundred litres of fresh water. Then he started tucking into the piles of alfalfa we had put out for him. After a while he seemed settled. The job was done.

It was congratulations all round and we went off to bed, satisfied that our new big boy was safe and sound.

I was asleep when the radio call eventually woke me.

'Standing by.'

'Mkhulu,' said the breathless guard at the *boma*, 'Gobisa's gone, he is out. He's gone.'

'What?'

'He is gone, Mkhulu, he went straight through the fence.'

'Straight through an 8,000-volt fence?' I replied, not believing what I was hearing. 'Are you sure? Was the power on?'

'Yes, Mkhulu, I checked the power; he smashed the fence into pieces.'

I dressed quickly and ran for the Land Rover. Ten minutes later I was standing at the *boma* in the dark, staring at a huge break in the fence by the light of my torch. The amount of damage was unbelievable. This was some elephant.

He was heading south-east, so with adrenalin pumping I woke up Andy, and we started searching for him. Vusi was out in another vehicle, David in another. Over the radio I heard Vusi waking staff and getting everybody up. We had to find Gobisa before he made the boundary and smashed his way out of the reserve. To compound matters, we found that the tracking device delivered with Gobisa had a part missing and wasn't working, so we were searching blind.

Eventually Vusi came on the radio and gave us the bad news. He had found the hole where Gobisa had burst through Thula Thula's electric boundary. It was our worst nightmare; he was heading straight towards the village. The problem, though, was that there were no roads where he was going, so we could not drive to him, and following an angry bull elephant on foot at night would be a death sentence in the making. Andy and I did a quick patch job on the hole in the fence and got the power going again so nothing else could get out of the reserve. But there was nothing further we could do. We would have to wait for morning.

At 2 a.m. the phone rang. It was a farmer, one of our neighbours about five miles away.

'You won't believe what's happened,' he said, getting straight to the point. 'I woke up and went outside to take a pee, and there was this bloody great elephant walking through my garden. I thought I was hallucinating for a moment. Is it one of yours?'

Well, at least we knew in which direction Gobisa was going. He had skirted the village and was heading east. I thanked him for the call and said we would be there in a few hours.

We were up before dawn, and the phones were already coming alive as the trail of destruction that Gobisa had left behind him started filtering through. It was one of the most incredible animal escapes I'd ever heard of. The elephant, still drugged from the journey in the back of the truck, had smashed his way out of Thula Thula and straight through two neighbouring reserves. That meant he had burst through six electrified fences, each packing 8,000 volts, in the space of a couple of hours. That he could do so in his semi-incapacitated state beggared belief. This has to be some sort of a pachyderm record.

I immediately phoned my good friend and possibly one of the finest wildlife capture experts around, Dave Cooper, who had been part of our Congo rhino rescue team that had been bulldozed into oblivion by bureaucracy.

Dave wasn't fazed by what I told him. But then, he never really is.

'That's bad news, Lawrence. But how's this for good luck? I have two transport trucks and a crane right here with me at the moment, and if we catch him today, I can bring him straight back to Thula Thula. Tomorrow will be too late – the truck will be gone. It's now or never.'

It was an incredible stroke of good fortune. To organize a top-flight elephant capture team can take days, if not weeks, and sadly it's sometimes easier just to shoot the animal on the run before someone gets killed. But here we had one ready and raring for instant action.

That was the only bit of good news we had received all day. There was no doubt KZN Wildlife Parks authorities would have to shoot Gobisa if we didn't bring him in. He was, after all, heading through populated areas.

Fortunately we were able to get Gobisa's tracking collar working enough so that we could follow his movements. David Bozas operated the controls, but although it was bleeping, which indicated that Gobisa was nearby, it was not indicating in which direction.

Dave Cooper managed to contact his helicopter pilot, Vere van Heerden, who – again, as absolute luck would have it – was available and could be airborne in a few hours. There is nothing like good friends who will go out of their way to help when you are really in the dwang. Darting an elephant from the air is a rare skill. One of Dave's previous pilots had been killed by the curse of low-level flying: electric cables. Another good friend of Dave's had recently leaned out of a helicopter to fire a dart, somehow without being attached securely to the chopper, and had plunged headlong to his death. The deaths of these good men shocked the game reserve community. Aerial bush capture is a rough, tough undertaking and there are very few who do it well.

Dave arrived in Vere's copter, followed shortly afterwards by the KZN Wildlife capture team who had driven down from the Umfolozi Game Reserve with the transport truck and crane. Andy and David Bozas were with me, and my sons Jason and Dylan came up from Durban to help, always happy for an excuse to be in the bush.

As soon as the capture team was in place, Dave and Vere took off again and the rescue was on.

We tried to follow the bleeping tracking collar from the Land Rover, but were getting nowhere. Every now and again Dave and Vere would hover low over us and we would point in the direction we thought Gobisa was heading. Then they would soar off, only to return later with Dave shaking his head in the cockpit.

The fact that there was no sign of Gobisa despite us receiving regular bleeps from the tracking collar was extremely confusing. Then Vere, one of the best bush pilots in the world, did something completely counter-intuitive. Flying just above us, he literally flipped the chopper over and went off in the opposite direction. He said that in his previous experiences with modern tracking devices they had sometimes given a reverse reading when held vertically by the user.

He was right.

'We've found him,' Dave's calm voice came in over the radio. 'But he's in some seriously thick bush. We have to get him closer to the road so the capture truck can get to him.'

We could see the helicopter about a half a mile away and there below it stood Gobisa, staring defiantly at the chopper as it came at him low, menacing and as noisy as a swarm of wasps on steroids.

This was bush flying at its very best, requiring steady nerves, deft handling and plenty of courage. Knowing that an elephant will almost always run from a helicopter, Vere was hovering noisily only ten or thirteen feet above the ground, trying to turn Gobisa around. Then Gobisa did something that was incredible. He flared his ears, trumpeted to the heavens – and charged straight at the helicopter. I caught my breath. The courage of the elephant was magnificent to watch. Vere yanked the controls to get out of the enraged elephant's way, as Gobisa swivelled on a coin to face them again.

Vere once again moved in, trying to nudge him closer to the road. Gobisa charged once more as Vere started dancing the chopper like a ballerina to keep out of the way. Neither Dave nor Vere, who between them have experienced pretty much all the South African bush can throw at you, had ever seen this before. Each time they came down at the elephant, he flared his ears, lifted his trunk and charged.

The capture team on the trucks was cheering each charge. Nobody had ever seen anything like it.

'Mkhulu – now this is an elephant,' one shouted to me.

Eventually Gobisa veered off and found the entrance to a ravine about a mile long and perhaps about twenty yards wide, and disappeared from our view. Dave could see by his mannerisms that Gobisa was instantly more comfortable in the protected ravine. He had trees above him and knew he was somewhere the vile giant wasp couldn't get to him.

Now Dave was facing a dilemma. If he darted him in the ravine we would never get him out. But if he didn't dart Gobisa today and get him to Thula Thula, the elephant would be shot by the Parks authorities on sight. It was a cruel catch-22.

Then Dave noticed a bit of a gap in the ravine, a level area from which we could operate. Gobisa was heading towards it. Perhaps there was a chance . . . it was a tight shot taken from a hovering helicopter, and the window of opportunity would be open for only a few seconds.

We heard the dart gun bark.

Dave's voice came over the radio as if discussing the weather. 'He's down. Bring the truck and equipment over.'

Fortunately, Gobisa fell well. But this was not just pure fluke. Dave had shot the dart into Gobisa's flank with a precision that you can only be born with. This was way beyond any textbook stuff.

We drove into the bush and reversed the truck to the edge of the rocky ravine. The capture teams immediately climbed down to the fallen giant. Andy, Dave and I, together with David Bozas and my two sons, Jason and Dylan, followed them.

'We'll have to pull him out with the crane,' said Dave, walking over from where the helicopter had landed between some trees. 'But first we have to clear a path. We have to get every rock, every tree, every obstacle out of the way to give us a clear route to pull him along.'

That was easier said than done. It was tough work, chain-sawing down trees and smashing rocks with hammers to clear a passage through which we could winch Gobisa free. It took time, and we were getting close to Gobisa's wake-up 'call'. Dave injected another dose of M99, the only drug that will keep an elephant sedated long enough to load it into a truck.

But it was taking us far longer than we thought, and all of a sudden Gobisa's ears began moving; the second tranquillizer was starting to wear off. Dave reluctantly injected him again, while everybody upped the pace.

'I can't just keep giving him *jovas* [injections],' said Dave, worry etched on his brow. 'It's too much; if I carry on he might die. We have to get him out now.'

I nodded. 'He'll be shot dead if we don't get him out of here. The authorities will never allow any elephant to be this close to human settlements.'

As if to reinforce that, a local famer arrived, his face brick-red, and it wasn't from sunburn. He was spitting mad.

'What do you guys think you're doing? I saw that elephant on the road earlier. It's going to smash some poor guy's car. What the hell is all this about?'

I explained our predicament, but for some reason he kept ranting on about how someone was going to get hurt on the road, which was half a mile away.

Eventually David Bozas had enough and stormed over to him.

'If you don't shut up you're the one who's going to get hurt,' he shouted at him at point-blank range. 'What the hell do you think we're trying to do? You think we're just playing around here? That we're doing this for fun?'

David's fists were balled and, knowing him, if the farmer so much as opened his mouth again he was going down. Discretion, though, is the better part of valour, and the man quickly apologized and walked away, muttering under his breath something about 'motorists being in danger'.

'David,' I said when it was over, 'I'm very disappointed in you.'

'Yes, I know, boss. I'm sorry, I'm really sorry, but I lost my temper. The guy was such an arsehole.'

I shook my head in elaborate mock-sadness.

'I'm disappointed because in the old days you would have just smacked that idiot. Now you mince up for a nice cosy little chat. What's all this touchy-feely stuff about?'

'*Yebo* – you're getting *madala* [old], David,' jibed one of the Zulu rangers.

David, whose nickname in Zulu is Escoro, which means boxer or fighter, burst out laughing.

He had said what we all thought, anyway.

CHAPTER THIRTY-EIGHT

By the time we returned from the confrontation with the farmer to the motionless grey hulk that was Gobisa, the rescue teams had wrapped broad nylon straps around his feet and were preparing to use the crane to drag him out of the ravine.

'This is the worst part,' said Dave Cooper. 'If he gets hurt by a rock he may crack a rib. Or if a tree stump snags him, he could be internally injured.'

As he spoke the crane started grinding. Gobisa lurched forward a couple of yards, then suddenly his tusk dug into the ground, his six-ton body pinned by a shaft of ivory. Andy and David grabbed shovels and quickly and carefully dug the tusk free. Dave, against all his instincts, reluctantly injected another sedative.

'This is the last one I can do,' he said. 'Otherwise I'll kill him. Absolutely no more!'

Slowly, inch by inch, fraction by fraction, Gobisa was winched towards the flatbed truck. Gradually he slid forward. He bounced over rocks, he flattened shrubs, he was pulled over stumps, but there was nothing we could do but keep winching, cross our fingers and hope for the best.

After what seemed an age, we got him to the edge of the truck. The crane straightened, took the weight and then winched him up high into the air. This proud bull elephant was now hanging upside down, dangling dangerously from his feet. It looked so undignified.

As they lowered him gently onto the vehicle's open deck and settled him in, the driver quickly keyed the ignition and gingerly moved forward.

It was a painful journey, slow and perilous, with rangers from the rescue team literally hanging on to the elephant as we crawled our way home.

I drove ahead to the *boma* with David, Jason and Dylan, while Andy flew in with Dave and Vere in the helicopter.

'Does your wife allow you to go in a helicopter since your accident?' I said, nudging the boys for effect as he got out. 'Our silence is going to cost you, big time.'

'But I was just a passenger,' he protested, 'and it was a very short flight.'

Suddenly we noticed that the repairs to the *boma* fence that were needed after the previous breakout hadn't been completed. The bottom strand of electricity had not been attached to the poles.

'What's the problem?' Andy asked, seeing my expression.

'They haven't secured the bottom electric strand. There's no way this *boma* will keep him in without it.'

'OK,' said David Bozas. 'Let's get the wire in.'

'There's no time,' I said.

'Like hell. Let's go, go, go!' he said, mimicking my way of spurring rangers on.

David grabbed a roll of cable, and with hammers, drills and curses he, Andy and the rest of the team got to work. Using the bare minimum of tools they somehow did it, wiring more than five hundred yards of fencing in about ten minutes. I looked at Andy with amazement. Here was a true business mogul, a captain of industry, not only getting his hands dirty with the rest, but leading the charge. But he's just that type of guy, working harder and faster than the toughest labourer and loving it, doing whatever he could to help the elephant. Perhaps he recognized a kindred spirit in Gobisa.

Gobisa arrived on the flatbed, surrounded by guards and rangers who no doubt would have had to jump for their lives if he suddenly woke up. The truck was too wide to get through the *boma* entrance, so now we had to break down a section of fence to ease it in. The crane gently hoisted Gobisa upside down off the truck and laid him on the ground in the centre of the *boma*. When the truck reversed out, we quickly put the fence back up, praying that the sedated elephant wouldn't suddenly stir.

We needn't have worried. Gobisa was out for the count, knocked flat by a succession of sedatives that would have killed most creatures on this planet. But it was something we had been forced to do. If we hadn't, he would have been shot dead and for that alone it was worth taking the risk.

In fact, the worry now was that instead of waking up too soon, he would never wake up at all.

Dave Cooper gave him the reverse injection.

Usually this is instantaneous. For example, after we had treated Nana's eye, as soon as the vets thrust in the needle we had to sprint for the Land Rovers. We had about a ten-second start.

But Gobisa was so drugged up that he didn't stir for a few minutes. We moved outside the *boma* fence and silently held our collective breath. Then his great head moved. Slowly it lifted as he took a look around. He started to stagger up, stumbling to his feet like a drunken sailor with the worst hangover imaginable. When he finally got upright, he stood there swaying gently.

Thank God he was back.

I thanked the capture team, and then bid goodbye to Dave and Vere, who left in the helicopter. Then I asked everyone else to move away from the *boma* so Gobisa wouldn't see a crowd of humans before him when he fully woke.

I watched as he stood unsteadily for a while before moving over to the drinking trough. He submerged his trunk and took the longest drink I have ever seen in my life. Elephants can go without water for days, but when they drink they do so in style, taking up to 200 litres in a single go. He drank and drank. He had been on the run for twenty-four hours, charged a helicopter and then taken a near-lethal dose of tranquillizers. No wonder he was a mite thirsty.

I walked up to the fence, talking to him as I had done to Nana when she and her family were first in the *boma* – the same *boma* he now stood in.

'Gobisa, this is your new home. There is plenty of food and water here. There are also lots of pretty girls here. You will have *askaris* that will follow and respect you here. They will love you as a father. You will have lots of children and a good life here.'

Gobisa of course didn't understand English, and I could not speak elephant, but intention and intonation can go a long way with understanding.

Gobisa looked at me, and suddenly I realized that he intended to run again. The message from him was loud and clear: 'I am leaving.' My heart jumped, but I tried to stay calm.

'OK, so you are going, then, but listen to me. If you go out of the next fence, if you do what you did before, and you go to where the helicopter was, they will kill you. You must not go past the next fence, you cannot go out of Thula Thula. Everything you need is here,' I repeated.

Many game rangers believe that elephants have some kind of telepathic ability, and I certainly hoped so, because he really needed to get the message!

He kept looking at me, then turned a fraction and, without warning, built up speed and hammered right into the fence with a strength that left me absolutely aghast. I could almost feel the pain myself as the voltage shuddered through him. Sparks flew and the thick poles and cables buckled.

And this is an over-drugged elephant, I thought. What could he do if he was fit and well?

I took out my 9mm pistol and fired three shots into the ground, but still he kept coming at the fence, directly in front of me. I was wasting my time with the shots, so I put the gun down, quickly moved away and watched, amazed, as he grabbed the top of the nearest pole with his trunk and kicked hard at the electric cable on the bottom of the fence. Despite the 8,000 volts surging through his six-ton body, he wouldn't let go. He kicked again. The *boma* fence, as sturdy a structure as you could wish, folded like rotten firewood and fell in a shower of sparks. Gobisa stamped over the torn heavy-duty wiring and smashed poles and kept running. I watched helplessly as he disappeared into the gloom.

I was stunned. After all he had been through, he still could knock down a fence that would hold almost anything else on this planet. He was gone, just like that. This truly was a special elephant.

But maybe, just maybe, he would stay within the reserve. It was our, and his, only chance.

I drove back to the lodge where Andy and the gang were at the bar chugging some well-deserved beers.

'We heard the shots,' said Andy. 'What happened?'

'He's gone.'

Then one of the rangers asked, 'What do you think?'

I didn't look up. 'I've got this ice-cold beer in front of me,' I replied. 'The only thing I'm thinking about at the moment is the next one.'

CHAPTER THIRTY-NINE

Luck was finally on our side.

This time Gobisa did not smash his way out of the reserve, as he had done the day before. He did not try to beat the pachyderm record of six electric fences in succession.

If he had, that would have been the end. He would have been shot on sight by the authorities. Instead he stayed away from the boundary fences and remained on the reserve, where he moved deep into a thickly wooded valley and went to ground like an outlaw.

I phoned Gobisa's original owners to let them know what had happened. They were astonished at his behaviour. He had never broken through an electric fence before, they told me. Well, they may have been surprised, but not as much as I was. He had expertly smashed through a succession of fences in the past twenty-four hours while suffering from the mother of all hangovers. Not bad for a novice escaper.

They offered to send out someone who knew Gobisa well, a man who had been in the bush working with elephants for forty-five years. His name was Ndlovu, which fittingly means 'elephant' in Zulu, and his tribe was also called the Ndlovu. All Zulu tribes have praise names – a *tagazela* – which is usually in honour of a famous ancestor, often an ancient chief of the tribe. The Ndlovu tribe's *tagazela* is Katcheni, which is what we called our new expert.

Katcheni looked every inch the tough veteran of the bush that he was. Short, sinewy and as hard and impressive as a tambotie tree, he turned out to be one of the most interesting people I have met. Katcheni had never seen the inside of a school; everything he had learned he had done so first-hand.

'Gobisa knows I am here,' he said as we shook hands Zulu style, with a shake and a thumb clasp. 'He knew when I got here. I too know where he is. His spirit is big.'

Incredibly, he then described Gobisa's exact hiding place. I was gobsmacked.

I took him down to meet David, who was keeping watch on the valley where Gobisa had gone to ground. David hadn't moved from his post, not even to come to the lodge for a drink of iced water in the midday sun. His sense of responsibility and loyalty wouldn't let him.

Katcheni asked David and I to show him Gobisa's spoor, and we discovered that he was an expert tracker, of which there were very few indeed left in Africa. He showed me how we could tell by the way Gobisa was dragging his hind feet that the effects of the sedative had not yet worn off. He could tell from the footprint depressions whether Gobisa had either stopped to listen, or whether he had stopped to catch scent drifting on the wind. You will never get that experience from any science book. It was fantastic to learn from him.

Gobisa had now truly gone into hiding, foraging at night and resting during the day, even covering his dung to try and disguise any hint of his presence. He was operating as a Special Forces soldier behind enemy lines. With good reason, as we were soon to find out.

The following day the wind carried Katcheni's scent into the ravine. Gobisa picked it up and came out. Katcheni was sitting in a Land Rover and Gobisa walked straight up, around the vehicle, and then back into the bush. David was outside the vehicle before he realized Gobisa was on top of them and had to move quickly, keeping the Land Rover between him and the huge elephant as he came round.

'He came out to greet me,' said Katcheni when I arrived shortly afterwards. 'He is happy I am here.'

Katcheni then outlined what had happened to Gobisa.

'You have to go inside his head,' he told me. 'Otherwise you will not know. Elephants have a very strong spirit.'

I nodded.

'Gobisa arrives in this strange place, and when he is put in the *boma* he smells elephants, and he knows immediately that he is trespassing in another bull's territory.'

As he said that I remembered seeing Mabula close to the *boma* when Gobisa arrived.

'He also knows that the dominant bull will come looking for him,' he continued, 'and then he will be in a fight for his life. But he is weak from the drugs, and he knows he cannot defend himself. He needs time to recover, so he decides to put distance between himself and the dominant bull until he feels strong again.

'But there is this barrier with electric teeth in front of him, the fence. He is scared of the pain from the fence, but he is even more scared of fighting a bull elephant, which may kill him. So he smashes his way out. Once he has been through one fence the others mean nothing, so he just keeps going until he finds a place where there is no sign of the other bull.

'Then, just when he thinks he has escaped, a terrifying machine comes at him from the sky and charges him again and again, never stopping. He has never seen a helicopter before. He tries to run, but it follows him, so he decides to stand and fight, and charges, but he cannot reach it. So he runs again and finds the ravine to hide in. Then he hears a bang from the dart gun and there is pain. He cannot stand any more, so he falls down.

'Then he wakes up in the same place he was before, in the same *boma*, back in the other bull's territory again. So he breaks out again. But this time, although he is still afraid of meeting the big bull elephant, he is even more afraid of the noisy machine that comes at him from the sky.

'He thinks to himself; I know elephants. But I do not know this machine. I will rather fight the elephant. But he is sick and needs to get better first, so he is hiding in the bush here. Every night he will come out for a while and learn more about where he is. He will smell the other elephants, and sniff their dung to see how many males there are, and how many females, and he will collect all the information he can about Mabula.'

I explained to Katcheni that when I realized Gobisa was about to break out, I told him to stay in Thula's boundaries, where he would be safe.

Katcheni nodded. To him, this was not even a discussion. He understood and repeated what he had said earlier: 'Elephants have a very strong spirit, and their spirit will find your spirit.'

Katcheni's summary of what would happen was uncannily accurate. Gobisa did everything exactly as the wise Zulu bush maestro predicted, coming out in the dark, sniffing the dung of the other elephants and getting closer to the herd. Every night he would foray further and further until he was barely half a mile from the main herd, watching and waiting.

'He will now know from his dung that the big elephant here is a youngster, and not as big as him,' said Katcheni a few days later. 'He will also know that there are beautiful girls and plenty of good food and water here. Soon he will come out and fight.'

But, just as Gobisa had sniffed out the herd, Mabula had sniffed out Gobisa. He was now aware that there was a strange big male in his domain. And he didn't like it.

Even though Gobisa was getting braver as his health returned, he still stayed in the bush in the valley during the day. Mabula would pace up and down the edge of the ravine, daring Gobisa to come out. He too was ready for a fight, and he would do anything he could to protect his newly won territory and his females.

There was going to be an almighty clash.

CHAPTER FORTY

It happened the following day.

Mabula had been pacing up and down the edge of the ravine as he did every day, when suddenly Gobisa decided the time was right and came out from the thick bush where he had been hiding. At last he felt he was strong and well enough to fight a deciding battle.

They stared at each other for a long while. I was at my house when I got a call over the radio from David simply saying, 'They're wrestling.'

I drove down as fast as I could. On the way I passed Frankie and Nana leading the herd in the opposite direction; they didn't want their precious family anywhere near this clash of the titans and were getting them as far away as possible.

It was a hugely impressive sight: slow, powerful, awesome and surpassing any other fight on this earth. It was as if two locomotives collided, then stopped, and collided again. The fight wasn't as short, sharp and savage as I thought it would be, but it certainly started that way before settling into an endurance competition of sorts.

The two giants stared malevolently at each other, circling, and then came at each other with enough force to give the planet a migraine.

They wrestled like giant sumo fighters. One would retreat, gain some traction and then lunge forward. Then the other would initiate contact. Supremacy was measured in yards gained and power displayed.

Although Mabula was a good eight inches shorter, and this was his first fight, he gave a hell of an account of himself, and while it was vital that Gobisa won, I was very proud of him.

Each clash lasted for a couple of muscle-jarring minutes. Every now and again, exhausted by the sheer intensity of it all, they would break for a drink of water. Sometimes during the longer breaks they would even eat.

Then resume. Then break. Then resume.

For forty-eight hours they did this, stopping only when it was too dark and resuming at dawn. The ferocity of some of the contacts still gives me a headache just recalling them.

Towards the end of the first day Katcheni, who was watching the fight with us, spoke.

'Gobisa is winning,' he said, and even though I loved Mabula, this is exactly what I wanted to hear. 'You will know it is over when he places his trunk on Mabula's *umthondo* [penis] and flicks it. He is saying, "This thing is finished. You will not need this any more, the females are mine now."'

That's exactly what happened.

During the fight the two younger bulls, Mandla and Ilanga, the *askaris*, had been standing on one side behind Mabula. As the tide ebbed against their champion they slowly eased over to Gobisa's side. And when Gobisa finally kept giving Mabula the derogatory flick, they were all standing behind the new patriarch. It was a classic case of 'The king is dead; long live the king'.

Katcheni came up to me. 'My work here is done. I must go home.'

I thanked him from my heart. It's good to know there are still such people around, true men of the wilderness. He had been invaluable. Although he had probably never read a book in his life, his knowledge of the bush was encyclopedic. Above all, he understood the spirituality of the wild, and especially of elephants, and I learned a lot from him. Like the elephants that he loved, Katcheni too had a strong spirit.

We shook hands. '*Hamba gahle umfowethu*,' I said – go well, my brother.

We now finally had a role model, and what a fine specimen he was. Gobisa took up the patriarchal position behind the herd, which not only showed his dominance but also ensured that he could sniff whenever a female came into oestrus and make sure that none of the *askaris* could sneak in for a bit of hanky-panky without him knowing.

However, one morning a week later, to our absolute astonishment, we saw Mabula tearing after Gobisa along the ridge overlooking our home. This thundering chase went on for nearly three miles, with Gobisa seemingly running for his life. Suddenly Mabula appeared to be the head honcho again.

We couldn't believe it. It appeared as though Gobisa had literally abandoned ship. No one could understand why, and our entire plan to provide a mature role model for the *askaris* was now in tatters. Would Mabula revert to his petulant teenage self? What role model would this prove to be for our young males?

Thankfully it didn't last for long. A few days later one of the females came into oestrus and Gobisa returned and fought Mabula violently to reclaim his dominance. Without a murmur, Mabula meekly rejoined the *askaris*. Once more it was a case of 'Long live the king'.

To this day one thing still amazes me. After his second escape from the *boma*, Gobisa broke down several internal fences in the reserve. But he never again approached an external fence, meaning he never went outside of the reserve again. The internal and external fences are identical, and he didn't know his way around, so how did he know which fences he could go through, and which he should not? Could it be that he understood me when I told him not to go out of Thula's boundary fences just before he smashed out of the *boma*? There is no doubt that I somehow connected with him at the time, I knew it and he felt it, and the fact is that against all odds he has respected the boundaries ever since.

Stranger things have happened in the bush, and maybe in time these things will prove to be not so mysterious at all.

CHAPTER FORTY-ONE

After Heidi's death, I was determined to get more rhino. Thula Thula was part of the ancestral breeding grounds of both black and white rhino, and I vowed that we would never allow that to change. We weren't going to be scared off by thugs with automatic weapons and helicopters; in fact, we would take the fight to them, and I had some ideas that could help swing the odds in our favour. Rough, tough anti-poaching strategies inside the reserve, combined with community involvement outside.

I put the word out that we were looking, and soon got a call from the Moholoholo wildlife rehabilitation centre in the northeast of South Africa asking if we would take in two orphaned babies.

Both had lost their mothers, one to a poacher and one to a fight with bull rhino. The first was discovered next to the butchered carcass of its dehorned mother, the other found wandering alone in the bush. Both were still suckling and barely alive.

I was pleased to take them and with a generous American donor to help us, we accepted them unhesitatingly. We may have lost in the Congo, but new battle lines were being drawn against the poachers in game reserves all over South Africa, and the fight to protect Thula Thula was just beginning.

These babies were symbolic to me, a reminder of what can happen when the world turns its back as it did in the Congo. Every day their lives would be in danger and protecting them would, I hoped, be a testing ground and perhaps even a blue-print for conservationists of the future. The only way forward is to defend our fellow travellers on this marvellous, but some-times insane, planet, as aggressively as we would protect our families. Or our countries.

In African conservation you seldom win any war. Instead you win breathing space to hope that sanity will prevail. Often it doesn't, and the killing starts again. As I write this, 440 rhino a year are killed in South Africa for their horns. That's a new dead rhino every nineteen hours. Poachers are being shot dead in what are becoming military-style contacts as the battle rages. Sadly, game rangers have also started dying in increasing num-bers as the violence ratchets up.

The two young rhinos, a male and a female, travelled to Thula Thula with Françoise and arrived one hot, arid afternoon. They were so cute they brought a smile even to the toughest ranger's face. They shuffled out of the truck like big armour-clad babies, unsure of their steps and looking to us for reassurance, their tiny myopic eyes blinking as they entered a strange new world. I felt like giving them a big hug as a welcome. I think all of us did.

They were already called Thabo, meaning happiness, and Nthombi, which is Zulu for girl, and we kept the names. They were our hope for the future, and they would have a permanent handler and armed guards with them around the clock. They would never walk a step in their lives without being watched.

Because the slaughter was on such a vast scale, you could not insure rhino any more. These increasingly scarce animals now cost a small fortune. The price of an adult white rhino is about $45,000 and a black rhino as much as $100,000. A dead rhino is not only a planetary tragedy; it is a fiscal wallop to conserva-tionists, who seldom have any black in their bank balances.

Their handler came with them to make sure they blended seamlessly into their new homes. She was a pretty young woman from Bristol in the UK, some 6,000 miles away, and looked like the classic English rose with her porcelain complexion and shiny cheeks. But that's where the similarity ended. Alyson McPhee was as African as the burning sun. Every morning she would wander off into the bush with the babies, as we called them, wearing shorts, T-shirt and rubber flip-flops, returning only at dusk. The bush and the rhino babies were her life. Alyson, a qualified veterinary nurse, loved the babies like her own, and God help anyone who came near them with anything but good in their heart. Thabo and Nthombi loved her in return, and when they were very young and still suckling, they would burst into her tent in the *boma* and take up residence when they weren't out in the bush. It was hilarious watching Alyson scrambling out of the way of these two prehistoric baby juggernauts.

Thabo and Nthombi were joined by two rescued baby warthogs that had also been orphaned and were released on Thula Thula by the same organization that gave us George, my favourite rogue bushbaby. The warthogs, which Alyson gave the very British names of Betty and Denise, were attracted by the milk that she fed the rhinos in big bowls, and soon learned to steal a share of the bounty. But this came at some risk, and on more than one occasion I saw a flying warthog as Betty or Denise somersaulted high into the air off the snout of an irritated rhino. They also had to be nimble to survive, for when the baby rhinos finished feasting they simply collapsed where they stood and went to sleep. A baby rhino weighs several hundred pounds and the warthogs, which usually ate between the rhinos' legs, as that's where all the scraps fell, had to move quickly to avoid being squashed flat enough to stick a stamp on and post first class. But a genuine friendship evolved between these orphans of vastly different species. We had built the baby warthogs an underground burrow where they slept to keep them safe from predators, and at dusk they would scurry down under, calling and agitating their rhino mates to follow them. You could virtually translate their squeals into – 'Hey, guys, it's dangerous at night; you'd better come down here with us where it is safe.' The fact that the burrow was barely a foot wide and the rhinos five times that obviously didn't enter the equation.

I chose Gumede, one of my trusted guards, to stay with Alyson and be in charge of protecting the rhinos during the day. Gumede was an incredible man who at sixty years old could climb trees as nimbly as a monkey. He would scale up the nearest one at the drop of a hat to scan the horizon if he sensed danger. If necessary, he would remain perched on top of a tall swaying marula for several hours. My legs used to get sore just watching him.

At night Alyson and Gumede were replaced by specialist game guards, tough men who would follow the rhinos wherever they roamed. They would be out in the bush among some of Africa's most dangerous animals in the black of night, which certainly takes both courage and keen bush skills. It was what had to be done, and I think Thabo and Nthombi are among the first rhinos in the world to have round-the-clock-protection in the wild.

Every day I would see them walking out with Alyson. Nearby, with his .303 always at the ready, was Gumede. Or more than likely he would be in a tree with his binoculars. For their own safety, the rhinos didn't know the night guards, so the guards always kept a bit of distance. They'd seek high points to do lookout, scanning for the torchlights of poachers, whereas during the day the babies would follow Alyson and Gumede as meekly as dogs with wagging tails.

However, there was one unbreakable rule: the guard on duty had to radio in every half-hour on the dot to tell us that all was OK. If not, or if we didn't receive a call exactly on schedule, a code red would instantly go out and every available ranger would grab his rifle and scramble for the nearest vehicle. It would be like an air raid in a war movie. That was the state of alertness that we had to be perpetually tuned into on Thula Thula, and I'm afraid that it is what front-line conservation has by force of dire circumstances come to today.

There was only ever one real lapse in security, and it was also the only time I saw a human being levitate. On this particular night the half hourly radio call didn't come in from one of the new guards, and on checking I found him fast asleep on the grass. It happened again the next night, and then, impossibly, despite my stern chastisement of him, it happened for a third night in succession. I can still recall the wonderfully content look on his sleeping face as I drew my 9mm pistol, placed it just above his ear, and fired three quick shots. And that's when he levitated. I mean he lifted right off the ground and seemed to hang in the air for an age before coming sharply back down to earth, whereupon he started running around like a headless chicken, shouting out to the heavens that he had been shot and would be dying shortly. He eventually saw me standing there laughing, and managed to gather himself before sitting on the ground and shaking his head in embarrassment. He has been with me ever since and has never again fallen asleep on night duty.

Eventually Betty and Denise, when almost fully grown, left to find warthog families of their own.

Sadly, Betty was taken by a hyena soon afterwards. Although I know this is the way of the bush, we were all tremendously saddened by her death.

However, Denise is still alive and I wonder if she recognizes her childhood mates when their paths cross, as Thabo and Nthombi wander across the plains just as their ancestors have done for millennia. I hope so.

Each day I watched our two rhinos grow. They seemed to do

so before my eyes, and will be adults soon. They are in robust health, beautiful specimens that will have beautiful children.

But to me, it's more than that. They are both iconic and symbolic; the hopes and dreams of the future of the wild.

They are also a constant reminder of what happened in Garamba, and what mankind can never let happen again.

CHAPTER FORTY-TWO

After our rescue of the Baghdad Zoo (as described in *Babylon's Ark*) during the Iraq invasion in 2003, we submitted a draft resolution to the UN in New York which is poignantly relevant to what was happening in the DRC. Named 'Wildlife in War Zones', it asks the UN to give wildlife areas, including game reserves, zoos and marine parks, the same status as schools and hospitals during times of conflict, and veterinarians and game rangers the same status as doctors and nurses, making them all illegitimate targets of war. There are so many endangered animals today that a war could prompt the extinction of a species – which is exactly what happened to the northern white rhino. For many species, zoos and game reserves are little Noah's arks, their last refuge, and they absolutely need to be protected.

Not only that, but battles that prompt the extinction or destruction of endangered species must be treated as war crimes. The same applies to the wilful destruction of the environment, such as I witnessed in Iraq during the zoo rescue, when Saddam Hussein set fire to the oil wells and the pollution reached Europe on the jet streams.

But the bottom line was that we had lost the fight to save the northern white rhino in the wild. I sometimes try to console myself with the obvious thought that we did the best we could and it was the intransigence of others that was to blame, but that would be a cop out. It is instead an indictment of us as human beings that this armour-plated behemoth, one of the ultimate survivors from the Cretaceous period, could now be wiped out thanks to the AK-47 and a bizarre craving to eat its horn in the Far East. There is no other way to put it. Until the leaders of some Asian countries, China, Vietnam and Thailand in particular, take responsibility for the terrible consequences of illicit horn buying, we will be in a fight to the death to save the last rhinos from extinction. And if they do not take responsibility, history will define these great nations not by their scientific achievements, but by the destruction of entire species for a superstitious medicine.

I had already decided that this patch of Zululand that we call Thula Thula would be where we make our own stand. We would join the good men and women in rhino reserves all over the country and dig in for the final battles.

Fortunately at Thula we have an incredible team, and we go into the future positively and with a deep sense of purpose.

Also I have *Nkosi* Biyela, the supreme tribal leader, on my side, as well as other chiefs and the local clans, whom we are educating with community forums showing that a live animal is far more economically valuable than a dead one. Indeed, my staff on their own initiative had visited their respective tribal *izinduna* headmen after Heidi was killed and asked them please to do something about it. They repeated the adage that the proceeds from a dead animal may feed one family for a couple of days – but a live rhino, with the tourism it attracts, feeds hundreds on a daily basis. In our area one job feeds eight people, so they have good reason to be concerned.

The *izinduna* listened. They agreed. I knew rhino hunters may still come from our local people. If they did, they risked ostracism. That alone was a major victory. But I also knew that a small percentage, the hardened criminals, didn't respect the police, or the chief, so the problem was never going to go away entirely.

However, as I've said before, it has never really been about tribesmen hunting the odd buck to feed a family. That is mere Bushveld shoplifting, and although we certainly don't condone it, we understand it.

Rhino and elephant poaching is a different matter altogether. This is done by big gangs, whether freelance gunmen hired by Asian thug businessmen or the local Boere Mafia, it doesn't matter. They are the cocaine barons of the illicit wildlife trade, organized criminals who have the resources, using sophisticated techniques, night-vision equipment and helicopters, and corrupt veterinarians to get what they want.

The difference from narcotics is that wildlife is unsustainable if poaching continues. You cannot replace a rhino that has been killed because their numbers are diminishing faster than they are being replenished. The exponential slaughter rate has nowhere to go except plummet to zero.

And then, when we thought it couldn't possibly get worse, it did.

Jean-Pierre Roux, a senior officer in the Hawks, South Africa's equivalent of the FBI, came out to meet me at Thula Thula regarding information on Heidi's death. Jean-Pierre, who was in the organized crime section of the Hawks specializing in endangered species, was fast becoming a folk hero among game rangers. Absolutely fearless, he was at home in the dirty underworld of the trade in rhino horn, and was taking the fight to the poachers and syndicates. Jean-Pierre hunted down and prosecuted poachers with a determination and commitment that helped lift everybody's spirits.

'I have just come back from the East,' he said, 'and the cops over there are trying to help us, but they've got their hands full. Prices are high, the demand is huge and the syndicates are ruthless.

'You already know that poachers have started poisoning rhino,' he said, 'lacing cabbages and oranges with herbicide and putting them out on rhino trails. That way there is no rifle shot to give them away. They are poisoning waterholes as well. They find a small pool where rhinos drink, fill it with poison and then just watch and follow the animal until it dies.'

'I have heard of this,' I said. 'It's shocking.'

'Now there are new developments. Poachers are leaving warning notes on rhino carcasses after they have taken the horns, saying they have laid ambushes and will kill anyone who tries to follow them.

'It gets much worse,' he continued. 'We recently caught a gang inside a major game reserve, and they were carrying hand grenades. Hand grenades, I tell you – we couldn't believe it. During the interrogation we found out that after they killed the rhino and took the horns, they were going to booby-trap the carcass with the hand grenades, to kill the follow-up rangers.'

I stared at him. 'If I hadn't heard it from you I wouldn't believe it. These are terror tactics.'

'It's not common knowledge, but it's true,' he said. 'The war against poachers is going to a whole new level, and it's going to get a lot worse before it gets better. If it ever does.'

There was a bit of good news, though. The four non-breeding captive northern whites in the Dvůr Králové Zoo in the Czech Republic were moved to a heavily protected holding area in Kenya, in the hope that natural surroundings would prompt mating. Many experts, though, believed that the opportunity to preserve a pure population of northern whites was gone, because of the limited genetic diversity of only four animals, and that they will eventually have to be bred with southern whites to at least preserve some of the genes.

I had unwittingly been dragged into this whole saga, thinking naively that all we had to do was provide money, resources and good old-fashioned determination to save a species. I had no idea of the bureaucracy, contempt, arrogance and hubris that we would encounter. I had no idea of the underlying causes of the myriad wars and conflicts in Africa that are also causing the collapse of conservation. And I had no real idea of the ruthlessness of rhino-poaching syndicates. It has been a bitter lesson.

And yet . . . and yet. The irony is that Africans are the original conservationists. The ancient inhabitants of this continent never hunted more than they needed. And they never hunted for trophies. That was total anathema, as animals had an intrinsic spiritual value. Animals were linked with deities. Every part of an animal killed was utilized to the full; its hide for clothes, its bones for tools, its sinews for bowstrings and, of course, its flesh for food. An animal was a gift from the gods.

Today that is all gone. A magnificent ancient creature is killed just for its horn, a fraction of its total mass, and the body is left to rot.

And while this book centres around the fight for the white rhino in Africa, the fate of its smaller cousin, the black rhino, hangs in the balance. With its imperial dignity and matchless courage, the black rhino enthrals and entrances like no other animal I have seen. It is estimated that there were around 1 million black rhinos in Africa in 1900. Then all hell broke loose and by 1970 there were only 65,000. By 1984 this had reduced to maybe about 10,000. Today there are only about 4,000 and, despite a tiny recovery, the species remains in great danger of going extinct.

While trying to save the northern whites, I got sucked into a maelstrom of which I had no inkling. By the time I discovered my life was in danger, or that I was in a situation I had absolutely no control over, it was usually too late. The fact that I survived is due either to fate or some very good friends out there; friends who live every day in some of the world's roughest neighbourhoods. Friends who live at the front line of the most important battle of the future: the battle for planet earth.

It was now two years since our baby rhinos, Thabo and Nthombi, had arrived, and the sun was setting low, a shimmering ball of fire in a sky-high display of vibrant reds, oranges and pinks and, on the fringes, the delicate mauves and deep purples of the night coming in. It was an iconic Zululand sunset, and it was closing a chapter of my life.

On the horizon I could just see the elephants. Nana was on the outskirts and, apart from her blindness in one eye, she was in robust health. I was glad we were in regular contact again, and it had become routine for her to detach herself from the rest of the herd whenever she heard my vehicle or smelled me. She was my muse; I would talk to her about anything and everything. Often without even verbalizing questions, I got answers.

Today, I couldn't see Gobisa, but I knew he would be nearby, as one of the females was coming on heat. He was proving to be a fine patriarch and his *askaris*, the young bulls Mabula, Mandla and Ilanga, were now well behaved. Their swagger had gone and they were learning manners. We hadn't had any vehicle charges for some time. Apart from the calming influence of Gobisa, this was also due to the fact that we were acquiring more and more land as the Royal Zulu game reserve project grew, so they had plenty of room to roam. Soon the dream of wilderness as far as the eye could see in every direction, with Thula Thula as the gateway, would become a reality.

Then there was a special treat. I caught a glimpse of movement and trained my binoculars. It was Thabo and Nthombi grazing contentedly. A few yards away was Gumede, his trusty .303 silhouetted by the fading light. For once he was on the ground, not up some tree endlessly scanning the horizon for danger.

This was the future of conservation in Africa: twenty-four-hour guards risking their lives with outdated weapons against machine guns and helicopters to protect critically threatened wild creatures. It was the best we could do with our limited resources. But it had to be done, and it was costing conservationists a fortune, even though these guards put their lives on the line for salaries that many in the West would not get out of bed for.

But that cost was in cash. The true cost will be the soul of the planet if we do not succeed. This world would be so much poorer for the loss of our fellow travellers that it may not even be worth being part of it.

Jeff, our half-Labrador, half-seal, came and sat by me at the view site outside our home. I wondered if he too was appreciating the magnificent scenario before us. He answered by nuzzling me and promptly falling asleep at my feet.

Then Françoise came out and put an arm around me. Gypsy was at her feet. Bijou, our little Maltese, had recently died. Tiny Bijou had the heart of a lion and had been as fiercely protective and loyal to her mistress as the wilderness king – she would have fought to the death for Françoise despite the fact that she weighed a mere five pounds. Françoise, who saw her as a child, grieved quietly and with dignity, and even I, who had been treated with lifelong disdain by the little poodle, missed her immensely.

'It is beautiful, is it not?' she said.

I nodded.

'It has been an interesting time. The rhinos, the Congo . . . and the children who are soldiers but do not want to be. The children who are now adults and want to go home.'

Again I nodded.

'It is so peaceful here. Look – there's Thabo and Nthombi. They are getting big and fat. It is so good.'

In her French way, she had said it all.

EPILOGUE
Lawrence's Legacy
by Graham Spence

March 2012

We got the call at 5 a.m. on 2 March 2012. My wife Terrie, who is also Lawrence's sister, took it. At our age every unusual hour call is a heart-stopper. I was instantly awake.

Terrie nodded and put the mobile phone down on the bedside table. She put her head in her hands. I knew what she was going to say.

'Lawrence is dead. He had a heart attack.'

I knew his health hadn't been good. But even so, Lawrence was indestructible – he had the constitution of an ox. I couldn't believe it.

Shock set in. I lay back, images flooding my mind.

Ah, Lawrence . . . Lawrence my friend, my brother, albeit not blood. You were the bravest I knew, and maybe ever will know.

In the process of writing three books with him, I won't say I got to know him even remotely more than most, as Lawrence was a professional enigma. He was as unpredictable as a rogue elephant. But boy, did we talk. There were long nights in Baghdad, England, Durban and, of course, the paradise that is Thula Thula. We talked non-stop. Sometimes like fools, sometimes like sages. The latter is our opinion, of course.

Some of it is recorded. For this book I have close on twenty-four hours of taped conversation as we both go off on tangents at the most flimsy excuse. There is stuff that has nothing to do with anything. There is stuff we thought profound at the time, but thankfully not for long. A lot is irreverent and irrelevant. Some is very good.

Sometimes, in the darkness before dawn, our only witness was a line of dead beer bottles. But not often; Lawrence preferred to party rather than to drink. But we were working, you understand.

I once committed a cardinal sin in Lawrence's eyes. It was in Baghdad in 2003, when I was working with him on the book *Babylon's Ark*. After two weeks I said I had to get back to my day job. He was aghast. 'This is where it's all happening,' he said. 'What is a day job? How boring is that?' I don't think he had consciously registered the concept of a 'day job' in his life. I pointed out that I had a wife and two kids back in England. The day job put food on the table.

Lawrence said he would get me out; in fact he said he would also go back home for a week himself, something he hadn't done for three months. There were no civilian flights from Baghdad, only military shuttles. To get on one required special persuasive skills, which Lawrence had in spades. How he did it, I do not know. We also had no visas, having snuck unofficially into Iraq, so as the plane landed at the Kuwaiti Air Force headquarters we slunk off the runway and jumped over a wall out of the direct vision of heavily-armed guards. We then sprinted down the road to rendezvous with the lift that Lawrence's friends had arranged to take us to the city airport.

We weren't out of the woods, or sands in this case. With all the foreign military around, Kuwaiti customs officials were itching to show Westerners who was boss. At the Kuwait City airport we therefore wanted to get out fast as neither of us had any documentary evidence of holidaying in this drab stretch of desert. If they'd known we'd been to Iraq without clearing their customs, we would have been jailed. No question. Lawrence persuaded an air hostess to escort him onto a flight about to leave for Dubai, where he would connect to Johannesburg. He was waved past soldiers like a VIP, while I waited all night in a London-bound queue. Then an aggressive uniformed Kuwaiti looked at my passport and started shouting. Alarmed to my bones, I took a deep breath and did what I knew Lawrence would do. Feigning carefree nonchalance I said I was sadly leaving this beautiful city – and thanks for the memories. Somehow, inspired by Lawrence, I made that plane. My wife's welcoming face at Heathrow London will remain with me for ever.

Today, almost a decade later, when dealing with life's unexpected challenges I ask: what would Lawrence do?

Indeed, there was no situation that Lawrence believed he could not talk his way out of – or more usually into – whether it were Lord's Resistance Army guerillas in feral Congo jungles; wildly unpredictable African bureaucracy; or Saddam Hussein supporters breathing fire down his neck. His amazing exploits are documented in the three books we wrote. Often I had to persuade him that an extremely brave or clever manoeuvre, performed with absolute grace under fire, should be kept in the text. 'Will people *really* be interested in that?' he used to ask me incredulously.

Yes Lawrence, they would.

But he would insist the funny bits were kept in, even though subjective humour can be a literary quicksand.

'Got to make people laugh, Graham,' he would say.

Lawrence knew how to make people laugh. We laughed often while writing these books, although I have to confess the way that Lawrence scrutinized the minutiae over at his desk in Thula Thula – re-reading again and again at 2 a.m. over a mug of coffee that could fly a jet and a lethal high-tar cigarette – drove me mad. But maybe that is what makes these books so focused.

We laughed over the titles. I proudly plead guilty to calling the first book *Babylon's Ark*; a name I made up in Baghdad before we had written a word. For the next book, thinking I was on a roll, I came up with the title *The Herd* – referring to elephants. Thankfully, our American editor, the immaculate Peter Joseph, who had the guts to take a chance on us African nonentities, gently pointed out that most readers would think we were referring to a bunch of cows. The name chosen was *The Elephant Whisperer*, a name neither of us was comfortable with as Lawrence seldom whispered. He talked in a booming bass. But the name struck a chord with readers and, as our editors pointed out, the elephants were whispering to Lawrence.

We wanted to call the book you have in your hand *Blood Horn*. But that was due to the adventurer in Lawrence. He wanted a daring sounding title. Maybe Lawrence would have hated me for saying this, but I think there is no doubt that he was innately a classic prototype adventurer more than anything else. One newspaper called him the Indiana Jones of Conservation, and that about sums him up. He did everything in life as a swash-buckler. That's how I will always remember him.

And yet, how do you explain that enigmatic quality? He had deliberately broken off contact with the elephant herd at Thula Thula as he wanted them to be truly wild. He wouldn't come out to greet them anymore at his and Françoise's humble cottage. Eventually they no longer came. After all, it was a bit out of the way of the best grazing, and to cap it all Lawrence wouldn't talk to them now.

But yet, but yet . . . The day after Lawrence died, the elephants, led by Nana, arrived at his house, in an eerie vigil that still gives me goose-bumps. A ranger took a video of that silent march-past that went viral on YouTube. A Google search 'elephants mourn Lawrence Anthony' gets over a million results.

As his son Dylan said, 'They had not visited the house for a year and a half and it must have taken them hours to make the journey. They all hung around for about two days before making their way back into the bush.'

Cynics may say that the animals were merely wandering past. Maybe the grasses were rich in that area at the time; it was, after all, the late summer rains. But we know better – don't we?

I'm glad we didn't use the *Blood Horn* title and thank Peter and our superb UK editor, Ingrid Connell, for showing us reason. They came up with *The Last Rhino*, but none of us knew that in the end that would also be a magnificent metaphor for Lawrence himself.

In my day job I am a journalist rather than a writer, although I still aim to be a full-time author. I like writing best about rare individuals who are still out there somewhere; the wild ones, the crazy ones, the mavericks, the passionate men and women who believe like monks in what they are doing. I wish I was one of them, but I know I am not.

Lawrence is. Or sadly now, was.

Ah, Lawrence . . . my friend, my brother.

Even when you drove us mad, we loved you.

October 2012

No one is completely irreplaceable. But Lawrence was more ir-replaceable than most, and the depth of the void in his passing is incalculable.

The question is this: how do you continue such an extraordinary legacy? How do you replicate such a force of nature? Well, you can't. But you can continue with the vision.

To Lawrence, conservation was a physical frontline presence; it was no game for sofa surfers. So when he died – way, way too young – there was no guidebook on how to be Lawrence Anthony. In fact, if there was, Lawrence would have thrown it into the furnace as he hated paperwork. However, although he was no genius with paperwork, he was a genius at getting people to follow him. He could inspire people like a prophet. He could get them to see his epiphanies; a crystal clear view of a world where the natural order of the universe is sacrosanct and none survive alone. Those whom he inspired are still out there living and breathing Lawrence's work.

The Zulu game rangers at Thula Thula continue with the passion fired by their revered Mkhulu. Bheki is there, so is Vusi and Promise. So too is the ever-vigilant Gumede, still climbing trees and scanning distant sun-scorched hilltops for poachers as he grips his battered .303.

He needs to. Despite twenty-four-hour security, poachers tried to kill Thabo and Nthombi just two weeks after Lawrence's death, even though the young rhinos have mere stumps for horns. They were repelled by Gumede and his team – men with bolt-action Second World War .303s against AK-47s. In the skirmish Thabo was shot in the leg. He is fine now, but today seven people are employed solely to guard Thabo and Nthombi around the clock. That, as Lawrence told me the last time I saw him, is what frontline conservation has become.

At the time of writing, the rhinos Thabo and Nthombi are three years old. They're growing at a rapid rate, weighing about a ton each. They are living hope for the future. Unlike their Northern cousins, they will not go silently into extinction. If they do, make no mistake; Lawrence's legacy will ensure that their disappearance will be seared on the conscience of the sentient world for ever.

Today, the elephants are thriving. So much so that Thula Thula management has had to implement a birth-control programme. The herd is now twenty-three members strong, an astonishing feat when you consider that the first six animals arrived at Thula Thula in 1997 with a suspended death sentence hanging over them, as recounted in *The Elephant Whisperer*. But the current herd is as many as the land can take until all fences are removed from the Thula Thula eastern gate at Buchanana to the Umfolozi Game Reserve 40km to the north-west, which will happen when the Royal Zulu is complete, creating a 500,000-acre game reserve.

But, having said that, the latest addition to the herd has just arrived; a beautiful and perfect calf, born on 11 September 2012. The rangers call her Andile which means 'They Increase' in Zulu and is as pithy a description of Lawrence's legacy as you will ever get.

After Andile was born an amazing thing happened. As soon as she could stand and had had her first suckle, the herd started moving towards the house where Lawrence had lived. However, when they reached the river it was in spate. The herd stopped and mulled. The behemoths could easily wade across the brown swirling waters, but something was preventing them. Rangers watched, wondering what had happened until, for the first time, they saw the baby and it became clear. The herd couldn't enter the swollen river because Andile was too tiny and would have drowned. The animals were clearly agitated and wanted to cross. It was a straight route to the main house. But they dared not.

Then the rangers understood. Nana and the herd had set off to introduce the new arrival, which had become a ritual when Lawrence was alive. Even though the elephants knew Lawrence was no longer around, as their silent vigil had shown on the day after his death, the ritual remains and probably always will. Cynics may say that's a coincidence; the animals were simply going to the river to drink. But we know better – don't we?

Gobisa is now the undisputed patriarch and Mandla his loyal *askari*. They hang out together, the pachyderm equivalent of dudes at the wilderness shopping mall, and as Lawrence had hoped, Gobisa the elder has taught the youngsters manners. They do not try to be macho juveniles, turning over vehicles, throwing their weight around just as some testosterone-fuelled teenagers without strong fatherly guidance sometimes do. They are now content in their enormous power.

*

The spearhead of Lawrence's legacy falls upon his two charismatic sons Jason and Dylan and his disciple David Bozas, who are at the forefront of the Royal Zulu game reserve project. They are joined by Lawrence's wife Françoise and Yvette Taylor, the energetic executive director of the conservation association that he founded, The Lawrence Anthony Earth Organization. Together, these five people are the keepers of the flame. It is what they do every day of their lives.

One of Lawrence's gifts was cementing friendships, invariably with a single handshake. In this case a close friend, Andy Ruhan, was also his business partner. Andy, an Irish businessman, who Lawrence describes in this book as being 'straight out of a Wilbur Smith novel', races souped-up cars for fun and thrives on action. He also has the financial muscle to make Lawrence's legacy work and is intimately involved in Lawrence's final project: the Moyana Game Reserve. His company, Bridgehouse Capital, aligned with The Lawrence Anthony Earth Organization and the Mayibuye Trust, representing the people who own the land, are responsible for creating this ambitious reserve at Camperdown, near Durban, which apparently is the closest Big Five game reserve to a city in the world. It's a bold step, establishing a wildly beautiful green lung in areas that can spiral out of control with so-called development. And even more boldly, putting elephant there. If that's not a symbolic halt to concrete encroachment then nothing is. David Bozas, who Dylan says is a Lawrence-replica, is in charge of running Moyana in conjunction with the Mayibuye Trust community leaders. Roughly translated from Zulu, Mayibuye means bringing back what was lost.

At the opening of the Moyana reserve in 2010, the Mayibuye Trust chairman, Welcome Maphanga, summed up the socio-environmental significance of this project perfectly. 'We have come the full circle since we were forcibly evicted from our land [by the previous apartheid government]. It has been a long hard road but we are back. Wild animals have always lived in our area and we used to hunt them. If you kill a wild animal it provides food for a week, but by protecting them today we create jobs for a lifetime.'

In short, the Moyana Game Reserve aims to provide local people with jobs and income through eco-tourism, while helping to secure the future of the region's wildlife from rampant development. That is Lawrence's vision.

But back to where it all began: Thula Thula. Jason, Dylan and Françoise are his successors, physically and spiritually. To visit the reserve today is an uncanny experience; the spirit of Lawrence is all-pervasive. It's as if you expect him to come bounding into the lodge at any time, his sweat-stained baseball cap with the Thula Thula elephant logo pulled low to keep the sun off his eyes; his wild red- and white-flecked beard awry and khaki bush-jacket dusted with the soul of Africa. Life goes on. That's how Lawrence would want it to.

Here, in her own words, is an update from Françoise:

I am working now at assisting meetings about the Royal Zulu with David Bozas and Vusi, our game reserve manager, who worked very closely with Lawrence with all the projects to extend Thula Thula. We had a meeting yesterday with the two local *Amakhosi* and their *Izinduna* [chiefs and head-men], as well as a conservation lawyer and a KwaZulu-Natal Wildlife representative to discuss the finer details of the Greater Fundimvelo Community Conservation Project. This will represent an extension of a further 3,000 hectares. So Thula Thula brings in a fully developed nature reserve to the project, while the communities bring in their land. KZN Wildlife will bring in game and commercial development will be put in place to generate job creation and income.

We are also raising funds to take in more rhino orphans from rehabilitation centres, such as Moholoholo in Limpopo, where we got Thabo and Nthombi. Last weekend there was an auction of one of these orphans, but the price went up to R200 000! The normal price is R100 000 [about $14,500]. Some people are now buying rhinos as an investment, to resell them for breeding in about five years' time when they estimate that the price of a rhino will be sky-high. So we need to raise funds to be able to buy more orphan rhinos.

We also carry on rehabilitating animals into the bush with CROW, the organization which gave us George the Bushbaby and Betty and Denise, the warthogs that grew up with Thabo and Nthombi.

Indeed. Life goes on.

Thula Thula is, and always will be, frontline conservation. Thula Thula is intrinsically what Lawrence was and where his heirs – from humble lodge room-sweepers to frontline rangers to blood family – continue to keep the vision alive. To understand that you just have to inhale the atavistically powerful African aura that embraces Thula Thula in a panorama of many colours, breathe in the beauty and the dust and see Thabo and Nthombi browsing in the savannah. You will also notice two people close by. One is white, Alyson McPhee, an English lass whose love for Africa and rhino is as fierce as a mother's; the other black, Gumede, wirily-muscled, whose love for God's own land is without condition.

Thabo and Nthombi are more than perfect specimens of their breed. They are symbols of Lawrence's last stand against poachers, where men clutching ancient rifles and shotguns stand ragged but firm against gangs shooting with automatic weapons and coming out of the sky in helicopters. The debt the world owes to these gallant warriors of the wild is unpayable.

Another aspect of Lawrence's legacy was that he irrevocably changed people's perceptions – and their lives – outside the perimeters of conservation. His Blackberry was choked with daily messages from people around the world saying exactly that. From the girl who said she now looked at her pet cat with different eyes, to those who pledged to live more in tune with the planet, their passion is directly due to the ignition he sparked. Many wrote with rage at rhino horn trafficking and mass poaching. Others wrote achingly heartfelt words thanking him for what he was doing. He replied to almost all of them.

When he spoke at gatherings, whether attended by celebrities, or the village book club, the audience listened rapt. The message was the same. For people who said 'I can't', Lawrence had a simple answer; 'you can'. Get involved. Join conservation movements that actually do something rather than relying on media gimmickry; lobby your local MP; plant a tree.

Or, most importantly, just go outside and look. Breathe. Through Lawrence, legions of people today now know that the wilderness is not somewhere out there. It's in your soul.

There is no doubt about Lawrence's global impact. That was shown in spades at the outpouring of anguish following his death. However, Lawrence believed he failed with the Northern White Rhino. That's why he vowed on the grave of Heidi that it would not happen to the Southern White on his watch and on his turf. For those who loved Lawrence, that vow is sacrosanct.

But yet . . . did he fail? Certainly he brought the plight of rhinos to international attention immeasurably beyond the prism of cold science and cerebral conservation. Perhaps these magnificent prehistoric beasts that have survived meteors, dinosaurs and ice ages are somehow, unbelievably, still out there. Perhaps, like Lawrence, their soul is indestructible. Indeed, the World Wildlife Fund reports that there have been some sightings, albeit unconfirmed, of Northern Whites deep in the forests of Southern Sudan.

Maybe, just maybe, there are still some hardy survivors. Some surly, gnarled, grumpy, magnificent, indomitable, scimitar-horned beast who – being an incurable romantic, I believe answers to the name of Lawrence – is refusing to surrender.

Maybe we have been granted a second chance. We cannot squander it. Then Lawrence's legacy will truly be complete.

PICTURE ACKNOWLEDGEMENTS

The author and publisher would like to thank the following for permission to reproduce the images used in this book:

Françoise Malby – page 1, top
Isabelle Marques – page 1, middle; page 7, top and middle
Marissa Lenting – page 2, top; page 8, top left and bottom
The Lawrence Anthony Foundation – page 2, bottom; page 6, bottom
Christopher Laurenz – page 3, top
Godfrey Ayoo – page 4, bottom
Suki Dhanda – page 5, top
Pieter Le Roux – page 5, bottom
Dylan Anthony – page 6, top
Alyson McPhee – page 7, bottom; page 8, top right

All other images provided courtesy of the author.

LAWRENCE ANTHONY was a highly respected South African conservationist and founder of The Lawrence Anthony Foundation, an independent international conservation and environmental organization with a strong scientific orientation. He was also the owner and head of conservation at the Thula Thula Exclusive Private Game Reserve in KwaZulu-Natal. He received the UN's Earth Day Medal for his rescue of Baghdad Zoo during the invasion of Iraq.

GRAHAM SPENCE is a freelance journalist and author who grew up in Africa and is now living in England.